Tartan Air Force

Tartan Air Force

SCOTLAND AND A CENTURY
OF MILITARY AVIATION

Deborah Lake

BIRLINN

This edition first published in 2009 by
Birlinn Limited
West Newington House
10 Newington Road
Edinburgh
EH9 1QS

www.birlinn.co.uk

ISBN13: 978 1 84158 806 3

British Library Cataloguing-in-Publication Data
A catalogue record for this book is available from the British Library

Typeset by HewerText (UK) Ltd
Printed and bound by CPI Cox & Wyman, Reading

CONTENTS

List of Illustrations   vii
Acknowledgements   ix
Foreword   xiii
Preface   1

 1 A Happy Invention   3
 2 Faltering Footsteps   14
 3 Experiments and Experience   26
 4 Bombs, Beardmore and Ghosts   39
 5 Gallant Gentlemen All   50
 6 Peace and Dismissal   65
 7 Not Cash But Courage   77
 8 In Business Again   94
 9 Dauntless in War   107
10 A Common Effort   123
11 Blizzards and Battleships   140
12 Grim Days, Valiant Heroes   157
13 U-Boats and Flak Ships   172
14 Peace and the Cold War   185
15 A Changing Age   206
16 Modern Times and After   223

Epilogue   239
Bibliography   243
Index   247

LIST OF ILLUSTRATIONS

1. Dunne's D1 Glider, Glen Tilt, 1907.
2. The cutting edge of the Royal Flying Corps: a contemporary postcard showing 2 Squadron's BE2 aircraft at Montrose in 1913
3. Isaac's Tribute. The flying services always strive to send off the departed in some style.
4. Sir David Henderson, architect of the Royal Flying Corps and, at one time, the oldest active pilot in the world.
5. Four BE2 biplanes of Number 2 Squadron at Stranraer, 1913 just before they flew to Ireland – the first time that the RFC left mainland Britain.
6. The first BE2C biplane completed by Beardmore's at Dalmuir.
7. A Sopwith 2F1, 'Ship's Camel', is pulled out of the Firth of Forth in 1918.
8. A Handley Page V/1500 heavy bomber at Inchinnan in 1918.
9. A Scottish-built aeroplane in India in 1918.
10. The R34 at the time of her Atlantic Flight in 1919.
11. Wopsie, the first cat to fly the Atlantic.
12. The officers of 602 (City of Glasgow) Squadron at the Palace Hotel, Southend in 1937.
13. The Marquess of Clydesdale, later the Duke of Hamilton, and David McIntyre before the Everest Flight in 1933.
14. The Houston Westland PV3 G-ACAZ approaches the Kangchenjunga Range during the 1933 Everest Flight Expedition.
15. Blenheim L1108 of 62 Squadron comes to grief at Abbotsinch during the 1938 Empire Exhibition.
16. An Avro Tutor trainer of 612 Squadron, Auxiliary Air Force, flying from Dyce in 1938.

17. Glasgow's first barrage balloon in 1939.
18. 'A' Flight of 602 Squadron pictured on 3 September 1939.
19. A Lockheed Hudson of 320 (Netherlands) Squadron takes off from Leuchars in 1941.
20. 'Aviatrixes' of the Air Transport Auxiliary preparing for their first delivery flight
21. John Hannah, VC.
22. Kenneth Campbell, VC.
23. Hugh Gordon Malcolm, VC.
24. William Reid, VC.
25. John Alexander Cruickshank, VC.
26. George Thompson, VC.
27. William Neil McKechnie, GC.
28. Eric Watt Bonar, GC.
29. John McIntosh McClymont, GC.
30. Winkie, the first winner of the PDSA Dickin Medal for bravery – the 'Animal VC'.
31. A line-up at Peterhead of Spitfires Mark Vc of 350 (Belgian) Squadron in 1944.
32. In 1944, Sergeant Cynthia Routh at Brackla negotiated a concession for her airwomen during the remarkably hot summer of that year – they could take off their jackets.
33. A Mosquito of the Banff Strike Wing in action shortly before the war's end.
34. Essential supplies being flown into West Berlin in Avro Yorks.
35. A de Havilland Vampire of 603 Squadron is re-armed for a training flight in 1956.
36. Flight Lieutenant Ian 'Beery' Weir of 8 Squadron at Lossiemouth celebrates his achievement at reaching 10,000 flying hours.
37. A 43 Squadron Phantom FG1 Leuchars escorts a Soviet Air Force Bear D away from the British coast.
38. and 39. From simple crosses in country churchyards to a fully fledged museum such as Montrose or East Fortune, memories remain of the men and women who served the Tartan Air Force: a memorial at St Fergus Church, Dyce and part of the present-day Montrose Heritage Centre.

ACKNOWLEDGEMENTS

History books depend on lots of help, be it from public archives and institutions or private individuals with a tale to tell.

Tartan Air Force has relied on both. In the public domain, I am greatly indebted to the library of Scotland's National War Museum at Edinburgh Castle and to the National Archives of Scotland. Ian Brown at the Museum of Flight at East Fortune has been extremely helpful as has Forbes Inglis of the Montrose Aviation Heritage Centre. The Imperial War Museum in London with its unparalleled collection of documents, sound recordings and images provided much useful material. By the same token, Peter Elliott and the Royal Air Force Museum at Hendon gave me a great deal of assistance as I ploughed my way through some of the more esoteric details of the Royal Air Force on Scottish soil. The National Newspaper Library produced everything for which I asked.

Much of the secondary material quoted in the Bibliography was promptly supplied by the Morpeth headquarters of the Northumberland County Library. They never once blenched at my increasingly obscure demands. One minor delight of the inter-library lending service is that books come from around the nation, from Elgin to Cornwall. To all of the above, I offer substantial thanks.

My task was made immeasurably more pleasant by the co-operation I received from Historic Scotland who arranged various visits for me. I also thank the Natural History Museum in London who provided me with a detailed discourse on the seeds of the zanonia microcarpa, a member of the cucurbitaceae plant family.

Dawn McNiven, the Media and Communications Officer at RAF Kinloss, provided me with a fine selection of material about that station. She answered my various inquiries with an ongoing patience despite her own busy workload. Squadron Leader Rob Deboys, Executive Officer of 43 Squadron at RAF Leuchars cracked a metaphorical whip to produce an account of fast jet flying in 2007 to round off the final chapter. I owe him.

Thanks go as well to Mary Guy, Librarian and Archivist of the Royal Air Force College, Cranwell, for her prompt response to my inquiries. Allison Wareham of the Royal Navy Library at Portsmouth wore out several copies of the *Navy List* by checking details; the National Maritime Museum also came to my aid on more than one occasion. I also acknowledge the courtesy of the respective editors of *Royal Air Force News*, *Navy News* and *Air Mail* for their assistance. Air Marshal Ian Macfadyen's immediate consent to my request for the Foreword to this book gave me much pleasure. He has made his own contribution to the history of the Royal Air Force; his acceptance does this title no little honour.

For the rest, I owe so many individuals a considerable debt.

Mike Parnell and Geoff Cooper did me the courtesy of reading an early draft and pointing out my various errors as well as contributing material. That said, any remaining mistakes and omissions are entirely my own work.

For the rest, the following all gave me much help. Some appear within the main text; others are paraphrased; a few may think they have been ignored. Not so. Everybody mentioned contributed to this book, directly and indirectly. My thanks thus go to Alf Allsop, Derek Armitage, Margaret Chaytor, Steve Collier, Jack Cornelius, Bernie Donders, Margaret Dove, Peter Dunne, Frank Fitzgerald, Reg Fry, Roy Evans, Harry Gummer, Paul Humphreys, Norman Jones, David Kelley, Garyth Lofthouse, Tom Lyness, Roy Maber, Gordon Maxwell, Nige Morton, Peter Payne, Arthur Pullin, Michael Peto-Shepherd, Gerry Raffé, Fred Roberts, Cynthia Routh, Carl Toulmin-Rothe, Ian Le Sueur, Philip Venn, Ron Waite, Harold Watling and John Wears, as well as a considerable number of correspondents who prefer the shade of anonymity. Modesty prevails, as always, in the Royal Air Force.

I am also indebted to copyright holders who have allowed me to quote passages. In some cases it has not been possible to contact the holder; if anybody feels their copyright has been inadvertently infringed, a correction will appear in subsequent editions of this book. I also thank my agent, Malcolm Imrie, for his unfailing encouragement. It's the more fortunate authors who can claim that their agent is also a friend. I am one of the luckier ones.

Peter Burns at Birlinn worked wonders to find many of the rarer illustrations in this book. In turn, Helen Osmani of National Museums Scotland and Andy Renwick of the Royal Air Force Museum ransacked their archives to meet some of my more hopeful requests. Their success can be seen by every reader. To their efforts, I add the pleasure of working with Andrew Simmons, Editorial Manager of Birlinn, who helped make this book a joy to produce.

Finally, I thank Vanessa Stead, who has firmly kept a household under control during the months in which this book has been in preparation, for her dedicated copy-reading and suggestions and for being an all-round good egg.

FOREWORD

As one whose ancestors came from Tiree, and who served for four years at RAF Leuchars, I am delighted to have been asked to write a foreword to this history of military flying in Scotland and of Scottish airmen. Leuchars will be well known to many readers as one of Scotland's premier air bases. Much less is known of the importance of Tiree as an RAF station in the Second World War, when aircraft flying from there provided many key weather forecasts for Allied airmen throughout Britain. Critically perhaps, the invasion of Normandy in 1944 was delayed as a direct result of meteorological forecasting operations from RAF Tiree. During that period, the island population tripled, approaching the levels when my great grandfather left in the 1850s. There are many such similar stories of unusual flying activities to be found within this book.

The Scots have had a reputation for toughness and bravery on the field of battle for many centuries, and also for their inventiveness. These qualities are all brought out in full measure, in association with an art of warfare that, as I write, is still not yet a hundred years old in Britain. Progress in the early years of aviation, after the Wright brothers' famous initial flights in December 1903, was painfully slow, mainly because the required power was not available. The Scots, nevertheless, were in the vanguard of European aviation, with early flying taking place near Tentsmuir Forest, right next to what is now RAF Leuchars. A fascination for flying, which was to grow rapidly as the technology became available, brought many Scots to prominence in the period leading up to and during The Great War.

Whether it was flying from land, or sea, Scotland continued to feature strongly and often pioneered new aviation ideas in the 1920s and '30s.

But it was in the 1939–1945 war that Scotland, and Scottish airmen, came really to the fore. The first RAF aerial combat in that war was by a Scottish-based aircraft, and six Scottish airmen earned the Victoria Cross during that global conflict. Rudolf Hess chose Scotland as the destination of his extraordinary journey from Hitler's side. A huge number of air bases were hastily built around Scottish shores. Some provided a platform for offshore operations against either the submarine threat, or for the remarkable offensive sweeps over Norway, which often involved almost unimaginably large numbers of aircraft. Others were key to the safe delivery of aircraft coming across the Atlantic from American factories. Sadly, only a few such airfields survive today.

Subsequently, during the Cold War, the main Scottish RAF air bases and radar stations were key players in operations which probed the strengths and weaknesses of Soviet aircraft and submarines. Today, although the radar sites are fewer, those same air bases remain open. These both reflect their continuing strategic importance and the wonderful opportunities for training over landscape that is often sparsely populated or the relatively quiet northern waters around Britain. Scotland therefore remains in the vanguard of training for the fight against today's threat – global terrorism.

This book brings out all that I have mentioned, and much more, in a most readable and often fascinating way. It is a proud history of bravery and achievement, sometimes against all odds. That tradition continues, as Scotland provides, in the twenty-first century, an important contribution to the extraordinary progress of military aviation.

Air Marshal I.D. Macfadyen CB, OBE
Station commander, RAF Leuchars 1985–87

June 2007

PREFACE

Although this book features aircraft, it is not a technical volume. Those who seek gripping information on how the Mark IV Puddlejumper became the Mark V Puddlejumper once Modification kit AM3571105/93581 was fitted must look elsewhere. This book is about people.

Scottish aviation, in all its forms, has a long history and this title deals with military flying. However, I am extremely conscious that it is, at best, a hasty skating over of one hundred years of history, since to cover every detail would require a volume twice the size of the Stone of Destiny and thrice as heavy.

Neither do I claim to mention every airfield, every unit, every aeroplane and every aviator that came to, or hails from, Scotland. Inevitably some will feel that I have ignored vital facts. I can only plead that it is not wilful; merely the result of marshalling thousands of pieces of information into a reasonably concise narrative within a given space.

Rather than provide a long table to explain arcane Service abbreviations, I have interpreted these in the text. I have further taken the cavalier approach that the reader needs no long list of metric and imperial equivalents and have generally employed the measurements familiar to the original user. The Luftwaffe dropped 250-kg bombs not 454-lb ones. In practice, it makes little difference if one doubles or halves the kilogram or pound weight to taste; for the record, a 12,000-lb 'Tallboy' blockbuster was just that, not a 5,448-kg bomb.

With its imperfections apologised for in advance, therefore, this is the story of men and women in uniform who flew, fought and supported the Tartan Air Force.

1

A Happy Invention

SECRECY was essential to protect the new invention. In 1907 politicians, civil servants, generals and admirals believed that spies and newspapermen were everywhere. Journalists from the more respectable papers, *The Times,* the *Morning Post,* the *Daily Telegraph,* and that bastion of Liberal thought, the *Manchester Guardian* normally behaved themselves responsibly; the rest, from the *Daily Mirror,* the *Daily Mail,* the *Daily Graphic* and others were simply scum who deserved a taste of the dog whip. Espionage was a greater problem. Spies from Germany certainly sought out British secrets. The French could not really be trusted and the Russians provided a distinct threat. So, a colonel spoke to a general. He murmured discreetly to a politician. Guarded words passed in Pall Mall. A Scottish nobleman offered secluded acres as a patriotic duty. The Marquess of Tullibardine, heir to the Duke of Atholl, agreed that Glen Tilt, part of the family's Perthshire estate, host the vital trials to test Britain's secret weapon – a heavier-than-air flying machine invented by Lieutenant John William Dunne who worked at the Balloon Factory at Farnborough in Hampshire.

Dunne saw active service in South Africa in the Boer War, both as a trooper in the Imperial Yeomanry and as a lieutenant in the Wiltshire Regiment. He learned at first hand that reconnaissance under long-range artillery fire presented dangerous problems and decided the complete answer was a powered machine for aerial scouting. As nobody had invented one, Dunne decided to design his own. Invalided home, he pushed his ideas at anybody whether they listened or not. In the England of 1902, flying was the preserve of the birds and balloonists, neither of much use in military matters. Birds did not read maps, while balloons flew wherever the wind pushed them.

Dunne had one advantage in pressing his views as his father was a recently retired army general, Sir John Hart Dunne, Colonel of the Wiltshire Regiment. He knew all about pulling strings and dutifully tugged every cord available for his son. The lieutenant did not stay idle. By 1904, Dunne had decided exactly what sort of machine the army needed. He believed military aircraft should be inherently stable to allow the crew to read maps, make sketches or take photographs without the worry of controlling the machine.

The lieutenant produced a series of models with swept-back V wings and no tail. Known as 'zanonias' after a fancied resemblance to the seeds of a relative of the cucumber plant, they had the desirable attribute of gliding steadily and gently to the ground. They looked little enough like swept-wing biplanes although modern eyes might discern the shape of a flying saucer. The models flew, and a delighted Dunne carried on.

By May 1904 Dunne was sure his design solved the control problem, since flying, he expounded, should be a simple technique, and easy to master. The machine must be able to fly in wind and rain, land safely if some vital component snapped in two and, in Dunne's phrase, 'be made to balance automatically by an aeronaut who has lost his nerve'.

Dunne had no practical flying experience of a petrol-engined, manned, controllable, heavier-than-air aircraft. The world held only two people who had: Orville and Wilbur Wright. Their invention, the Flyer, did not meet Dunne's strict control requirements, and several years after their first flight in December 1903, the Flyer had hardly changed. Describing it as 'an exceedingly simple apparatus', the 1910 *Aero Manual* went on:

> The operator sits to the left of the engine, counter-balancing its weight, and has a wooden lever in each hand, the left-hand lever raising or lowering the forward elevation planes, and the right-hand lever having a double movement, forward and rearward, to turn the rear vertical rudder, thus giving lateral movement to the machine, and to left and right in order to bend the wing tips to facilitate turning and maintain lateral balance.

Dunne made little progress with the authorities until Colonel John Edward Capper became interested. He headed the Royal Engineers' Balloon Factory at Farnborough, and in the enigmatic way of the military, this placed him under the control of the Directorate of Fortifications and Works.

Capper knew mechanical flight was possible, since he saw it with his own eyes in America where he met the Wrights, and was utterly convinced that Great Britain must control the air just as it did the oceans. The enthusiastic colonel decided that Dunne was the very man to open the skies for the nation.

Matters came together neatly, when in April 1906, Lieutenant Dunne went permanently on to half pay because of continuing ill-health. In the same month, Capper became Superintendent of the Balloon Factory and invited Dunne, now free of any regimental duties, to join him at Farnborough to design Britain's first military aeroplane.

Capper personally authorised Dunne to start work on 7 June 1906, before official approval arrived. Seven days later, the War Office confirmed his appointment. The colonel, anxious to acquire sufficient funding for the scheme, told his superiors that the Balloon Factory would soon provide a far better flying machine than the Wright Brothers had managed. Dunne produced a grown-up version of his models, the Dunne D1. It was a glider, launched by the simple process of propelling it downhill on a trolley. When it reached flying speed, the D1 took to the air before it flew evenly back to earth just like a zanonia seed.

Dunne and Capper agreed that the very idea of inherent stability was so important that secret trials were essential. Scores of inventors busily tried to rival the Wrights. Like the taciturn Americans, they had to crack the problem of control in the air. The last thing Capper wanted was Dunne's solution being copied without restraint, so he made discreet inquiries. During the Boer War, he had become friendly with the Duke of Atholl's heir, the Marquess of Tullibardine. Plenty of land existed on the Duke's distant Perthshire estate. Further, the Duke's tenants would provide a bodyguard and patrol service. Capper lost no time in arranging to move the flimsy D1 and its even more secret successors, to Scotland.

In July 1907, six sappers from the Kite Section of the Royal Engineers, in unaccustomed civilian clothing, took a train north under the command of Lieutenant Francis Westland, in a rather better cut suit. The soldiers guarded a sealed goods wagon, filled with packing cases that held Britain's secret weapon. After them came John Dunne, promoted to captain, his civilian assistant, Percy Gurr and a carpenter named Smith. At Blair Atholl, the tenantry put up wooden sheds to house the gliders. Soldiers of the Scottish Horse provided a row of tents for sappers and civilians.

The experiments were so secret that nobody kept any written records, unlike the Wrights who meticulously recorded every single attempt they made. Dunne and his team worked less formally and only contradictory eye-witness accounts remain.

Somewhere around the end of August, Dunne sent a message to Farnborough that two gliders were ready for trials, a monoplane and a biplane. Colonel Capper, together with Louis Dwarris Lancelot Gibbs, a newly commissioned officer of the Duke of Connaught's Own Hampshire and Isle of Wight Regiment, a militia component of the Royal Garrison Artillery, set off for Perthshire. Gibbs subsequently transferred to the Royal Field Artillery, the militia being an acceptable back-door route into regular service for those who preferred to avoid the rigours of Sandhurst.

Gibbs was to pilot the biplane, since Capper believed that Dunne's health was too frail to undergo the strain of actually flying. The lieutenant, an experienced skier, had the assumed advantages of a well-developed sense of balance as well as familiarity with the landscape rushing by at speed. Capper intended to fly the monoplane himself. The *Daily Express* then gave Capper's desire for secrecy a serious knock when its issue of 6 September 1907 told its readers all about the experimental work at the Balloon Factory. A lighter-than-air section took care of balloons and airships. Man-lifting kites were the responsibility of a second department. Most thrilling of all was the Aeroplane Section:

> The aeroplanes are of a new and interesting type. All the parts have been made separately so that only the highest officials who have the plans in their possession know what the completed figure will resemble.

Capper should not have been surprised, as his demands for secrecy did not extend as far as his own discretion. Friends and acquaintances all knew that Dunne's machine was 'far away ahead of the Wrights'. In the meantime, the Special Correspondent of the *Express* set out for Blair Atholl.

Capper always claimed that he made the first man-carrying trial. Amongst the more important witnesses were the Master-General of the Ordnance, Major-General C. F. Hadden, Colonel R. M. Ruck from the Directorate of Fortifications and Works, the Marquess of Tullibardine and a devoted Mrs Capper. Lurking in the background were the sappers and estate workers. One further guest mentioned as being present, allegedly in a private capacity, was Richard Burdon Haldane, the Secretary of State for War. Government funds financed the venture. The Edinburgh-born Minister, son of a Writer to the Signet, Haldane liked to know how the money was spent.

Haldane had a mind as sharp as Jack the Ripper's razor. A lawyer himself, with a formidable intellect, he did much to prepare the British Army for the twentieth century. A corpulent man, described by contemporaries as 'more round than oval', he created one moment of pleasure for onlookers during an inspection of Portsmouth Dockyard. James Graham, marquess, son and heir of the Duke of Montrose, recorded:

> when Lord Haldane, Minister for War, came down to see a submarine, never having seen one before, we took him out to one of the early 'A' type. The Admiral went down the conning tower first; Lord Haldane, who was very stout, tried to follow but got stuck in the conning tower, and could not get up or down. I heard Admiral Fisher say from below: 'He's got us damned well corked – pull the bloody cork!' It took a lot of work to do this; a derrick had to be rigged to get Lord Haldane out.

Dunne's monoplane came out for the trial. It was nothing more complicated than a run-and-jump contraption which would fly when the pilot reached sufficient speed. Dunne himself, aware of the wind's danger, kept testing its strength with a white handkerchief. Colonel John Capper prepared himself by putting on a fencer's mask to protect his face if he crashed.

The wind dropped, the air calmed and the colonel ran furiously downhill, his legs pumping madly, but the glider remained earthbound. After several attempts, the trolley from Farnborough came out. The colonel and the machine settled down at the top of an inclined ramp. Sturdy arms pushed the contraption down the ramp. It gathered speed and rose triumphantly into the air. The machine sailed forward for a short distance, touched the ground, bounced, stalled on one wing, tilted over and flipped upside down into a convenient drystone wall. Capper's flying time was eight seconds. The wreckage moved as Mrs Capper and the onlookers rushed forward. Capper emerged, blood pouring from his ear where the protective mask had dug into his flesh. Otherwise, he was uninjured except for a few knocks and bruises.

In his subsequent report to the Department of Fortifications, the good colonel put the brightest gloss on the episode. Conceding that the machine had been in the air only a short time, he pointed out that the test 'though to an unskilled eye merely disastrous' in fact proved that Dunne's calculations were basically correct. Although the monoplane was a crumpled heap of wood and fabric, the experimenters agreed to rebuild the machine as a powered aeroplane. Two 12-horsepower Buchet engines crouched in a wooden crate for the very purpose.

The experiments continued and the trials went on. At one point, Tullibardine himself was commandeered as a pilot, the intention being to launch him off a cliff on an instant solo flight. The heir to the Atholl Estates gazed over the edge: far below was a ground-sheet on which the local doctor was carefully spreading out his instruments. An errant gust of wind that overturned the glider saved the Atholl dukedom from disaster and the marquess never made the flight.

Capper corresponded with friends. On 27 September the Special Correspondent of the *Daily Express* showed he snooped to some purpose in Perthshire. Powerful field glasses and a ready purse gave the news-paper a scoop:

BRITAIN'S FIRST AEROPLANE EXPERIMENTS WITH
AERIAL FIGHTING MACHINE
SUCCESS ASSURED
WORK IN SECRECY IN THE HIGHLANDS

Experiments have been carried on for more than a week . . . with the new aeroplane for the British Government, which it is believed will surpass any other machine of the kind in existence . . . It has no gas bag, and is built on the heavier-than-air principle. Its lifting power is derived from motors . . . It is essentially a fighting machine.

In a second article, the reporter revealed that he himself had seen the machine, albeit through binoculars. 'So confident are the inventors of the new aeroplane of its success,' he wrote, 'and of its superiority over all of its predecessors that they are sparing neither pains nor expense to maintain absolute secrecy. Sentries,' he added, 'are posted in the flanking hills.'

The following day, the paper carried a further report. The marquess, bitterly opposed to the Liberal Government, hardly hindered the busy reporter who told the readership:

> The trials are hampered by the parsimony of the Government . . . But for the generosity of the Marquess of Tullibardine, who has granted the site and paid all the expenses of cartage, the aeroplane would not have gone beyond Lydd, where it was arranged originally for the experiments to take place . . . All that ingenuity, experience, and mechanical skill can devise has been brought into operation but another £5,000 or £6,000 is wanted to ensure a definite triumph.

A further £5,000 to gain mastery of the air for Britain and the Empire might not seem a great deal of money. It was, though, twice the amount the War Office had allocated for all experiments with powered flight. Lieutenant Gibbs tried to fly the biplane glider but it buried its nose into the ground at take-off. The two wrecked machines went back into their packing cases. The party returned to Farnborough. Richard Haldane was not impressed.

In 1908 the Wright Brothers, tired of European claims they were charlatans, decided to silence the doubters. Wilbur Wright, with their improved Model A flying machine, arrived in Europe. In early September, the Blair Atholl experiments resumed with some urgency, because the Americans had to be beaten. In contrast to the previous year, Dunne's team made notes of their efforts. Once again, they tried out both machines as gliders. Convinced they had a winning design, they fixed the engines to the aeroplane. Efficiency was not the main characteristic of the Buchet: the 12-horsepower output of each engine shrank to a total of 16 horsepower when the two ran together, partly because of inefficient propellers, partly because each crankshaft spindle had two pulleys with belts. These led outwards to a propeller and inwards to a large flywheel. Swinging the flywheel started the engines. It proved extremely difficult to persuade both engines to run at the same time.

Dunne's biplane had garnered a real undercarriage that used bicycle forks and castored pairs of oil sprung wheels. The pilot sat on the lower wing and used 'elevons' to climb and descend with separate levers for turning right or left. Gibbs returned as the pilot, and by the end of October, the Dunne aeroplane made several jumps and hops. In December, it finally bounced into the air, flew just above the grass for

40 yards and returned smartly to earth. A mere three months earlier, Wilbur Wright had flown the Model A for 1 hour 31 minutes and 25 seconds.

Haldane promptly turned off the money tap, since he hated inefficiency. He felt that Dunne, Capper and the Balloon Factory were bumbling amateurs and that academic science and rational principles were the way to produce an aeroplane. He claimed that Germany 'was building up the structure of an Air Service on a foundation of science'. Dunne's experiments cost the public £2,500. In Haldane's admired Germany, the Government had spent £400,000 on aviation in the same period.

Haldane tightened his grip on the development of military aviation. He was a member of a newly formed sub-committee of the Committee of Imperial Defence. This was charged with reporting on 'the dangers to which we should be exposed on sea or on land by any development in aerial navigation reasonably probable in the near future'. It was also to investigate the advantages of aeroplanes and airships as well as decide how much should be spent on aerial experiments and who should conduct them, which all suited Haldane very well.

With much guile and careful planning, Haldane moved the committee his way. The Balloon Factory at Farnborough was re-cast to Haldane's own design. Capper hung on until 1910, while Dunne received his marching orders. He was no scientific engineer and suffered accordingly. He later did build aeroplanes that flew, and flew well, but he was firmly a civilian without War Office attachments.

Scotland's connection with military flying did not end with the departure of John Dunne. As a sport or hobby, it may have been a rich man's pastime but there were Scots who took to the skies like born-again birds. Captain Bertram Dickson was one. Born in Edinburgh on the day of the winter solstice, 21 December 1873, Dickson became a second lieutenant in the Royal Horse Artillery, the cream of the British Army's gunners, in November 1894. Three years later, his promotion to lieutenant appeared in the *London Gazette*.

In 1899, Dickson was in South Africa, fighting in the Boer War, where he caught typhoid fever. Lucky to survive, he recovered in time to command the Royal Horse Artillery detachment at the opening of the very first Australian Parliament by the Duke of York on 9 May 1901. That same year, Dickson, newly promoted to captain, was selected for 'special service' and was posted to Mombasa, where he served on a boundary commission in Patagonia, hunted big game in East Africa and went on to Kurdistan. Detached for service with the Foreign Office, as British Consul at Van in Eastern Turkey, Dickson appraised the local situation with a military eye. He produced detailed reports, as good political officers did, on everything he thought would interest sharp minds in Whitehall. Dickson travelled, spending time on the Persian Frontier, until worsening health finally forced him back to Europe.

The summer of 1909 brought Captain Bertram Dickson to aviation for Europe buzzed with excitement at flying exploits. He went to a widely advertised aviation show at Reims, which enthralled him. Not being short of the occasional shilling, he bought a Farman biplane, because, as he explained, the clear air above ground would improve his physical condition. On 19 April 1910 Captain Bertram Dickson of Edinburgh became the first Scot to gain an aviator's certificate, Aero Club de France Certificate Number 71, awarded on 12 May 1910. With the certificate, he was able to enter flying meetings himself. Dickson won first prize at Tours in his Farman, powered by a 50-horsepower Gnôme engine. He beat the local French competitors to such effect that he also collected the Schneider Cup, a handsome prize donated by a wealthy businessman, himself a pilot and balloonist. Victor Schneider subsequently inaugurated the Schneider Trophy for seaplanes.

The Scottish artilleryman had won the first important international prize gained by a Briton, and less than a month later, on 6 June 1910, he set a world duration record by flying 61 miles. As Dickson was still on sick leave, in receipt of full pay, his exploits did not endear him to the Treasury. On 3 August 1910 Dickson left the Army on half pay.

Three days later, the captain was a star performer at the first Scottish International Aviation Meeting at Lanark. More than 250,000 people flocked to see 22 aviators from Europe and the United States. Even more exotically, Jorge Chavez, a Peruvian, took part in his Blériot XI. The meeting was doubly exciting for 15-year-old Grahame Donald, son of a local doctor. The aviator Samuel Cody, whose machine did not fly too well, actually stayed in Lanark as the doctor's guest. Donald was hooked.

Dickson – the 'Flying Scot', as one journalist inevitably called him – had struck up a close association with the Bristol and Colonial Aircraft Company. In September 1910 he was placed on the Reserve of Officers, a useful move just days before the Autumn Manoeuvres began. The two traditional enemies, Redland and Blueland, engaged in an epic struggle across much of Salisbury Plain. The Bristol Company had established itself on the plain itself, at Larkhill. As the national press reported on the annual exercise at length, and the company wanted publicity and War Office contracts, it was no surprise that Captain Bertram Dickson, helpfully equipped with a Bristol Boxkite, offered his services to the army. Whether officialdom agreed is doubtful, but what is certain is that Dickson flew a reconnaissance on behalf of Red Force.

The Boxkite was an improved version of Dickson's own Farman. The pilot sat unprotected, exposed to wind, rain, snow and sun, in a chair on the lower wing. Dickson made his flight on the chill autumn morning of 21 September. He found the Blue Army, advancing steadily between Amesbury and Salisbury, and returned to report their position to the Red headquarters. Airborne once more, he found the 'enemy', saw a nearby house with an interesting telephone wire leading from it, and landed in the adjacent field to report his news. Corporal Arthur Edwards of the North Somerset Yeomanry, part of the Blue Army, took action:

Soon the Boxkite again appeared, circled overhead and landed two fields away from us. We immediately galloped over, and although too late to stop Captain Dickson from 'phoning information to his Headquarters, were able to capture the aircraft, so putting it out of action until the operation was over.

Dickson's exploit attracted much comment. Later that afternoon, the Home Secretary, one Winston S. Churchill, who was at the manoeuvres in a curiously undefined capacity, turned up to look at the Boxkite and speak with Dickson. Churchill, as was his wont, wore a uniform, appearing as a major of the Oxfordshire Yeomanry.

The newspapers buzzed with comment. In London, Robert Loraine, a well-known actor and ardent pilot who was the first to fly across the Irish Sea, at once offered his services to the Blue Force. Lieutenant Louis Lancelot Gibbs, now an officer in the Royal Field Artillery, appeared with a Farman aeroplane to join Dickson. Colonel John Capper arrived with the *Beta* non-rigid airship to help Loraine. Despite excited comment in the press, the aviators achieved little, since inexperience and bad weather combined to reduce their efforts to a token. As a colonel sniffily wrote later, 'one or two aeroplanes that had nominally shared in the proceedings had played no practical part in the campaign, either strategically or tactically. Alike by the forces engaged and by the spectators, they had been regarded as interesting curiosities'.

Dickson left England to head for the Milano Circuito Aereo Internazionale, or Milan Aviation Meeting. Bertram was invited as a famous aviator to demonstrate a gliding descent without power, a technique generally regarded as hideously dangerous. On 2 October he took off to entertain the crowd, climbing high above the throng before switching off the engine. He did not see the Antoinette of a Frenchman, René Thomas, below him. Thomas did not look upwards and the two aircraft hit each other in the first mid-air collision in history. Both men survived but the Scotsman received serious injuries.

Dickson died at Loch Rosque Castle on 28 September 1913. Most ascribed his death to the delayed effects of the Milan crash but the cause was, officially, a stroke. He lies at Cnoc na Bhain near Achnasheen, a tiny settlement 40 miles north-west of Inverness, beneath a regular low-flying route for today's military aircrew.

2

Faltering Footsteps

The *Daily Mail* had no doubts. On 11 July 1908 its headlines bellowed a stark and terrible warning:

COMMAND OF THE AIR
GERMANY AS THE AERIAL POWER
TEUTONIC VISION
A LANDING OF 350,000 MEN

Frederick Wile, an American journalist, represented Lord Northcliffe's newspaper in Berlin. His sensational article came from an interview with Rudolf Martin, a principal adviser to the Kaiser and the German Government. Martin nursed a dislike of Britain – to which, in common with many Europeans, he habitually referred as 'England' – and boasted to the American:

In a world war, Germany would have to spend two hundred millions sterling in motor-airships, and a similar amount in aeroplanes, to transport 350,000 men in half an hour during the night from Calais to Dover. Even today the landing of a large German army in England is a mere matter of money. I am opposed to a war between Germany and England, but should it break out today, it would last at least two years, for we would conclude no peace until a German army had occupied London.

In my judgement it would take two years for us to build motor-airships enough simultaneously to throw 350,000 men into Dover via Calais. During the same night, of course, a second transport of 350,000 men could follow.

Martin further claimed the latest Zeppelins could carry 100 men. The invasion force therefore needed 3,500 airships. The two-year production schedule required five airships to be made every day, a task beyond even the German manufacturing colossus.

Other newspapers jumped into the debate despite the dubious arithmetic. Journalists referred ominously to the estimated 50,000 German waiters in the country, many of whom apparently worked at hotels near railway stations. German landlords ran public houses close to British military camps. German officers in plain clothes were said to skulk around the country with binoculars and sketch pads recording 'every inch of our surface through a military microscope'. General Sir William Nicholson, Chief of the Imperial General Staff, had no truck with such alarmist nonsense. The *Daily Mail* for 23 July 1908 carried a semi-official riposte:

In the highest military circles in Great Britain it is accepted that so far airships are a failure.

The military authorities have had experts employed in watching the flights of the various airships and aeroplanes, and the impression is that for a long time to come there is nothing to be feared from them . . .

The Army Council is . . . thoroughly aware of all that is taking place both on the Continent and in America in aerostatics.

Consultations have been held at the War Office with expert artillerists as to how aerial attacks can be best met, and the plan of campaign in which the principal feature will be the use of high-angle fire with high-explosive shells has been evolved.

The military authorities point to the fact that nowhere has any machine designed for flight in the air proved effective . . . All this points to a lack of practical working in the various designs . . . When it is possible to cross the Channel, say with a party of excursionists, and to land at any fixed point, the War Office may be prepared to regard recent experiments seriously.

The public was temporarily reassured, believing the authorities knew what to do. And if the statement ignored the Wright Brothers, so be it, since they were Americans and a long way away.

On Sunday 25 July 1909, just one year and two days after the War Office had dismissed aeroplanes out of hand, Louis Blériot flew from

Calais to the Northfall Cliffs at Dover. As usual, a man from the *Daily Mail* was on hand to interview the policeman who had heard a whirring noise above his head:

> I looked up and saw something like a huge butterfly dart across the sky. I telephoned to the police station, and then ran as hard as I could. I came across the flying man in the meadow and he shook my hand in both of his. It was wonderful.

The 37-year-old Frenchman was not a cheap flight day-tripper; even so, blushes covered the War Office face. Nicholson allegedly proclaimed that flying was 'a useless and expensive fad, advocated by a few individuals whose ideas are unworthy of attention'. The First Sea Lord, Sir Arthur Knyvet Wilson, reputedly concluded that the Admiralty's aeroplane requirement would be two machines.

The War Office, however, took action in 1911. The Balloon Factory, headed by Mervyn Joseph Pius O'Gorman, Haldane's chosen replacement for Colonel John Capper, became the Army Aircraft Factory with the extra responsibility of giving some experience to officers interested in flying. Shortly afterwards, Whitehall authorised an Air Battalion of 14 officers and 176 men. Officers from any regiment were invited to volunteer for the new unit. The necessary RE sappers, volunteers or otherwise, transferred to aeronautical duties. Although the authorities had already conceded that officers might learn to fly at their own expense, the Air Battalion insisted on a six month probationary period to test their aptitude.

Britain's first air arm had a headquarters and two self-contained companies. One looked after kites and balloons. The other handled aeroplanes. To the delight of the more sceptical military minds, the Air Battalion officially formed on All Fools Day 1911. The Admiralty quickly set up a rival Naval Air Organisation. They established a flying school, conveniently close to the coast at Eastchurch in Kent, which opened in November 1911.

From the very beginning, the Air Battalion suffered from a lack of trained pilots, observers and aeroplanes. It had a mere 12 aircraft, in a mixture of types, that were slow and often dangerous. In contrast, the French Army already employed over 200 aeroplanes for the control of artillery fire, aerial reconnaissance and photography.

As part of its ongoing experiments, a balloon detachment of the Air Battalion had arrived at St Andrews in the summer of 1911. With a keen eye for the ground, they set up camp in Tentsmuir Forest near Leuchars. Military aviation had returned to Scotland.

Criticism grew, since British aerial strength was clearly inferior to that of other nations. The Government came under increasing pressure. As hard-pressed politicians often do, they referred the whole question elsewhere. It went to the standing sub-committee of the Committee of Imperial Defence, chaired by Haldane, now a Viscount. The committee was 'to consider the future development of aerial navigation both for Naval and Military purposes, the means which might be taken to secure . . . an efficient Air Service, and also whether steps should be taken to form a corps of aviators for Naval and Military purposes, or otherwise to co-ordinate the study of aviation in the Navy and Army'.

The Flying Corps Committee, as it was rapidly called, got to work without delay. It comprised Colonel John Edward Bernard Seely, chairman, a former yeomanry officer and Boer War veteran turned politician, Brigadier General David Henderson, a Glaswegian whose early service was with the Argyll and Sutherland Highlanders, Captain Frederick Hugh Sykes, a cavalryman in the 15th Hussars, and Major Duncan Sayre MacInnes of the Royal Engineers, a Canadian of Scottish ancestry. Henderson enjoyed the distinction of being the oldest qualified pilot in the world. He held Royal Aero Club Certificate 118 which he gained weeks earlier at the age of 49. Sykes, too, was a pilot. He held Certificate 96.

Colonel Seely had no illusions. Under pressure to produce a swift report, he told his fellow board members: 'At the present time in this country we have, as far as I know, of actual flying men in the Army about eleven, and of actual flying men in the Navy about eight, and France has about two hundred and sixty-three, so we are what you might call behind.'

Four principles guided the committee. Any new organisation should make use of all the country's aeronautical resources; it should not only meet immediate needs but be sufficiently flexible to allow for expansion; that both the Army and the Navy required an adequate supply of properly trained pilots; that the new technology should embrace private manufacturing companies because, just as the Royal Navy needed private shipyards, so an air service needed a vibrant aircraft industry. With these clear signposts to mark the way, the committee called for evidence.

Captain Bertram Dickson, injured, unable to fly, responded. He foresaw, in the event of war, that each side would use aircraft not only for reconnaissance but to stop their enemy from getting information.

This would lead to 'a war in the air, for the supremacy of the air, by armed aeroplanes against each other'.

The committee produced its recommendations. It proposed a new and independent service, the Flying Corps, with a Naval Wing and a Military Wing. There should be a Central Flying School to instruct all service aviators. The Army Air Factory should serve both wings under the new name of the Royal Aircraft Factory. Finally, a permanent 'Air Committee' should be formed with representatives from the Royal Navy and the Army. The Cabinet approved the proposals in early April 1912, with no reference to Parliament and without a vote. King George V accordingly signed the Royal Flying Corps into being on 13 April 1912.

The idea of a separate service found no support amongst the senior officers of the Army and the Navy. The Admiralty quickly went its own way. Egged on by the enthusiastic civilian First Lord, Winston Churchill, the Navy established the headquarters of the Naval Wing at Eastchurch alongside their Flying School. The Admiralty soon dropped the title 'Royal Flying Corps – Naval Wing' from official documents and unilaterally invented the 'Royal Naval Air Service'. Not even the Cabinet was asked for approval when the Admiralty formalised the name on 1 July 1914.

The Military Wing soon became simply the Royal Flying Corps. With no responsibility for aeroplanes in proximity to ships, the RFC went its own way. The idea of an independent service vanished entirely and the War Office first placed the RFC under the Directorate of Military Training. They then created a separate Directorate of Military Aeronautics in September 1913. The RFC retained a quasi-independence in financial affairs under its Director, Brigadier General David Henderson, instead of the Financial Member of the Army Council.

Born on 11 August 1862, Henderson was the youngest son of David Henderson, a shipbuilder, and his wife, Jane Pitcairn. Although he studied engineering at Glasgow University, he joined the Army in 1883. After action in the Sudan in 1898, he saw more active service in the South African War. Wounded during the Siege of Ladysmith, he eventually became Lord Kitchener's director of military intelligence. He revamped the system, collating all reports to compile, on a daily basis, a map of the distribution of enemy forces.

In 1903 he went to the War Office. His book, *Field Intelligence: Its Principles and Practice*, which appeared in 1904, greatly enhanced his reputation. He followed this in 1907 with *The Art of Reconnaissance*, a title that became a training manual. In 1911, Henderson gained his pilot's certificate. With the zeal of the convert, he became a passionate believer in air power and the use of aircraft in reconnaissance. When he took over the military wing, he controlled recruitment, training, and equipment. The one-time engineering student had to turn the new organisation into a credible military force.

Permanent bases were an immediate priority. The Flying Corps Committee had decreed that the Squadron, with three flights of four aircraft each, was the operational unit of the Flying Corps. The Military Wing had an establishment of seven aeroplane squadrons and one airship and man-carrying kite squadron. They all required landing grounds with a quota of cooks, mechanics and clerks. Everyone needed a bed, a roof over the head and something to eat.

The RFC created twelve 'Air Stations'. Most were located close to Army garrisons in the South of England. One, though, served Scotland. Montrose, fifteen miles north of Arbroath, became the first permanent Scottish military aerodrome. On 26 February 1913 the first aeroplanes arrived. Number 2 Squadron came north from Farnborough to settle first in temporary lodgings at Upper Dysart to the south of the town before they moved to Broomfield in January 1914.

The squadron commander, Major Charles Burke, decided that five of the squadron's aeroplanes would fly from Farnborough to Montrose. In what became an endurance test, five aircraft set out on 13 February 1913 when Captain Charles Alexander Holcombe Longcroft and Captain John Becke, both in BE2a aircraft, and Captain George Dawes, Lieutenant Francis Waldron and Lieutenant Philip William Lee Herbert in Maurice Farman Longhorns clambered into the air. Their 450-mile journey took 13 days. They were followed every mile of the way by a collection of mechanics in motor lorries.

Their first stop was at Towcester. Only Becke arrived on time. Longcroft landed at Littlemore, near Oxford. Unable to find accommodation, he spent the night at the local lunatic asylum. Eventually, all the aircraft arrived at Towcester, from whence they set out for Newark and York. At both places, they signed autographs or posed for photographs. By 22 February, the five aviators were en route for Newcastle. However, fog and haze hampered navigation and only two aircraft made it to the landing-ground at Gosforth Park. Even they had to land several times to ask for directions of a nature that advised them to 'turn right at the Red Lion and follow the road to the Black Horse'. The directions were simple enough to follow on the ground but more difficult from the air. They reached Edinburgh on 25 February and Montrose the following day. Both times, the pilots and the ground crew received a tumultuous reception as well as 'liberal entertainment'.

Number 2 – 'Second To None' – was the first aeroplane squadron in the whole Royal Flying Corps and proud of it. While Number 1 Squadron messed about with airships, balloons and kites, not proper flying machines at all, the officers and men at Montrose set about proving aeroplanes were more than toys. The squadron, like all the others in the RFC, trained for the reconnaissance role. Generally reckoned to be a better leader of men than he was a pilot, Major Burke determined his squadron would be the top of the class. Burke was not especially popular and few rated him as clever. He was, though, personally brave and indifferent to ridicule with a single-minded tenacity. He became widely known for his 'maxims': some were general, others dealt specifically with flying. 'Waiting about on an aerodrome,' Burke opined, 'has spoilt more pilots than everything else put together.'

With a mixture of aircraft, the squadron established its reputation with a series of headline-catching flights. They flew about 1,000 miles a week. Their BE2 aircraft came from a design created by the Royal Aircraft Factory. Lieutenant Dunne's philosophy lived on for the BE2, soon to be universally known as the 'Quirk', was stable and generally well tempered. It flew amiably enough with the pilot's hands away from the controls and was ideal, everyone believed, for reconnaissance work.

On 19 August 1913 Captain Charles Longcroft broke the British record for a flight in a straight line with a passenger, covering the 287 miles from Farnborough to Montrose, non-stop. His companion was the commander of the Military Wing, Lieutenant Colonel Frederick Sykes, one of the members of the sub-committee that recommended the formation of the RFC. A special fuel tank under the front cockpit gave the BE2a enough endurance to stay in the air for 7 hours and 40 minutes.

Two weeks later, on 2 September 1913, Longcroft led five machines across the Irish Sea to Rathbone Camp at Limerick. For the first time, a unit of the Royal Flying Corps flew overseas. Cylindrical air bags were fitted under the wings as a crude form of flotation gear but they did nothing to improve the BE2's hardly vigorous performance. At sea level, unburdened with air bags, the BE could manage a maximum of 70 miles per hour with a climb rate of less than 1,000 feet every minute.

The Army Aircraft Factory licensed production of the BE2 to private manufacturers, amongst them the Bristol and Colonial Company that had employed Bertram Dickson. One of their aeroplanes, 218, Longcroft's usual aircraft, was extensively modified to take a 54-gallon fuel tank. Designed by Air Mechanic First-Class H. C. S. Bullock it fitted into the front cockpit where the observer normally sat. A special fairing reduced wind resistance. With this, on 22 November 1913, Longcroft broke his previous record by flying 650 miles without landing, from Montrose to Portsmouth and then to Farnborough. The Royal Aero Club awarded him the Britannia Trophy for the 'most meritorious flight of 1913'.

Number 2 Squadron flew in every kind of weather, and a popular pastime, when the wind was high, was the 'tortoise race'. The squadron had some Maurice Farman biplanes on charge which were slow and under-powered and which actually went backwards if pointed into a fierce wind. The pilot blown back the fastest or furthest over a given course was the winner. With aircraft like these, it was no surprise when a Parliamentary Commission found that a large proportion of the aircraft available were unsuitable for military purposes.

Despite their imperfect aircraft, the squadron trained hard. Many of the ground crew were given familiarisation flights; warrant officers and non-commissioned officers received flying instruction. With an insight ahead of its time, BE2a 228 flew with dual controls, possibly the first military aircraft to have them. A popular training run involved the 30-mile trip south to St Andrews, across the Firth of Tay, where a three-mile stretch of firm, level sand proved ideal for practising take-offs and landings. The local garage was happy enough to supply petrol against signature – one of Burke's Maxims was that prompt payment of small tradesmen was essential – although spectators wandering in front of approaching aircraft were a constant hazard.

Desmond Lucius Arthur, a grey-eyed Irishman with jet-black hair, an officer in the Royal Munster Fusiliers, joined 2 Squadron on 17 April 1913. He qualified as a pilot at Brooklands, gaining Royal Aero Club certificate 233, on 18 June 1912. After this, he went to the Central Flying School. At the end of the course, with a total of 25 hours' flying time, the pilot joined his squadron.

On the morning of 27 May 1913, Arthur climbed into the wood and fabric BE2a, distinguished from every other 'Quirk' in the squadron only by the number painted on the tail. It was a rare beast for 205 was truly an Army Aircraft Factory aeroplane. Built there, it was briefly the prototype BE5 before alteration back to BE2 standard. In its service, it had enjoyed the benefit of three different engines.

The BE2a climbed out over Lunan Bay and thirty minutes later, spectators saw 205 descend in a serene 360-degree spiral. Desmond Arthur then began a right hand turn, still descending. The upper right wing collapsed, the varnished wooden struts gave way and wing fabric fluttered as the BE2 jerked in the air. Some claimed to see a puff of smoke as the engine note accelerated.

The collapsed wing pitched the aircraft fiercely nose down. Arthur, a dark shape with flailing arms and legs, fell away from the wreckage. The aircraft crashed some 160 yards from where its pilot hit the ground, 200 yards from Lunan Bay Station. It was a long way down and aviators fell only once – nobody wore a parachute in 1913.

The Royal Aero Club's Public Safety and Accidents Investigation Committee quickly reached an inescapable conclusion. The main rear spar, about 12 inches from the wingtip, broke in flight. The fracture probably happened because of careless ground handling. The wing might have banged against a hangar door or dropped when it was being moved in the workshop or being fitted back onto the aircraft.

Worse, the wing collapsed because of a botched, shoddy repair that was both unauthorised and concealed. A 7½-inch-long taper splice held the broken spar in place. Thinly, inadequately glued, it was held in place with a whipcord binding. Any competent tradesman would then varnish the binding or treat it with cobbler's wax, but this was not done and a patch of new fabric simply covered the mend. In effect, somebody had broken the wing spar through carelessness and instead of taking the rap, the culprit cobbled a repair to conceal the damage.

Arthur's death clouded the squadron. Its pilots knew, however, that there is rarely time to overly mourn the departed: it serves little purpose and the dead do not return. In the way of those who follow a calling in which life is fragile, the pilots attributed the accident to the machinations of Isaac in reference to the good Doctor Newton, apple-watcher, mathematician, part-time alchemist, inventor of the cat flap and Member of Parliament whose sole contribution to democratic debate was a request that a window be opened. To the RFC, his 'mathematical principles of natural philosophy' could be neatly condensed – 'what goes up must come down'.

The Admiralty viewed aeroplanes differently from the Army. The premise was startlingly uncomplicated: the British Army did not fight on home soil, a position that it enjoyed by courtesy of the Royal Navy who defended Great Britain. By extension, defending the country against air assault was the Navy's job, not the Army's. The Admiralty considered that defence was not merely a matter of large numbers of grey-painted ships sailing back and forth along the three-mile limit. In time of war, Britain's defences began at the enemy coast. The admirals knew the best form of defence is attack.

The Royal Naval Air Service immediately applied the doctrine to military aviation. As a first step, in October 1912, the Admiralty started a chain of seaplane and airship stations along the eastern coast. Eastchurch was an obvious start. The Navy steadily worked its way northward. In the first months of 1913, Cromarty became the first seaplane station in Scotland. With only three aircraft, it operated more on enthusiasm than on great numbers.

On 1 January 1914 the Admiralty assumed control of all service airships. The Military Wing's 1 Squadron thankfully handed over its dirigibles and man-lifting kites and converted to aeroplanes. The pre-1914 Navy claimed that airships offered considerable advantages over contemporary aeroplanes, since they remained airborne longer, had a longer range and carried heavy wireless equipment for transmitting and receiving messages. Airships could drop bombs and use machine-guns, a task beyond the aeroplane crews. In 1909, the Treasury agreed £35,000 for the construction of an airship to challenge the German Zeppelins. The Admiralty accepted a tender from Vickers of Barrow-in-Furness on 7 May 1909. Work began in immense secrecy and almost two years to the day, the huge airship was brought out to her mooring mast at Cavendish Dock. She was popularly called the *Mayfly* with no apparent irony.

His Majesty's Naval Airship Number One measured 512 feet in length with a diameter of 48 feet to give a capacity of 663,518 cubic feet. It took 46,000 square yards of watertight silk fabric to cover the frame of duraluminum alloy that contained 17 rubberised fabric gas-bags that held the ship's hydrogen. It was driven by 2 Wolseley motors, each of 180-horsepower. Control was exercised by a collection of vertical and horizontal rudders at her stern.

She remained at her mast for four days then passed her mooring tests after which, still moored, she underwent her engine trials. It became horribly clear she was too heavy for her engines to lift her into the air and she went back into her shed. On 24 September 1911, she emerged once more into the daylight. A beam-side gust of wind laid her over but she righted and the handling crew pivoted the ship to point her nose back towards the dock. A moment passed before a sharp, sudden cracking noise amidships announced she had broken her back as she took the shape of an inverted letter 'V'. When the crew in the aft gondola dived overboard, the stern shot upwards. One senior officer, gazing on the wreckage, commented simply, 'It is the work of a lunatic.' His remark is understandable.

The RNAS experiments with aeroplanes continued. They fitted floats to several of the machines to practise landing and taking-off at sea, close to ships. At Rosyth, in 1912, they spent hours attempting to detect submarines from the air in the murky tidal waters of the Firth. The naval aviators experimented with bombing. They investigated methods of bringing down airships, generally regarded as the most likely machines to attack Britain.

The Royal Navy cherished the idea of flying aeroplanes directly from ships and the very first such flight came on 10 January 1912. Lieutenant Charles Samson trundled his Short S38 along a wooden ramp built on the forecastle of the battleship HMS *Africa*. After a run of 100 feet, Samson got airborne from the anchored vessel. The ramp then went to a sister ship, HMS *Hibernia*. Samson repeated the feat on 2 May 1912 while the battleship steamed into wind. The well-used ramp continued its progress to HMS *London*. On 4 July, Lieutenant Cecil 'Molly' Malone took off after a 25-feet run as *London* nosed into a force 3 wind.

Samson and Malone had shown it was possible to take off from a ship although nobody could land on one. William Beardmore & Company of Glasgow had the answer. They submitted a plan for a 'Parent Ship for naval aeroplanes'. Beardmore's design visualised a ship of 15,000 tons, some 430 feet long with a deck that would be 110 feet wide. On each side of the deck, a 220-feet-long hangar, 30 feet wide, would take 3 aircraft. The forecastle would have 140 feet of unobstructed deck for take-offs. Landings would be made on 70 feet of free space on the quarterdeck.

James Graham, the Montrose heir and a director of the company, inspired much of the design. Despite his considerable influence, the Scottish blueprint for the world's first aircraft carrier never made it past the Admiralty. One major problem was the wasted space in the two hangars, since aeroplane stowage took up an inordinate amount of room and nobody had built an aeroplane with folding wings. The Beardmore design was doomed when their Lordships contemplated the expense of building a specialised ship before anybody had proper experience of operating aeroplanes at sea.

The Admiralty compromised and adapted HMS *Hermes* as a parent ship for the RNAS. Suitably modified, she carried two seaplanes on her quarterdeck while a 100-feet-long forecastle ramp allowed an aircraft to take off. Recommissioned on 7 May 1913, *Hermes* spent a mere nine months in her unusual role. After that, her forecastle ramp came off and she reverted to her role as a cruiser.

Graham's design came out of the Admiralty safe during the First World War. On 6 October 1916 work began to build the world's first complete naval aircraft carrier in the world. An unfinished hull at Beardmore's Dalmuir yard, on which Graham had, coincidentally, based his original conception, eventually emerged as HMS *Argus*. Launched on 2 December 1917, she served for 29 years and 3 days.

At the beginning of 1914, six coastal air stations guarded Britain. Scotland's single station, Cromarty, was joined by Dundee in April 1914. The defence of the realm against air attack was in a parlous state. The RNAS had only two aeroplanes and one airship actually fitted with a machine gun. One of those, a Lewis gun, was on loan from a retired army officer. All other aircraft made do with a rifle. The only other suggested means of destroying a German airship from the air was to drop a grenade on it – but few of these existed. At Hendon, designated as the station to defend London, the armoury had only twelve grenades for use.

From 18 to 22 July 1914, King George V reviewed the Fleet at Spithead. Nearly all the RNAS aircraft available, something less than 30, took part in a mass fly past, supplemented by 3 airships. They flew low over the ranks of warships, an act that encouraged some spectators to believe aircraft did not fly high. After the review, the RNAS dispersed to its bases. On 29 July they received instructions that scouting and patrolling were secondary to the defence of the country. They had 130 officers, some 700 men, 39 landplanes, 52 seaplanes and 7 airships with which to fight the enemy.

As July stuttered into August, Winston Churchill ordered mobilisation of the Grand Fleet. By the time German cavalry trotted across the Belgian border, the Grand Fleet was snug in harbour at Scapa Flow with a penny packet of aircraft at Cromarty. Scotland was a backwater in the two years that followed the formation of the two wings of the Royal Flying Corps. Only three military bases operated in the country. That would change. The Great War had arrived.

3

Experiments and Experience

The outbreak of war sent 2 Squadron hurrying south. Major Burke, with his customary precision, had orders for just such an emergency. Each pilot should carry a revolver, a roll of tools, a water-bottle containing boiled water, a spare pair of goggles, a small stove, some biscuits and cold meat, a packet of 'soup-making material' and a pair of binoculars.

The squadron set off on 3 August and after some en-route excitements, all aircraft safely reached Dover. The ground crews and squadron transport left Montrose by rail on the morning of 8 August and they arrived that evening at Govan, close to Glasgow. Men and stores boarded the ss *Dogra* for Boulogne.

Lieutenant Hubert Dunsterville Harvey-Kelly of the squadron became the first RFC pilot to arrive in France when he landed at Amiens at 0820 on 13 August 1914. Amongst the squadron pilots, three came from Scottish regiments. Captain Alexander Ross-Hume was a Cameronian, the Argyll and Sutherland Highlanders supplied Lieutenant Dudley Crosbie while Lieutenant Claud Farie had moved to the Flying Corps from the Highland Light Infantry.

The Royal Flying Corps, under the command of Brigadier General Sir David Henderson, KCB, DSO, went to war with 105 officers, 755 men, 63 aeroplanes and 4 vehicles. The numbers included not only a Headquarters, Numbers 2, 3, 4 and 5 Squadrons; Henderson also had an 'Aircraft Park', to serve as the travelling base of the squadrons with 12 officers, 162 men, 4 motorcycles and 12 spare aeroplanes.

Once 2 Squadron left for France, a deserted Montrose waited. The departed officers had fastened their room doors with sealing wax and on every door a notice instructed that nothing should be disturbed while the occupant was away at the war. Montrose was not alone, as in the whole country a mere 116 machines remained. Only 20 aircraft at the Central Flying School were usable and the scrap heap beckoned for the rest.

The RFC ordered large quantities of the very latest version of the BE. The BE2c was, like its immediate predecessors, inherently stable in flight but with a marginally better performance. At sea level, with a 70-horsepower Renault engine roaring at full throttle, the BE2c managed an exhilarating 75 miles per hour, but unfortunately, it was still in the prototype stage.

The Royal Aircraft Factory Drawing Office hastily completed the plans and contracts for 178 machines went to Bristol, Vickers and Armstrong-Whitworth. A rapid follow-up order went to companies that had no experience with aeroplanes. These included the respectable firm of G. & J. Weir of Glasgow, founded in 1873 by the brothers George and James Weir as a marine engineering and maintenance company. In 1914, its managing director was William George Weir, James's son, born in a top flat on 12 May 1877 at Albert Crescent, Crosshill, Glasgow.

A family connection to Robert Burns, albeit by a liaison on the wrong side of the blanket, had not produced a dreamy-eyed poet. He was a shrewd and hard-headed businessman whose ideas about industrial relations can be politely described as robust. He fervently believed in payment by results, an attitude that became anathema to the burgeoning Socialism of his workers. Dismissive of collective bargaining, Weir saw no earthly reason why others did not follow his own example of hard work and self-sufficiency.

At the age of sixteen, Weir entered the family firm and five years later, he became a director. Another four years elapsed before he became managing director at the advanced age of twenty-five. The company bloomed and blossomed, aided by its patents on such engineering marvels as a feed-pump, and by Weir's spectacular skills. His workers may not have loved him but he pushed the business into pole position when it came to the making and selling of condensers, fire pumps, bilge pumps, feed pumps, oil pumps, air-pumps, evaporators and distilling machinery. A ruthless dedication to standardisation, his own determination and tenacity allied with a prodigious appetite for work ensured competitors trailed in Weir's wake. The company were no stranger to military contracts and in 1913, two-thirds of their work was involved with warships. Building aeroplanes was simply another job to be done, and

Weir himself relished the challenge. By the end of the war, G. & J. Weir had assembled 1,427 aeroplanes.

In 1913 William Beardmore & Company Limited bought a licence to make the 120-horsepower Austro-Daimler aero-engine. They tooled up in time to meet the demands of war. By 1915 Beardmore's had increased the engine's performance to 160 horsepower. In due course they turned out over 2,500 of the standard engine as well as working on further variants. Shortly before August 1914 Beardmore's forked out for another licence, this time for the Deutsche Flugzeuge Werke seaplane. Hostilities intervened. The aircraft was never made but the experience netted contracts to build military aeroplanes. Production began at Dalmuir in the first months of 1915.

The Battle of Mons on 20 August 1914, followed by the fierce fight at Le Cateau and the slow, desperate retreat to the Marne, changed British ideas about a quick and easy victory. Kitchener, aware like the canny Sir Douglas Haig, that the war was destined to be long and bitter, issued his call for volunteers. By early 1915, Kitchener's Army had 30 divisions. To support them, the Directorate of Military Aeronautics decided the RFC needed 50 new squadrons, an estimate which met with incredulity in Whitehall. The memorandum reached Kitchener, and he scrawled across it, 'Double this. K.' The financial tap turned on fully, but air forces are not produced overnight. They need machines, men, pilots, observers, mechanics, clerks and cooks.

For the RNAS, the situation was a little different. Their prime task was the defence of Britain, although few believed in a mass attack by German airships. Rudolf Martin's wild predictions, so trumpeted in the *Daily Mail*, proved hollow when war actually came. The combined might of the German Army and Naval Airship Divisions came to a definite eleven machines. Only seven could be used for warlike operations.

In September 1914 the Admiralty formally assumed responsibility for protecting the country against air raids and Winston Churchill immediately issued typical instructions. The RNAS was:

1 to attack enemy aircraft and airships as close as possible to their point of departure as well as at their bases;
2 to provide an intercepting force of aircraft on the east coast;
3 to concentrate anti-aircraft defence at vulnerable points of a military nature rather than round towns;
4 to defend London and other large towns by a black-out.

Pre-war decisions added extra tasks to the RNAS role. A clear need existed for tactical reconnaissance of the enemy fleet albeit the bases were two hundred miles across the sea. The war could be lost or won if Sir John Jellicoe, commanding the Grand Fleet, had no knowledge or, worse, wrong information about the enemy should they put to sea. In an ideal world, the RNAS would have the aircraft for the job in hand, but they did not.

Military flying expanded slowly during the first few months of the conflict. Aviation may have gone to war but warfare had hardly come to flying and air combats were relatively infrequent. When they did occur, they were matters of rifle shots exchanged between opposing reconnaissance aircraft. The importance of aeroplanes steadily grew for tasks such as observation, artillery co-operation, photography and bombing. Both sides tried to shoot down their inquisitive opponents by anti-aircraft fire, a chancy procedure that gobbled up enormous amounts of ammunition. The idea of destroying them in air-to-air combat took time to develop, as neither fighting aeroplanes nor suitable armament were readily available.

Sir David Henderson had no doubt that air fighting would dominate the future of the RFC. He foresaw a time 'which will ultimately end in great battles in the air, in which hundreds, and possibly thousands, of men may be engaged at heights varying from 10,000 to 20,000 feet'. As early as September 1914, Henderson sent a telegram to the British authorities:

> There are no aeroplanes with the Royal Flying Corps really suitable for carrying machine-guns; grenades and bombs are therefore at present most suitable. If suitable aeroplanes are available, machine-guns are better undoubtedly. Request you endeavour to supply efficient fighting machines as soon as possible.

For the Royal Naval Air Service based in Britain, a new threat quickly emerged that changed the whole nature of their existence: the U-boats arrived. The first sighting, close to Scapa Flow, just days after war began caused near panic in the Grand Fleet. The idea that German submarines had the range and ability to reach the Orkneys had been dismissed before the war. More dismay followed when reports flowed in of U-boats off the west coast of Scotland. For all its efforts, the Royal Navy had no answer to the menace from beneath the waves.

The underwater threat caused an immediate reaction in the Navy. Hasty plans produced a string of aerodromes around the coast. The SS-class airship came from the fertile brain of Sir John 'Jacky' Fisher, the First Sea Lord. On 28 February 1915, ten days after the German declaration that the waters around the British Isles were a war zone in which U-boats would sink any enemy ships they found and where neutrals sailed at their peril, 'Chinese Jack' sent for his senior RNAS airship officers. He demanded small, fairly fast airships to hunt down this new enemy and, he added, he wanted them at once.

The Navy already owned airships. They inherited some from the Military Wing but they also had one, His Majesty's Naval Airship Number 2, designed by a Welshman, Ernest Thompson Willows. Number 1 was the lamentable *Mayfly*. Unlike that wretched machine, Number 2 was non-rigid. Rigging controlled the shape of the envelope.

Resourceful naval engineers attached the fuselage and engine of a BE2c aeroplane to the Willows ship to produce the prototype Submarine Scout airship. Fisher demanded an airship and he had it within three weeks. SS1, which later met her end when she hit telegraph wires on the road between Dover and Folkestone and burst into flames, had a speed of between 40 and 50 miles per hour, carried a wireless transmitter as well as 160 pounds weight of bombs and could stay airborne for eight hours.

A prototype was one thing, mass production quite another, and every part of the Army and Royal Navy needed and demanded more supplies. Orders for everything from bootlaces to battleships strained the industries of the nation. Fisher's airships were another drain on stretched resources. Necessity improved the design both to withstand the wear and tear of service and for easier manufacture. Eventually, a waterproof clothing manufacturer took on the job of making the envelope and rigging. The cars in which the crew sat became the responsibility of a firm of shop-fitters.

The first station on the west coast was Luce Bay, later known as West Freugh, which opened on 15 July 1915, with sheds to take four small ss type airships. A portable shed, for emergency use, was located at Larne on the Irish coast for the use of the Luce Bay ships.

Until Christmas 1914, the RFC did little more than make up its losses. Only 24 aircraft arrived in France from Britain during the last four months of 1914. All had French engines. A further 26 came direct from French factories. By the start of 1915, supplies of aircraft increased enough to allow the formation of new squadrons, usually from a cadre of experienced pilots withdrawn from the front lines and newly qualified aviators. As the army on the ground increased in size, so the demand for more RFC units grew. By 31 May 1915, the RFC had swallowed 535 new aircraft. Some 300 had been lost, worn out or destroyed. Expansion was on the way though, since orders existed for 2,260 new machines. The growth of the RFC was not merely a matter of more soldiers needing aerial reconnaissance. As aircraft developed, as engines became more powerful, the scope of the aeroplane expanded.

New training units sprang up, and the RFC reclaimed Montrose in July 1915. Number 6 Reserve Squadron, a training unit, was the first occupant. As winter closed in, it was clear that the weather was often unsuitable for elementary flying training. The permanent staff and the equipment of the reserve squadron metamorphosed on 25 September 1915 into 25 Squadron, Royal Flying Corps under the command of Major Felton Vessey Holt DSO of the Oxfordshire and Buckinghamshire Light Infantry. The elementary training aircraft gave way to the BE2c and for three months or so, the squadron served as a replacement pool, sending pilots to France as needed. Finally, on 31 December 1915 the Squadron moved south to Norfolk.

If the Royal Flying Corps considered Scotland nothing more than a training camp, the RNAS had a different opinion, since with the Grand Fleet at Scapa Flow, the RNAS had a specific job to do. Already labouring under the burden that the surface Navy believed RNAS stood for 'Really Not A Sailor', naval aviators faced enormous difficulties. In 1913, the Admiralty decreed that the first two duties of naval aircraft were distance reconnaissance work with the fleet at sea and reconnaissance 'off the enemy coast working from detached cruisers or special "aeroplane ships"'.

This admirable precept was difficult to accomplish with the aircraft of 1914. Some ships received launching decks, but these helped little. Although the first successful take-off from a ship was made in 1911, it continued to be a risky procedure with under-powered aircraft. Worse, aeroplanes could not land on the small launching decks. Seaplanes were no answer, since stopping to lower an aeroplane into the water did not appeal to sea-going officers once U-boats prowled the seas. Anyway, aircraft with floats had limitations. In a calm sea, they had problems getting 'on the step' to take off. In rougher water, the aircraft capsized when their floats broke.

31

Ships altered to carry aircraft did little good unless they could keep pace with the rest of the Fleet, which required steaming at 30 knots for hours on end. Fleet reconnaissance foundered on a lack of suitable aircraft and ships. Other priorities also intervened. The first, and most obvious one, was to patrol the seas in an attempt to deter the U-boats while the second was the defence of Great Britain against air attack.

Despite these demands, the Navy plugged away at the problem, and in October 1914, the Admiralty bought the Cunard transatlantic liner *Campania* to fit out as a seaplane carrier. At 20,000 tons, with a full speed better than 20 knots, she offered pace and space and, altered by Cammell Laird, she entered service in April 1915. Above her forecastle sat a 120-feet-long 'flying deck'. For the first time in the war, aeroplanes served with the Grand Fleet. With Jellicoe's encouragement, trials began at Scapa Flow.

In the south of England, the Royal Navy had carried out successful trials of gunnery spotting and the results went to Jellicoe in the Orkneys on 23 July. He replied that no seaplane had managed to fly off *Campania* so the prospect of gunnery observation for the fleet was a problem. During fleet exercises the previous month, the seaplane carrier's role had been less than useful. In a rolling sea, she experienced delays and difficulties in hoisting out her aircraft. When they did reach the water, the floats broke away and the seaplanes sank. Only one aircraft became airborne. Moreover, the pilot made a careful but futile reconnaissance, since his wireless transmitter did not work.

Sir John believed that the only solution to the problem was an aircraft that could take off from a ship. The *Campania* experiments had failed, a result which put the Navy firmly into a dark box. Jellicoe, always something of a Job's comforter, noted that air spotting would be the preserve of the German High Seas Fleet with Zeppelins in the event of a major naval battle:

> We, on the other hand, will be powerless to carry out aerial spotting, but I am afraid we shall also be unable to prevent the Germans doing so by means of their Zeppelins since our seaplanes are incapable of engaging the Zeppelins owing to their insufficient lifting power, and our aerial guns will not be able to reach them. In view of the remarkable accuracy with which aerial spotting can be carried out, this matter is one of the most serious import to which I invite their Lordships' earnest attention. I regret that I am unable to propose

any means of meeting this menace, unless it be by the use of aeroplanes, rising from the deck of *Campania*, capable of climbing above the Zeppelins, and able to land on the water and be supported sufficiently long by air bags to allow the rescue of the pilots.

A few days later, on 6 August 1915, as *Campania* steamed at 17 knots into a brisk Orkney wind, Flight Lieutenant William Lawrie Welsh of the Royal Naval Air Service took his Sopwith Schneider single-seater into the air with just seven feet of 'flying platform' to spare. Welsh's aeroplane, as its name suggests, was a version of Sopwith's triumphant entry in the 1914 Schneider Trophy contest. Small, light, with one of the best engines around, the take-off could not be emulated by a heavier aircraft. Doubts about the value of the ship rumbled through Whitehall and Scapa Flow. Finally, she returned to Merseyside, to Cammell Laird, for a longer flight deck, while her seaplanes went ashore to Scapa. The summer days were long and the pilots, when not on patrol in a hunt for U-boats, experimented. Taking off from a ship had been licked – now the problem was to land safely.

The economy moved to a war footing, and the Government, aware that words were not enough, appointed civilian businessmen to sort out problems. David Lloyd George, as Minister for Munitions, wanted men who could clear bottlenecks and increase production. In July 1915 he appointed William Douglas Weir to look after Scottish industry as the unpaid director of munitions for Scotland.

At Rosyth, Vice Admiral Sir David Beatty fretted. In command of the Battle Cruiser Fleet, he firmly believed that, if the British Grand Fleet and the German High Seas Fleet met in battle, Zeppelins would give the enemy a huge advantage. Dreadnought guns hurled high explosive shells fifteen miles. The fall of shot was difficult to see from even the topmost mast of a warship. From the air, though, it was simplicity itself to tell gunners of their accuracy.

The Navy had used a balloon, tethered to a ship, to control artillery fire at Gallipoli. At Dover, Rear Admiral Reginald Bacon employed a balloon as an artillery spotter when bombarding the U-boat harbours at Ostend and Zeebrugge. Beatty decided that the Grand Fleet needed one as well and wasted no time in submitting a proposal to Sir John Jellicoe at Scapa Flow. 'They could,' Beatty pointed out, 'be sent up in weather where it would not be possible to launch a seaplane; probably in weather that would be prohibitive for Zeppelins.'

Beatty was not an ideal subordinate, believing Jellicoe to be too cautious by far and making no secret of his opinion. Sir John, though, had already taken action and the Admiralty had suggested the same thing in May. The Admiral replied that the fitting out of a fast balloon-carrying ship could not be justified for fleet work as the scheme was unproven. He suggested that the Navy experiment at Scapa Flow with *Campania*, carrying out tests to see if the idea was practicable.

A balloon station arrived and aside from its obvious task, it was later pressed into service to make a fake Zeppelin gasbag. This was fastened to an armed trawler to give the impression of a downed airship. Sailors in German uniforms heightened the ruse. Any passing U-boat, in theory, would immediately surface to help and the trawler would then open fire at close range. Thankfully, this plan, that breached several articles of the Geneva Convention, was dropped after the unlikely combination proved less than manageable in anything other than a flat calm.

Jellicoe passed Beatty's plea to the Admiralty who responded, with perhaps a slight touch of acerbity, that a new balloon ship, *City of Oxford*, would be put at Jellicoe's disposal when she completed her refit. Jellicoe's own words returned to him for the Admiralty pointed out that a high-speed balloon ship could not be justified until experiments proved its value. As a final rejoinder, their Lordships drew Jellicoe's attention to the fact that the Navy were meeting urgent demands for kite balloons from the army on the Western Front.

This did not satisfy Beatty, and on 23 September 1915 he wrote again to press for a balloon ship, since scouting before a fleet action was essential. If aeroplanes could not do the job, then a balloon would have to.

Jellicoe responded and 9 Kite Balloon Section of the Royal Naval Air Service set up shop at Rosyth. Sir David could arrange and organise his own experiments. Beatty jumped at the chance, giving the job to Rear Admiral the Honourable Horace Lambert Alexander Hood, in command of the 3rd Battle Cruiser Squadron. Hood, generally recognised as one of the best brains in the whole Royal Navy, wasted no time. A seaplane carrier, HMS *Engadine*, arrived on 24 October 1915. Three days later, the inflated balloon was bagged down on top of the seaplane hangar on the ship.

Engadine sailed while two volunteers clambered into the wicker basket. Once the ship cleared the Forth Bridge, handlers let out the cable and the balloon shot up to 2,000 feet as *Engadine's* engines drove her up to 18½ knots. The observers reported that all was well. *Engadine* changed course sharply, once, twice, three times and the balloon followed meekly.

On 29 October 1915, a more drastic test took place. Ballast went into the basket instead of volunteers. The deck winch spewed out cable as the balloon shot skywards in heavy seas. The seaplane carrier edged up to 22 knots, rolling and pitching as she rode the waves as the balloon rose serenely on its cable. The crew hauled it down, launched it once more, hauled it down, then let it rise again to 3,000 feet. Finally, back on deck, careful examination of the fabric and rigging showed that the balloon was totally unharmed. The experiments were an undoubted success and Hood reported to Beatty:

> I hope that a proper ship may be fitted without delay and if possible one that may have the speed to accompany the Battle Cruiser Fleet ... I think I have proved the value of the kite balloon for reconnaissance purposes; in a suitable vessel the strategic and tactical value will be very great; at 3,000 feet there will be a radius of vision of 60 miles and the communication will not be of the sketchy kind in use from aeroplanes, but will be conversation by telephone from a skilled observer sitting comfortably in a basket, to a responsible officer in the balloon ship, who with efficient W/T and all signal books and codes at hand, will rapidly signal by the most efficient method the information that may well win or lose the Dominion of the World.

Beatty forwarded Hood's observations to Whitehall with the comment that 'the advantage that the enemy has hitherto possessed by the aid of his Zeppelins in obtaining early information of the position, composition, disposition and course and speed of our Fleet will by the use of the kite balloons be in a great measure nullified'. Any disadvantages of lack of speed compared to that of a German airship was countered by the fact that the balloon was more mobile, could not be driven off by gunfire and could be launched or brought down in a strong wind. With a final flourish, he suggested that *Campania* lose some of her aircraft to balloons.

Jellicoe himself preferred to see a new balloon carrier in the Fleet, adapted from a fast merchant ship. That did not happen. Warfare poses choices. The Admiralty had far too much need of such vessels elsewhere. Finally, they decided to modify *Campania* to take an inflated balloon.

Despite the enthusiasm, the Grand Fleet met the High Seas Fleet at the Battle of Jutland the following year without the benefit of observation balloons riding in the sky. HMS *Invincible*, Hood's flagship, went down with the loss of all her crew, bar six.

In August 1915, Sir David Henderson handed over the RFC in France to Brigadier General Hugh Trenchard. Sir David returned to the War Office and retained overall control of the Flying Corps and military aeronautics. Hugh Trenchard had rather shallower Scottish roots than his predecessor. Born in Taunton on 3 February 1873, the son of a country solicitor, his connection with Scotland came from his mother, Georgina, daughter of John McDowall Skene, a Royal Navy captain. She claimed kinship with the Gordons and Lumsdens of Aberdeenshire.

Trenchard scraped into the army by way of the militia, passing the entrance exam, eighth from bottom, at his third attempt. 'Last resorts' like Trenchard went to any regiment that would take them. With a slight Scottish connection, he found himself in the 2nd Battalion of the Royal Scots Fusiliers, then serving in India. He fought with distinction in South Africa during the Boer War as the leader of a mounted company until a Boer ambush left him with severe wounds in the chest and spine. He not only had a useless left lung but was also unable to walk without sticks. Capricious fate sent him to Switzerland to recuperate. His own obstinate insistence on attempting the Cresta Run on a hired toboggan resulted in an inevitable crash. He soared over the banking, bounced twice and landed in a snowdrift thirty feet below. The crash pushed his spinal cord back into place and, remarkably, he was able to walk again, unaided.

By 1912, Trenchard, thirty-nine years old, close to becoming one of a myriad of unpromoted majors, decided to learn to fly at the suggestion of a colleague. He was nearly at the maximum age, forty, for a qualified pilot to transfer to the Flying Corps. In practice, he had four weeks to gain his certificate. He went to Brooklands and, although an indifferent pilot, passed the tests after a total of 64 minutes' flying time spread over thirteen days. He then joined the Central Flying School, where his foghorn voice quickly earned him the nickname of 'Boom'.

Hugh Trenchard became General Officer Commanding the RFC in France in time for the intensive period of planning that preceded the Battle of Loos. He spent much of his time visiting squadrons mapping the sector where the attack was planned. One morning, after visiting 3 Squadron at Auchel, a kilted soldier waylaid Trenchard and his ADC,

Captain Maurice Baring. After a smart salute, the private recited his service to date before finishing with the statement that he wanted to become a pilot in the RFC.

Trenchard showed no emotion. He merely asked the soldier's unit.

'The London Scottish, sir.'

'Take a note of that, Baring. Now, do you hold a Royal Aero Club certificate?'

The soldier produced a piece of paper: Certificate 591.

'You say you applied to join the RFC?'

'Repeatedly, sir, but my CO won't forward the application.'

'Have you an application form on you?'

Trenchard took the proffered piece of grubby, folded paper, produced from a tunic pocket. He handed it to his ADC. 'You'll hear more about this,' he commented. The soldier was unsure if that were a threat or a promise.

Trenchard beckoned to an NCO who stood, respectfully, some yards away.

'If there's transport going this soldier's way, see that he gets a lift.'

Private Donald William Clappen, a pre-war apprentice with the Blériot Aviation Company at Hendon, had time to reflect on his temerity. The driver of the truck that took him back to his unit wondered at his nerve, treating a general as if he were a recruiting sergeant.

Years later, Clappen remembered:

Three weeks later, at roll call, I was instructed to report to the orderly room. I had just come out of the trenches with the remnants of my battalion after the chaos of Loos. Within three hours I was on the train for Boulogne to report to the War Office and start training as a pilot.

Less than twelve months after, Clappen flew at the front with 45 Squadron. He eventually retired from the Royal Air Force as an Air Commodore.

Before the war began, it was realised that the best position for a machine-gun on an aeroplane was where it could fire forward, ahead of the aircraft. Pusher aircraft, those with an engine at the rear, appeared. With tractor aeroplanes, whose engines were in the front, the propeller had a nasty habit of obstructing the bullets.

One technically crude solution involved bolting metal plates to the wooden propeller. This novel approach briefly produced exciting results, as haphazard bullets clanged into space or, occasionally, the engine. Another, more sophisticated technique, mounted a Lewis gun on the top wing of a biplane so that it fired over the propeller. A cable from the trigger to the cockpit allowed the pilot to fire the gun and the ammunition came from a drum mounted on top of the gun. To change the drum in flight added further diversion to combat flying.

The solution was a mechanism that regulated the machine-gun to fire through the propeller arc. The Germans got there first. Nevertheless, it took time, even so, for air fighting to develop, since the first enemy fighters were not introduced for offensive purposes. Their role was to protect the reconnaissance two-seaters. It was the winter of 1915 when, finally, the 'Fokker Scourge' cut a swathe through the RFC. It changed everything. The battle for air supremacy brought Scotland – and Scots – an even greater role to play.

4

Bombs, Beardmore and Ghosts

Work flowed to Scotland from the Admiralty, the War Office and the Aero Contracts Commission. The Clyde shipyards, already busy with warships, turned to aeroplanes as well and most sub-contracted the work. Cabinet-makers, shopfitters, coach-builders and small engineering firms grappled with the problems of the flying machine. Scottish aeroplanes came from some unlikely workshops as a result, including the Glasgow Corporation Tram Depot at Coplawhill.

February 1916 saw Home Defence pass from the Admiralty back to the War Office. The RFC had a total of eight aircraft standing by for the job, all of which were in the south. A hastily organised Home Defence Wing, with seven squadrons, took over. The naval airship crews in Scotland had the unglamorous task of patrolling vast expanses of water in the hope of sighting and sinking a U-boat. They had little success. Easily seen, slowness was a hallmark of the airship. At an attack speed of often less than 50 miles per hour, even the most lethargic U-boat crew submerged before the patrolling gasbag arrived. Although their presence deterred, airship crews spent fruitless hours inspecting the flotsam and jetsam of the waters around Scotland. The ability to remain stationary did have some value. RNAS men enjoyed fresh fish at meal times. Simple financial transactions between airships and trawlers, made easy by a basket on the end of a long rope, produced a welcome variety of diet.

The belief that only England attracted Zeppelins received a nasty bruise on the night of 2 April 1916. An attack on 'England North', as the Airship Division of the Kaiserliche Marine called Scotland, was no new idea. A bombing raid on Rosyth Dockyard and the Firth of Forth was first planned for the night of 5 March 1916 but fearsomely bad weather stopped the attempt. The Kaiserliche Marine tried again, and soon after noon on 2 April 1916 two airships took off from Nordholz, near Bremerhaven, into a sky layered with cloud the colour of hammered pewter. L14 was in the hands of Kapitänleutnant Oskar Böcker and his crew. Kapitänleutnant Martin Dietrich commanded L22. They headed across the sea, fighting a strong wind from out of the north, to join two other raiders, Kapitänleutnant Heinrich Mathy in L13 and Kapitänleutnant Werner Peterson commanding L16. Their targets were Rosyth Dockyard and Naval Base, the Forth Bridge and the firth where the Heavy Cruiser Fleet rode at anchor.

Mathy, plagued by engine trouble, never made the start and turned L13 around to head back to Germany. A swift flurry of morse confirmed the successful rendezvous of the three remaining raiders to headquarters and the attack was under way. The stammered dots and dashes, in German Navy code, pulsed into the headphones of Royal Navy wireless operators, who waited patiently for just such signals. Within minutes the transcript reached Room 40 at the Admiralty, the Navy's intelligence gatherers. Considerably aided by possession of the Kaiserliche Marine's codebooks, they quickly broke the message. In Rosyth, in Edinburgh, as far north as Scapa Flow, the warning flashed out that an enemy air raid was expected.

The three Zeppelins throbbed steadily towards Britain as darkness crept over the water. In the increasing wind, the three lost sight of each other. They continued on, each alone. Around 2115, Martin Dietrich and the crew of L22 crossed the coast at Berwick-upon-Tweed which they confidently identified as Newcastle-upon-Tyne. Bombs fell on darkened pastures as Dietrich delivered a blow to the British war effort. The airship headed north to follow the coast towards the Forth and Edinburgh. At about 2350, the remaining bombs dropped somewhere in the region of the city. For Dietrich, it was almost immaterial whether he caused death and damage as he believed every attack reminded the beef-swallowers that their precious island was no longer immune. Peterson in L16 never reached Scotland, arriving some eight miles north of Blyth at 2300 and steering south to drop his bombs with stunning accuracy on empty fields. After ninety minutes of wandering, Peterson headed back across the North Sea.

Kapitänleutnant Böcker had more success. A former merchant navy officer with the Hamburg–Amerika Line, he had visited Leith before the war. L14 reached Scotland at around 2130 just off St Abb's Head, close to Eyemouth, where the coastline changes from heading north to run to the west towards Edinburgh. Böcker stayed clear of land as he flew parallel to the shore. Keen eyes spotted the Zeppelin out to sea. At East Fortune, the RNAS took a hand. Flight Sub Lieutenant George Aubrey Cox took off in Avro 504C 8588, optimistically referred to as a 'Zeppelin Chaser', in a gallant attempt to intercept the raider. The thick cloud that covered the area soon hid L14. Cox returned to East Fortune out of luck. The landing in the miserable dark on a field lit only with paraffin flares was not a success and Cox ended up in hospital, badly injured.

Somewhere around 2300, Böcker reached the mouth of the Forth and cruised slowly inland to look for the Forth Bridge. The cloud, and a series of searchlights poking their beams upward, defeated him. Glimpsing the lights of Leith through the murk, the Kapitänleutnant positioned his airship over Edinburgh. With no definite target in mind, Böcker gave the command to the crewman standing by the release switch.

'Los!' – 4,200 pounds of bombs fell in an apparently aimless pattern as L14 cruised across the city. Thirteen people died from the bombs and a further twenty-four were injured. The Zeppelin attack wrecked several houses and damaged three hotels as well as Waverley railway station. One bomb smacked into the cliff face below the walls of Edinburgh Castle itself which, unsurprisingly, survived. In a splendid gesture of defiance, the One O'Clock Gun fired a single blank shot, the sound reverberating through the streets.

At Leith, a stray bomb smashed into a whisky warehouse owned by Innes and Grieves, and ruptured vats poured out the spirit onto the street. Local citizens scorned the remote chance of another bomb landing near them to scoop up the bounty. A myriad of containers came into service and a few anxious souls even drank up there and then. The recumbent forms of the less careful remained for the police to collect once the Zeppelin droned away into the darkness. Böcker departed at about 0100, passing close to Dunbar as he headed back to Germany. The *Edinburgh Citizen* for 7 April 1916 expressed suitable outrage at the invasion:

a realisation of what our brave soldiers daily have to face was one of the things taught by the Scottish visitation. Many a man must have felt that the soldier had the easier task after all to face, for he was doing his bit in the great scheme by which we trust the nations will be able to put an end to this present-day barbarism. Whilst under Zeppelin bombardment the non-combatant was doomed to helpless inactivity. There would have been some relief in the possibility of doing something, however small, against the cowardly attackers of women and children. The Germans need not think that they will terrorise the people of this country into the making of peace. The crushing out of the spirit that has unblushingly defied all international laws must be effected, for it would be a sin to generations yet to come were this generation to permit of the possibility of a repetition of a like carnival of crime to this that is being enacted under the excuse of national necessity.

The Zeppelin raid spurred the hasty formation of Scotland's second operational squadron on 15 April 1916 at Stirling. Number 43 Squadron, designated for Home Defence, sprang from a nucleus of 19 Reserve Squadron at Montrose. The commanding officer was William Sholto Douglas, a name steeped in Scottish history from the Earls of Morton to the Queensbury family.

Sholto's Scottish roots though were hardly robust, since his nearest blood kin actually born in Scotland was a maternal grandmother who came from Glasgow. His father, an English vicar, was himself the son of another English clergyman. He reputedly fathered eighteen children, at least eight of them outside marriage. The firmly legitimate Sholto Douglas was born in Oxford. Educated entirely in England, his posting to Montrose, early in 1916, was the first time in his twenty-two years that he put a foot on Scottish earth.

Number 43 Squadron set up shop in a field near Falleninch Farm, close to Raploch to the west of the town. Stirling Castle towered above the aerodrome. It was possibly an historic choice. Four centuries earlier, in 1507, an Italian monk, John Damion, announced that he would fly to Paris. Damion fastened a pair of feathered wings to his arms and the waiting crowd watched as he stepped into space from the castle battlements. His arms waved madly as he plunged disastrously towards the unyielding earth.

Early pilots had a saying that any landing from which they walked away was a good one. Monk John did not make a good landing and, if reports are accurate, he broke his thigh. Unwilling to confess to pilot error, he apparently claimed that his fall occurred because he used chicken feathers instead of those of the eagle. Even though he had clearly isolated a substantial design fault, no record suggests that John Damion ever limped up to the battlements for another go.

The men of the new squadron found Stirling extremely agreeable. Most of the population of Britain had never seen an aeroplane so 43 Squadron's aircraft, 'whirring flying machines' in the words of the *Stirling Observer*, attracted gawping visitors from around the district. Every member of the squadron enjoyed an exciting social life. The pilots, distinguished by their woven badge of outstretched wings, reported remarkably thrilling progress, not confined to scones-and-jam teas, amongst the female population.

One month later, the Kaiserliche Marine tried another raid which met with even less success. Only two airships reached Scotland and a brisk south-easterly wind made navigation tricky. Once again, the star of the night was Kapitänleutnant Böcker with L14. His course-keeping, in foul weather, was less accurate than on his earlier visit. Peering through the gloom, he mistook the Tay for the Firth of Forth. Isolated lights on the ground became illuminated battlecruisers and his bombs fell to earth to shake an innocent farmhouse and kill a cow.

The other Zeppelin to find the right country was L20, under the command of Kapitänleutnant Franz Stabbert. Blown northwards by the wind, Stabbert was close to Loch Ness when he saw a small cluster of lights. Bombs tumbled from the Zeppelin on what was clearly a bustling industrial centre as the bemused inhabitants of Craig Castle pondered why German bombs fell on dark woods and meadows. Stabbert, determinedly not lost, but definitely uncertain of his position, wove a course across the Highlands. Finally, he found Peterhead which he identified as the Firth of Forth. Relieved, with a light heart, he set a course for home. However, the wind blew them further to the north and the airship finally crashed in a Norwegian fjord.

The authorities hastily opened a new airfield at Turnhouse to protect Edinburgh. It became the base of 26 Reserve Squadron, another training unit. Its proximity to the capital made it an extremely popular posting.

With the primary task of Home Defence passed to the Army, the Admiralty reorganised their air service. The RNAS had become a convenient umbrella organisation that included a fine collection of miscellaneous operations. These included 15 armoured car squadrons, 3 armoured trains that trundled along the rail lines of France and an anti-aircraft section of 24 officers and 1,500 men for use against marauding Zeppelins. All these were swiftly handed over to the Army.

As a corollary, naval air stations became the responsibility of the senior naval officer in their area. 'It will be of the greatest possible importance,' commented Arthur Balfour, who had succeeded Churchill as the First Lord of the Admiralty, 'to bring them into the regular routine of day-to-day naval work, and organise them for naval purposes as if they were destroyers or submarines.'

This admirable sentiment caused problems, for Naval discipline took little note of the temperament of early aviators. The Admiralty, following principles established long before Nelson suffered sea-sickness, appointed new men to the top RNAS jobs. Their Lordships chose officers distinguished for their rank, their seniority and sea-going experience rather than any knowledge of aviation. Efficiency in the air found itself on the Admiralty's sacrificial altar for non-conformists. Balfour then approved a monument to disaster. The new men decided that a fleet of rigid airships, British versions of the Zeppelins, would serve the Navy better than a swarm of aircraft. The decision soaked up money and blew away time, as Scotland duly learned.

The demands of war increased, and Scottish industry put both muscle and brains to work. By the middle of 1916, Beardmore's had transformed the Austro-Daimler aero-engine into a beast that developed more than 230 horsepower. They also had their own aviation department and within months they had produced plans for a single-engined, two-seat long-range bomber. Only a prototype, the WB I, saw the light of day.

Their WB II, a development of the BE2c that the firm built under contract, fared no better. It tackled a major problem of the BE2c in which the observer sat in the front cockpit. The Beardmore aircraft, that used only the wings and struts of the original aircraft, reversed the arrangement to give the observer a much better field of fire. With a more aerodynamic fuselage and a 200 horsepower engine, the WB II promised much but only one ever took to the air.

Beardmore benefited from the Admiralty's desire for rigid airships. Vickers, chosen as the main contractor, designed the 23-class, then farmed out the tedious business of making it. Building girder-framed airships as opposed to string and fabric aeroplanes is a business that demands large amounts of space as well as a construction time of many months. Large airships enjoy a gestation period suitable to an elephant. Work on an airship shed at Inchinnan began in January 1916. The firm had no experience in the field of rigids and Vickers accordingly flooded their sub-contractor with drawings, materials and advice. Work began on His Majesty's Airship Number 24r on 21 July 1916.

Manufacturing was not the only contribution. The Scottish nation has never hesitated to spill its blood when their land demanded, and on every fighting front of the War, Scots participated, bleeding and dying. In July 1916, Scots went forward on the first day of the month in the great endeavour of the Battle of the Somme. Amongst the men of the RFC who supported them was one Lieutenant Ian Henry David Henderson, son of Sir David himself. He scored his first victory on 25 August 1916 in a rackety BE12, the 'fighter' version of the BE2. Generals, like others, lived with fears for their nearest kin.

The RFC needed aerial gunners as well as observers for the new breed of aircraft that reached the front. They needed mechanics, fitters, riggers, clerks, photographers, cooks and a host of others to keep the squadrons airborne. For every man who fought amongst the clouds, ten more served on the ground. Without them, there was no air service.

Volunteers stepped forward. Norman MacMillan, a lieutenant in the Highland Light Infantry was one. James Alexander Weatherhead Binnie, from the same regiment, was another. From the Middle East, where he had fought at Gallipoli, came a nephew of Lord Lovat, Gerald Joseph Constable Maxwell.

Not everybody joined as a would-be pilot, since the Flying Corps wanted men who could shoot straight to serve in the two-seaters. Soldiers, stuck in the trenches, could be in a clean bed with blankets inside a day if they joined the RFC as gunners. But not every man who presented himself met with universal approval, as one pilot recalled of a new arrival in early 1917:

We occasionally got specimens such as my completely fearless Scottish infantry lieutenant: full of guts and ignorance, highly belligerent and trigger-happy; he itched to shoot at anything, everything, or nothing, regardless of range. In one dogfight in which our Sopwiths received unexpected reinforcements from some FEs from No. 20 Squadron, he opened fire on one of the FEs merely because it looked different, and I had to kick the rudder hard to throw his aim off. The only things I ever knew him to hit for certain were our own tail, rudder and wing tips.

In the fading light of an autumn evening in 1916, Lieutenant Desmond Arthur, the Munster Fusilier from County Clare, returned to Montrose. More precisely, Charles Grey Grey, editor of the weekly magazine *The Aeroplane* claimed that he did. The station was now the home of 18 Reserve Squadron. New buildings dotted the airfield while a smart officers' mess housed the pupils and administrative officers. The flying instructors chose not to live cheek by jowl with the trainees but in the original officers' mess used by 2 Squadron.

According to Grey, a flight commander, Captain Cyril Foggin, saw a figure in flying kit in front of him as he walked back to the instructors' mess as dusk fell. Foggin watched the pilot reach the door but he did not open it. When Foggin reached the entrance, the door was closed. The other man had vanished.

Foggin put the incident down to imagination or strain but a few days later, he saw the figure again, walking towards the same door. Once more, the pilot vanished when he reached it. Foggin witnessed the apparition twice more. To see a phantom once is fancy; to observe it four times is derangement, as far as doctors are concerned. Other instructors sensed or saw things. One woke to witness, in fading firelight, a man seated in a chair at the end of the bed. He disappeared as the instructor leaned forward to ask what he wanted. The stories multiplied that a presence lurked in the mess. Several people saw it, calm, simply reading a newspaper, oblivious until anyone approached then vanishing. The tale leaked out to reach Grey.

Idiosyncratic, monocled, controversial, opinionated, the magazine editor loathed the Royal Aircraft Factory and all its works, believing passionately in an independent air service and a private aircraft industry. Grey never hesitated to bend the facts for his own purposes. The journalist righteously claimed he did not dismiss the rumours of the Montrose Ghost as the result of jangled nerves amongst overworked instructors. He looked for an explanation and an obvious one, if the thought of an unhappy ghost rang true, was that the presence was that of a student who crashed on his first solo. Grey claimed he dismissed this as facile, since the shade of a student would surely haunt his own mess for preference. The phantom seemed perfectly at home in the old 2 Squadron mess. Grey seized on the apparent fact that the ghost was first seen in October 1916 with its last appearance in January 1917. Using these two dates as ammunition, Grey constructed a barrage of criticism. The ghost, he declared in his trenchant manner, was the spirit of Lieutenant Desmond Arthur. He had known the little Irishman and declared him to be a 'singularly lovable person, though distinctly weird'. He was also 'psychic' in Grey's opinion.

The editor latched on to the campaign of a maverick, self-publicising, right-wing MP, Noel Pemberton Billing, who, for a wager, had gained his pilot's certificate in the course of a single day. Billing left the RNAS in early 1916 to stand for Parliament. His complaints about the way the air war was fought attracted wide attention and he revelled in his own description of 'first air member'. Like Grey, idiosyncratic, monocled, controversial and opinionated, the pilot-turned-politician believed passionately in an independent air service, a private aircraft industry, reprisal raids against German cities and the closure of the Royal Aircraft Factory. He relentlessly bent the truth when it suited his purpose and headed the company named after himself, an enterprise that made generally eccentric aeroplanes. He was, in short, an aircraft manufacturer who wanted military contracts.

Grey and Pemberton Billing could have been Siamese twins in their beliefs, aside from the coincidental flaunting of a monocle in the right eye. Neither ever hesitated to use any story to advance their ideas, and on various occasions Grey's cantankerous articles made him many enemies, as did Pemberton Billing's wild accusations. The MP forced an inquiry into the conduct of the RFC and RNAS because 'certain officers had been murdered rather than killed by the carelessness, incompetence or ignorance of their senior officers or of the technical side of those two services'.

The Government had no great concerns about the RNAS. The Admiralty favoured private makers, and they could fight their own corner, but the RFC was a different story. The BE2 formed the bulk of the observation squadrons on the Western Front, its construction favoured over competing products from the private sector. Slow, ungainly, unwieldy, cumbersome, ill-armed, the 'Quirk' was easy game for the eager young guns of the German Air Service.

Pemberton Billing was trouble, alleging that the Royal Aircraft Factory was a haven of inefficiency, maintaining its aeroplanes were deathtraps, poorly designed and badly built, a claim not entirely without merit. He further made the specific charge that Desmond Arthur was 'killed on some type of BE machine which had been repaired by the Royal Aircraft Factory. The repaired part broke at 4,000 feet up, and the pilot was pitched out'. In his enthusiasm, Pemberton Billing ignored any other possibility as to when and how the wing was damaged, since inconvenient facts ran a poor second to his opinions.

The Government decided on a policy of containment. The simplest way to destroy Pemberton Billing was to prove him a liar on one specific point. They set up a sub-committee to investigate the claims. On 3 August 1916, it issued an interim report designed to destroy the MP's credibility. The sub-committee made its own fatal error when they quoted the wrong day as the date of Arthur's crash. To compound matters, they overlooked the Royal Aero Club report. In what was intended as a public beheading of Pemberton Billing, the sub-committee intoned:

> There was a suggestion made at the time that there had been a patch on the outside of the right wing of the plane, and that someone had broken the tip of the wing, then repaired it, and put a patch on the repaired part. The suggestion being that this was done by someone with a view to hiding some damage which he had done to the machine. The matter was closely enquired into at the time by a Committee, of which Mr H. T. Baker, MP, was Chairman. The Committee have had the notes of the whole of the evidence . . . There are some 23 witnesses. The suggestion depends on the unsupported evidence of one man out of these 23 witnesses . . .
>
> A perusal of the transcript of the notes of evidence leads to the conclusion that the suggestion of the patch is quite unfounded.

C. G. Grey argued this comment meant that, if there was no cobbled repair, the crash must have been caused by 'stunting' or dangerous flying. Arthur's restless spirit therefore appeared to pressure his friends to reveal the truth. Charles Grey Grey failed to explain why Arthur did not haunt Montrose when the original Baker Report appeared but that would have spoiled the story.

The Committee's Report appeared just before Christmas Eve, 1916. It carried an important addendum. Two members of the Committee, Messrs Bright and Butcher, an engineer and a lawyer respectively, had learned of the Royal Aero Club investigation. They dissociated themselves from the findings of the Interim Report, since the Government inquiry was clearly a sham.

Accordingly, Desmond Arthur's honour and competence were not besmirched, and once again, he could rest easy in his grave at Sleepy-hillock Cemetery, close by Montrose aerodrome. Certainly, the journalist claimed that Arthur's ghost was never seen again after January 1917. For Charles Grey Grey, Desmond Arthur, phantom or not, had served his purpose.

In France, the sixteen miles of battle front between the Ancre and Somme Rivers witnessed the grim arithmetic of mounting losses until the fighting ground to a halt as the weather worsened. The Flying Corps learned the hard way that the Germans fought like fury – as the days grew shorter, enemy aggression increased. The war in the air became a race for supplies, a race that the RFC was losing. Flying Corps supplies were dealt with by an Air Board apparently more concerned with its own political gains than the needs of the fighting men at the front. As the Somme battle ground its way into history, political wheeling and dealing led to the downfall of the Asquith Government and David Lloyd George became Prime Minister.

For the RFC squadrons on the Western Front, who lost twenty-seven aircraft in December 1916, Whitehall antics meant little. But a significant change had occurred and a new man went to the Air Board with fresh powers to get things done. Lord Cowdray wasted no time in words. The Board moved into new offices in the Strand at the Hotel Cecil. With them went two men from the Ministry of Munitions who had taken over responsibility for supplying both the RFC and the RNAS. One of them was a taciturn Glaswegian – William George Weir. Things were about to change for the better.

5

Gallant Gentlemen All

Within months, Weir's exceptional abilities as an organiser cleared the production log jams that threatened to cripple the RFC in the first months of 1917. The Scottish infantry lieutenant who so concerned his pilot with inaccurate shooting was no isolated example. In January 1917, the RFC opened its School of Aerial Gunnery at Loch Doon. The aircraft were largely the faithful BE2c, machines only slightly less advanced than those at the Front.

More airfields with new squadrons were set up. Donibristle in Fife, just two miles east of the Rosyth naval base, came into use as a landing ground for 77 Squadron. An acquisitive RNAS grabbed it in August 1917 as a 'ship's aeroplane base'. A rail line from the Firth of Forth and a lane that led to the water's edge made it ideal as a storage and repair base, and it also became a Salvage Park for Turnhouse aircraft.

The Navy still worried about the idea of flying aircraft from ships, and in August 1917 a new type of fixed platform, weighing a mere 2 tons, came into operation with some of the light cruisers. The platform produced a runway scarcely 36 feet in length. Mounted on the forecastle, it extended from the foremast to just in front of the forward gun mountings. But the major problem with platforms remained: once the aircraft had left the ship, it had either to find an aerodrome or splash into the sea.

One of the first ships to receive the new platform was HMS *Yarmouth* of the 3rd Cruiser Squadron at Rosyth. The Clydeside Yard of the London and Glasgow Company had finished the near 6,000-ton ship in April 1912 at a cost of nearly £400,000. In June 1917, Flight Commander Frederick Joseph Rutland took off successfully from a 20-feet platform on the ship's forecastle. *Yarmouth* joined the 1st Light Cruiser Squadron and destroyer escorts when they left on a minelaying operation on 18

August. As dusk fell, *Yarmouth* went to sea with her newly acquired pilot, Flight Sub Lieutenant Bernard Arthur Smart, and a Sopwith Pup single-seat fighter, serial N6430. This was the first in a series built under Admiralty contract by William Beardmore & Co. at Dalmuir. Destined for shipboard use, the Admiralty demanded airbags in the rear of the fuselage. Beardmore's Pups were easily distinguished from those produced by other contractors. The elevators were striped blue, white and red, top and bottom, to enhance the national markings.

The flotilla headed towards the German coast, and by the night of 20 August *Yarmouth* was close off the Dogger Bank, near to the route taken by Zeppelin reconnaissance patrols. With luck, Smart had the chance of a successful interception. At dawn on 21 August 1917, Bernard Smart checked over his Pup. All control surfaces gave full and free movement and the Le Rhône rotary engine spluttered into life, roaring up to its maximum 80 horsepower. Smart blipped the switch, turning the engine on, off, on, off, listening to its response. Satisfied, he turned to his single machine-gun. The Lewis chattered off a dozen or so rounds, and since Smart could do no more he went below to wait.

At 0500, one of the workhorses of the German Navy Flying Service, a Friedrichshafen 33e, poked an intrusive nose towards the bunch of cruisers. She swiftly turned for home once she reported the presence of the British ships, followed by a cluster of exploding shells from the cruisers. Thirty minutes later, look-outs spotted a Zeppelin to the southwest, heading north, and Smart quickly returned to his Pup. The blue, white and red roundels and rudder stripes caught the bright morning light. Smart asked his mechanics to find some grey paint to tone down the vivid colours, since anything bright might alert a watching Zeppelin crewman. Minutes ticked by and the airship maintained a respectful distance of seven miles from the cruiser group, flying back and forth on a parallel course.

HMS *Yarmouth* requested permission to move out of line to launch the fighter and Smart settled himself in the cockpit along with helmet, goggles, two lifebelts and a flask of medicinal brandy in case he ditched. He tightened the lapstrap and checked the instruments as the minutes dragged by. Ahead of him stretched a mere 16 feet of platform, beyond which was rather more North Sea. The cruiser turned into a Force 2 wind and the Pup trembled gently as her flying surfaces felt the light breeze. The airspeed indicator remained obstinately still. Smart asked for more speed but the wind delivered only a few knots. Unless the airflow over the wings was fierce enough, the Pup would not make it into the air.

The stokers responded to the clanging telegraph from the bridge and the cruiser's bow bit into the water. The Le Rhône roared into life and Smart raised his arm as the signal that he was ready to go. A pull on the release cord that held the Pup in position and she jumped forward, lifting into the air well clear of the end of the platform. A layer of strato-cumulus ribboned across the sky to the right and Smart climbed hard to reach its cover. With a full fuel load of 19 gallons, the 1,300-lb weight Pup ascended at under 1,000 feet a minute. The silver cigar-shaped Zeppelin was high above him at about 7,000 feet and Smart took a swift compass bearing on her in case she also slid behind the clouds. He climbed, the airspeed decaying gently to about 60 miles per hour as the Zeppelin signalled her base at Tondern: 'L23. Enemy chasing.'

The Pup clambered through the puffy clouds. At 9,000 feet, Smart levelled off. The speed increased and at around 100 miles per hour, the Pup managed almost twice the maximum speed of the airship. Some 3,000 feet below, Oberleutnant zur See Bernhard Dinter of the Imperial Navy's Airship Division ordered a turn for home. Smart eased forward the control column. The altimeter unwound gently to 8,000 feet. With speed and height advantage, the Pup stayed in a blind spot above the airship. Nobody in the control gondola slung beneath its bulk could see the Scots-built Sopwith.

The slipstream howled through the wing wires as the Pup went into a full-throated dive. The Zeppelin grew in Smart's vision as he pointed the aeroplane towards L23's stern, and with his speed at 150 miles per hour, Smart pulled back the control column. Pups did not like full dives but his aeroplane came out at the same altitude, 250 yards from the Zeppelin. Smart fired and the incendiary bullets sailed harmlessly over the top of the envelope. There was another dive, another zoom and a second try. The Lewis gun again chattered in anger as the Pup closed to less than 40 yards from the target. Smart saw his incendiary bullets curl away slowly before they hit the airship's after section. Five, six, perhaps even seven shots pierced the hull before he shoved the stick to avoid a collision. The Pup hurtled towards the earth and Smart pulled out at 3,000 feet. He looked back to see flames at the airship's stern roaring into the sky, a burning mass of fabric, falling towards the sea, the untouched nose pointing upwards at a 45-degree angle. Her four propellers spun uselessly as fire raged through the 585-feet-long frame.

Smart saw a single parachute blossom before the mass of blazing aluminium hit the water off Lodbjerg in Denmark, 500 miles from her base. It was L23's 101st flight and none of the crew survived. The sea was empty of ships and the Pup turned away from the burning hulk on the water. Smart followed the reciprocal course to his outward leg. In theory, he must eventually sight his own side. If he didn't see them within the next 45 minutes, the sanctuary of a neutral Denmark beckoned. At last, he caught a glimpse of the long, grey shapes on his port side, hurrying towards the plume of blackened grey that marked the graves of L23 and her crew.

Smart prepared to ditch close to a pair of vigilant destroyers. He cut off the Le Rhône and settled the Pup into a long curving glide. As the sea rose gently towards him, he eased back, back, back on the control column until the Pup stalled gently onto the water. Straps already undone, Smart hauled himself hastily out of the cockpit. The engine-heavy nose dipped downward with only the rear, supported by its airbags, staying clear of the water. Smart splashed clear of the cockpit to grab the tail, holding on grimly while a boat from HMS *Prince*, a three-funnelled Moon-class destroyer, rowed hastily to his aid. Flight Sub Lieutenant Smart collected a Distinguished Service Order. A new Pup and pilot arrived for HMS *Yarmouth* and Smart went to HMS *Furious* on which great things were happening for the Navy's aviators.

HMS *Furious* was with the rest of the Grand Fleet at Scapa Flow. She had begun life in 1915 as a large light cruiser and had originally been built as part of a shallow-draught fleet designed to attack Germany's Baltic coast. When this scheme collapsed, her superior speed of nearly 32 knots, and size made her a prime candidate to carry aeroplanes to war and she soon acquired a flying-off deck. At Smoogroo, the naval airfield close to Scapa, where the pilots from *Furious* landed after their deck take-offs, the challenge of landing back on the ship finally went to the test. It was infinitely more impressive than ditching into the sea with its attendant discomforts and superior to tamely returning to land. After a few experiments that involved rolling wheels along the distance available on the launching deck, another Scottish-built Pup from Beardmores, N6452, took part in a slice of history. The RNAS pilots reckoned that it would be possible to land back on *Furious* if the wind speed exceeded 25 knots.

Squadron Commander Edwin Harris Dunning, the ship's senior pilot, took off from HMS *Furious* on 2 August 1917. The ship, even in the majestic space of Scapa Flow, did not have enough room to work up to maximum speed. Even so, she reached 26 knots and headed into a steady 21-knot wind. The combined speed of 47 knots was tantalisingly close to a Pup's normal landing speed.

The layout of *Furious* prevented Dunning from simply lining up on the floating runway and landing. He had to fly alongside the ship before side-slipping in front of the bridge and onto the deck. Only a fool or someone with no imagination would consider it simple – and only a brave man, and a skilled pilot, would try it. The Pup was suitably modified with rope handles under the tail and wings. Dunning flew parallel to the ship, edged across and onto the deck. A deck party, made up mostly of his fellow officers, grabbed the handles as the Pup's wheels kissed the deck. The aeroplane rolled to a halt and another milestone had been achieved. An aircraft had taken off from a ship and returned safely to it.

Five days later, Dunning tried again in a gusting wind and made two successful landings but slightly damaged the elevator. He changed aircraft for a third attempt, using his original Pup. This time, he misjudged his approach, side-slipping from a greater height and the Pup landed too far along the deck. The waiting crew had no chance to catch the rope toggles. Dunning waved them away as they chased after him, then flicked the blip switch to restart the engine. It fired, the Pup lifted briefly to go round again but the engine choked. N6452 stalled onto the deck with a thump and the right tyre deflated. Dunning was helpless at the controls as the Pup veered to its right to topple into the sea. *Furious*, clipping along at close to 30 knots, could do nothing to help. No safety boat was on hand and it took *Furious* 20 minutes to turn round to reach the scene but nothing could be done. Presumably knocked unconscious when the aircraft hit the water, Edwin Harris Dunning drowned in the cockpit before he could struggle free.

William Beardmore's Aviation Department had a bright idea. The Sopwith Pup contracts, and the aeroplane's use as a ship-borne fighter, suggested that a substantial modification to make it more suitable for operations at sea would win Admiralty favour. The trials on HMS *Furious* suggested that an aircraft designed for the job could help win the war by destroying Zeppelins. The WB III soon appeared. Based solidly on the Pup, it incorporated folding wings and undercarriage together with the popular air bags. If the aircraft did ditch, the pilot could jettison the undercarriage, make a simple splash-down and wait for rescuers. The Admiralty placed orders for one hundred aircraft. Fifty-five of them reached the RNAS but the pilots did not fall in love with the creation. The Pup, everybody agreed, was a delight to fly, responsive, free from tricks and able to operate as high as 15,000 feet, an altitude much favoured by German airships. However, Beardmore's modifications seriously affected the flying qualities of the original Pup. As the complaints flooded in, the Admiralty changed its mind. Although at least fifty-five machines were delivered, with about thirty reaching the Fleet, many went straight into store. One achieved a minor distinction. Captain W. W. Wakefield flew it under the Forth Bridge on 28 August 1918. The Japanese Navy evaluated a further two but they failed to place an order.

Hot on the heels of the WB III came the WB IV, another shipboard biplane fighter. This employed the detachable undercarriage as well as a flotation chamber in the front half of the fuselage. In a particularly ingenious flight of fancy, the powerful 200-horsepower Hispano-Suiza engine sat behind the pilot. A long shaft ran from the engine, between the pilot's legs, to the front of the aeroplane to drive the propeller. The pilot thus enjoyed a remarkably fine view as the cockpit was in front of the wings. The WB IV was a rather better aeroplane than the WB III but it suffered from a major disadvantage, being pitted against the superlative Sopwith Camel in the race for orders. As a fighting aircraft, the Camel was infinitely better. As a final mark of disapproval, the Navy considered the Hispano-Suiza, itself a magnificent engine, much too complicated for shipboard use. The death knell of the design sounded when the single prototype underwent ditching trials on 27 September 1917 and the buoyancy chamber collapsed.

Dalmuir refused to be disheartened. They produced the WB V, a more conventional aeroplane, with the Hispano-Suiza engine mounted traditionally in the nose. Once again, they stuck with the jettisonable undercarriage. Again the WB V, designed for flying from ships, had flotation bags, this time fitted along the leading edges of the lower wings. Aware that fire-power was all-important in a fighter, Beardmore's designed the aircraft to take a quick-firing 37-mm gun, whose performance was such that the test pilots allegedly refused to fire the creature in flight. It quickly gave way to a standard Vickers. Two machines, possibly three, were built for evaluation but no orders followed. Beardmore's had the consolation of large contracts to build the Navy version of the Camel. One aircraft they made, N6812, with the trademark striped elevators, shot down Zeppelin L53 on 11 August 1918. The pilot, Lieutenant Stuart Culley, took off from a lighter, towed at speed, behind HMS *Redoubt*, a Harwich-based destroyer. In the words of the *London Gazette* citation for his Distinguished Service Order, Culley 'ascended to a height of 19,000 feet, at which altitude he attacked an enemy airship, and brought it down in flames completely destroyed. This was a most difficult undertaking involving great personal risk, and the highest praise is due . . . for the gallantry and skill he displayed'. The original recommendation was for the Victoria Cross. Culley ditched his Scottish-made Camel close to *Redoubt*. It survived the crash and, recovered, it hangs today in the Imperial War Museum in London with a restored paint job that retains the Beardmore elevator stripes.

From East Fortune, five Coastal Class airships patrolled over the Forth and Tay to protect the battle-cruisers at Rosyth. Flying boats and seaplanes from Dundee reinforced their efforts. One of the more flamboyant Naval pilots spent some time at Dundee. A fellow pilot, Grahame Donald, the schoolboy who had been at Lanark, recounted an exploit of Squadron Commander Christopher Draper:

> He used to fly quite regularly through the Tay Bridge, which is not like the Forth Bridge. The Tay Bridge was built on stone pillars quite reasonably wide apart. He used to fly through that quite gaily. One day he challenged me to follow him through. So I followed just a comfortable distance behind. As he went through, it struck me that he'd dashed little clearance on his wingtips. It struck me that it wasn't enough for me anyway. So I may as well admit here and now, I funked it at the last moment. I was on the old Short biplane and I just pulled her right up and went over the bridge, not through.
>
> So when we got back to the station, Christopher said 'Well, you managed it all right? I had to admit to him that I funked it. He said, 'What?! What?'
>
> I said, 'No, I funked it.'
>
> He said, 'Why?'
>
> 'Well,' I said, 'what clearance did you have at your wingtips?'
>
> 'Oh, About a foot and a half, I should think – each wing – three feet overall.'
>
> I said, 'You know, from a rough guess, I think the old Short

seaplane's five or six feet wider span than the Avro. which you were flying. If I hadn't have funked it, you know, I'd have knocked the Tay Bridge down and you'd have got the blame!'

Both the RFC and the RNAS realised that better training was the key to success against a resolute enemy, since all too many British pilots went to war with only the sketchiest preparation. The sole requirement for a new frontline pilot in 1916, for example, was that he should have spent at least fifteen hours in the air and have been 'encouraged in trick flying and to be given every opportunity to practise fighting manoeuvres'.

By early 1917 it was clear that this was not adequate. Amongst other ventures, the RFC opened Number 1 School of Aerial Fighting at Ayr which used the racecourse as its aerodrome. Pilots destined to fly single-seater fighters went for intensive instruction and their teachers had all completed at least one operational tour on the Western Front. The commanding officer, just to emphasise the point, was Lieutenant Colonel Lionel Wilmot Brabazon Rees. A brilliant pilot, he walked with a pronounced limp from an old wound and below his flying badge, he wore the sombre ribbon of the Victoria Cross. Equipped with Camels, the obsolescent de Havilland 2 and a handful of other aircraft, the school set about teaching its pupils how to fly, fight and survive.

On 11 May 1918 the school moved to Turnberry, 20 miles south of Ayr, with the slightly amended name of Number 1 School of Aerial Fighting and Gunnery as it absorbed Number 2 Auxiliary School of Aerial Gunnery that had been there since January 1917. The courses expanded to include fighter-reconnaissance pilots, their gunners and day bomber crews, and it provided the last stage of training before posting to an operational squadron.

On 28 October 1917, 535 feet of spanking-new rigid airship made its first flight. Beardmores had finally completed their Vickers contract. His Majesty's Airship 24r flew from her shed at Inchinnan to East Fortune. British airships took a long time to build and so 12 months was not uncommon. The Zeppelin works managed much better: 12 weeks was more their mark. Beardmore's vessel was hideously overweight, a characteristic allegedly caused by shipbuilding techniques with the use of extra-strong rivets and fastenings. Her move to East Fortune had become urgent. The Inchinnan shed was needed for a new airship, the R34. In a desperate attempt to obtain lift, all the fixtures and fittings from the after gondola were removed. This took out one of her 4 Rolls-Royce

250-horsepower engines and its associated propeller together with the emergency controls. So lightened, HMA24r managed to clear the hills between her construction shed and East Fortune, although her top speed was a miserly 30 miles per hour.

Even with the engine back in position, the essential weakness and fallibility of the design meant she could not go faster than 38 miles per hour. On one occasion, when her port engine failed in a stiff wind, she made no progress over the ground. Like the Farman aeroplanes at Montrose four years earlier, she even achieved the distinction of moving slowly backwards when her engines were set to full ahead. By the time she was written off, at the end of December 1919, she had flown a grand total of 164 hours and 38 minutes.

Inchinnan was already working on another airship, the R27. The Admiralty modified the original Vickers design to produce what was officially the 23X class. Construction began on 16 March 1917 and completion came the following June. After a short life of less than 90 hours' flying time, R27 caught fire on 16 August 1918 when safely in her shed at Howden. Garaged with three blimps, non-rigid ships, she went up in flames when a spark from some wireless equipment on a blimp ignited a pool of spilt petrol.

With R24r out of the way, Beardmores began work on the R34, bigger and better than the 23 class in all its forms, for in December 1917, it seemed the war would go on for ever. As the German U-boats sank more and more ships throughout 1917, privation followed. In genteel tea-rooms of Edinburgh, dismayed matrons struggled without the consolation of scones, muffins, tea cakes and fancy pastries. Sugar bowls disappeared from tables. Afternoon tea as an occasion suffered further when the authorities decreed that no customer could be charged more than sixpence a meal between three o'clock and six o'clock unless meat, fish or eggs were served. No customer should be allowed more than two ounces of bread, cake or biscuit.

Squadron Commander Dunning's short-lived experiments, with those of his successors, sent HMS *Furious* back to the shipyard. She emerged with a 50-feet-wide landing-on deck from her stern for half her 600-feet length. A hoist lift, duplicated at the forward section, served hangar space below decks for 16 Sopwith Camels. She had become the world's first aircraft carrier.

Pilots quickly discovered that landing on *Furious* remained a hazardous affair. The light biplane Camels found it difficult to cope with the turbulence created from the superstructure when the ship steamed at speed. In thirteen attempts, nine aircraft crashed. It took flush decks, heavier aeroplanes and more powerful engines to solve that problem. Nonetheless, the arrival of a fast floating aerodrome gave the Navy the chance to realise a long-held dream.

A long and protracted battle in Whitehall finally led to the amalgamation of the two flying services into one new organisation, the Royal Air Force, on 1 April 1918. The same jokes made about the Air Battalion, also founded on April Fool's Day, made a fresh appearance. To avoid confusion with initials, the Royal Aircraft Factory became an Establishment, but the RFC and RNAS hardly noticed the change. The biggest difference was that officers and men could be sent to any flying unit. At the Kirkwall seaplane station on the Orkneys, the change was evident:

Our parades would have delighted lovers of comic opera ... These were early days in the life of the Royal Air Force, and uniforms varied from the light blue of the Commanding Officer, through the khaki uniform of the Foot Guards (Adjutant) to the dark blue of the Royal Navy and every combination one could think of, not forgetting the Royal Flying Corps with forage cap ... Except for the shoulder flash, I could have been in the Royal Field Artillery, with splendid riding breeches and puttees done up cavalry style.

The decision to authorise a light blue uniform for airmen was taken months in advance of the formation of the RAF by the Air Organisation Committee, chaired by Lieutenant General Jan Smuts. One of its most dynamic members was Lieutenant General Sir David Henderson who had watched his brainchild grow in stature in six short years. The committee pursued everything from uniforms and ranks to flags and pennants for senior officers.

The 'light blue' proved to be sky blue. Gold lace rings around the tunic cuffs denoted rank while the flying badge was a masterpiece of gold embroidery. The general effect, according to one pilot whose commanding officer appeared in the new outfit, was that a Siamese admiral had joined the squadron. The sky blue gave way to the modern blue-grey in September 1919.

Sir David Henderson wanted new ranks for the Air Force and suggested rank titles taken mostly from the Army and Navy which went to the other two services for approval. The War Office responded with the acerbic comment that the new organisation should have its own distinctive titles, adding waspishly that the suggested list gave senior officers Naval titles while junior officers made do with Army ones.

The Admiralty, equally stubborn, objected to the use of any Naval titles at all even if prefixed with 'Air'. They suggested army ranks be used exclusively and, failing that, the upstart should produce its own names, suggestive of the air. Whether Sir David and his fellow Glaswegian, Sir William Weir, helped compile the new list is unknown. It included the ranks of Reeve, Banneret, Fourth Ardian up to First Ardian. An alternative list featured Flight Ardian, Squadron Ardian and Wing Ardian. Ardian lost much of its romance when the Committee learned that it came from two Gaelic words. 'Ard' translated as chief. 'Ian' or 'eun' created a hiatus. It means 'bird'. Senior officers felt their dignity compromised with the title 'Fourth Chief Bird'.

In the end, the committee submitted their initial list to the War Cabinet. That body, presumably unencumbered with such matters as prosecuting the war effort, agreed with the Admiralty that Air Force officers would temporarily use army ranks, a decision that considerably irritated former RNAS men. Henderson resigned from the Air Council in April 1918 when the RAF came into being. He loathed the political intrigue that had permeated the Air Ministry, knavery that meant there was no place for him in the Royal Air Force. Sir David went back to France.

On board HMS *Furious* on 17 July 1918, the naval aviators vaguely ignored their new ranks. Sporting dazzle camouflage to fool any wandering U-boat, the world's first aircraft carrier put to sea from Rosyth, accompanied by a gaggle of destroyers as escorts and five light cruisers. The flotilla neatly summarised Scotland's contribution to the war. *Furious* carried a dozen Sopwith 'Ship's' Camels, most of them marked by the elevator stripes that showed they came from Beardmore's at Dalmuir. Of the five escorting cruisers, Beardmore had made three on the Clyde, HMS *Galatea*, HMS *Royalist* and HMS *Inconstant*. Only *Caledon* and *Phaeton* originated in English yards. Five battleships of the Royal Sovereign Class in the 1st Battle Squadron of the Grand Fleet gave area support. The only battleships with a single funnel, *Royal Sovereign* herself, *Revenge*, *Ramillies*, another Beardmore ship, *Royal Oak* and *Resolution* were followed by their own attendant cruisers and a swarm of destroyers.

Furious headed for the German coast. Operation *F7* had begun. Its single, simple aim was to destroy the Zeppelin sheds at Tondern, in Schleswig-Holstein, close to the German–Danish border. The Admiralty dearly wanted to put the airships out of business. During four years of war, several attempts had been made to attack them, in the tradition of Francis Drake fighting the Spanish, in their own safe havens. Success had been hard to come by and gallantry had not overcome the problems of inadequate aeroplanes operating at the limit of their range. By mid-1918, German airships no longer posed a real threat. German bombing raids had become the province of the aeroplane although the Zeppelin remained a potent symbol in the minds of the admirals. The modifications to HMS *Furious* brought a gleam to the eyes of admirals and aviators alike. The carrier could approach the enemy shore to launch its 2F1 Camels, each armed with two 50-lb bombs, within their fighting range. Fuel would be tight but sufficient as long as there were no diversions – such as angry German fighters. The RNAS may well have become the Royal Air Force but nobody doubted that this was a naval affair. No sky-blue uniforms polluted the deck of HMS *Furious*.

Seven pilots trained at Turnhouse for the mission, all former RNAS pilots, despite their reluctant acceptance of RAF ranks. Captain William Douglas Jackson, Captain William Forster Dickson and Lieutenant Norman Edmundson Williams comprised the first attack. The second consisted of Captain Bernard Arthur Smart, the killer of L23, Captain Thomas Kenwood Thyne, Lieutenant Samuel Dawson and Lieutenant Walter Albert Yeulett. Two previous attempts to attack Tondern had been called off when *Furious* was at sea and so every pilot hoped that this one would succeed. They practised dropping bombs on a painted target on the ground and given that precision bombing from a single-seat biplane with frisky habits is more guesswork than science, the rehearsals went well.

Airships are huge creatures requiring enormous hangars and Tondern had one of the biggest, a tempting target for any Camel pilot who made it that far. With a penchant for order, every German Navy airship base named its hangars so that the first two letters identified the base. The German Imperial Navy at Tondern dutifully called the largest hangar *Toska*. Gigantic, it measured 225 metres in length, rose 67 metres high with a width of 40 metres. The British pilots preferred to think of a staggering 730 feet in length, rising to 220 feet high with 130 feet of width. This gargantuan construction could comfortably take two of the latest and largest of the Kaiserliche Marine's Zeppelins. Two smaller hangars, *Tobias* and *Toni*, each 180 metres by 40 metres by 31 metres, clung close by. Each housed a single airship within their roughly 600 feet by 130 feet height and 100 feet width.

In the cold half-light of a dawning day on 19 July 1918, the seven pilots prepared for an 0300 take-off.

'Switches off!'

Cold-fingered mechanics primed engine cylinders.

'Switches on!'

Hands grasped the wooden propeller of Jackson's aircraft.

'Contact!'

A heave, the prop swung, the engine caught, fired, settled into a roar. The smell of burnt castor oil, used as the engine lubricant, drifted across the deck. Satisfied, Jackson nodded. A jerk and the holding toggle fell clear and he was away safely.

By 0320, the first flight was on its way. Limited fuel did not allow the pilots to circle and pick up formation. That was done on the way to the target and at 0322, the second flight launched. Captain Bernard Smart went first, his aircraft sporting a distinctive blue and white chequered engine cowling. The three remaining aircraft followed him and they, too, grouped into a loose formation as they headed toward the enemy coast.

Thyne's engine lost power soon after take-off and frantic action with the gravity feed did nothing to help. Finally, he gave up, turned round to head back to *Furious*, his engine working in fits and starts. He found the flotilla and ditched successfully. Picked up by an eager destroyer, Thyne was safe although, in its hurry, the destroyer sent his aircraft to the bottom when it ran into the floating Camel.

Ninety miles to fly and Jackson led his two companions to 5,000 feet. With the coast of Denmark identified, the three Sopwiths turned east, climbed steadily until they reached 6,000 feet. The Friesian Islands lay below and to find Tondern was a simple matter of a compass course and a helpful road. Without radio, the three pilots relied on visual signals. Jackson had briefed his flight that he would wave a red flag when he sighted the target but when the time came, he couldn't find the flag. Camels were tricky beasts to fly and grovelling on the floor to locate it did not appeal. In the end, a pointing hand worked just as well.

Dickson went in first, diving down to 700 feet before he released his first bomb on what he thought was a Zeppelin hangar. It landed, if local reports are accurate, in the Tondern market square. Falling out of the sky at around 150 miles per hour, adrenalin pumping, the three pilots confused the sheds. They seem to have mistaken *Toska* for the two smaller hangars and thought that the other two were one big building. Despite this, the appearance of flames and smoke rising as high as 1,000 feet was a clear triumph.

Elated, all three pilots, who had lost contact during the action, headed individually for safety. The intention was to join up off the coast before making for the safety of the flotilla. Landing-on was forbidden and all pilots had to ditch. William Dickson arrived off the lighthouse at Lyndvig at 0445. A helpful destroyer with a fluttering white ensign ploughed through the sea beneath him. Dickson killed his height, circled neatly, landed on the water and waited for HMS *Violent* to collect him.

Jackson arrived at the meeting point at 0455 to gaze at an empty sky and sea, but his troubles worsened when the engine misfired, coughed, stopped. Fuel was not reaching the Bentley. Jackson switched to gravity feed and climbed. Every pilot knew that height was money in the bank – the higher the aeroplane, the further one could see and the further one could glide. With its light wing loading, the Camel went a long way without power. Jackson reached 10,000 feet but a cloud layer stopped him looking out to sea. At 0535, he ran out of fuel. Turning, Jackson headed for Denmark, gliding serenely down towards neutral ground. With no power, there is only one chance at landing, so Jackson touched down in a field close to the village of Bramminge. The Camel bounced along until stopped by a fence and somersaulted with a neat grace. William Douglas Jackson crawled free of the wreckage, flare pistol in hand. One minute later, Sopwith Camel N6771, made at Dalmuir, delivered to Turnhouse on 13 April 1918, went up in flames.

Norman Williams also landed in Denmark, at Scallinger, close to Esbjerg. The local police arrived before he had a chance to destroy his Camel and he and his aeroplane were interned. At 0445, the second flight arrived at Tondern to find *Toska* under a pall of smoke, blazing merrily, the flames much helped by the presence inside of two airships, L54 and L60. Jackson had also hit *Tobias* and damaged a balloon. Smart and his men arrived in excellent time to receive a helping of anti-aircraft fire from some understandably annoyed Kaiserliche Marine gunners.

The Camels released their bombs at 800 feet then Smart dived to almost ground level to escape their attentions. He high-tailed it back towards the fleet, his Bentley engine becoming decidedly more temperamental as the minutes passed. Soon after 0600, a relieved Smart splashed into the water close to *Furious*. Lieutenant Samuel Dawson landed at Holmslands Klit in Denmark. He was unable to set fire to N6823, delivered from Beardmore's less than a month earlier, so decided to leg it to freedom. The Danish police stopped him at the railway station on his way to Kolding. Dawson had thoughtfully put on civilian clothes under his flying clothing but his lack of fluent Danish gave him away. An affable escort took him to Esjberg to rejoin his fellow flyers.

Walter Albert Yeulett, known as Toby to his friends and relations, failed to return. His Camel washed ashore near Norre Havrvig, in West Jutland, on 24 July. Four days later, his body was found on the beach near Holmsland. Recommendations for immediate gallantry awards, including the newly instituted Distinguished Flying Cross, went from Rear Admiral Richard Fortescue Phillimore to London. Like every other British distinction, with the exception of the Victoria Cross and a Mention in Despatches, the DFC could not be awarded posthumously, but as long as the award was approved before death was confirmed, it stood. Mid-morning on 19 July 1918 only three pilots out of seven had regained *Furious*. The remaining four could be dead and so approval quickly arrived. On 20 September 1918 the *London Gazette* announced the award of the Distinguished Flying Cross to Captain William Douglas Jackson, Lieutenant Samuel Dawson and Lieutenant Walter Albert Yeulett of the Royal Air Force.

Captain Bernard Arthur Smart received a bar to his Distinguished Service Order; William Dickson gained the award for the first time. Only Thomas Thyne, forced back by engine trouble, did not receive an honour. The three interned pilots, carefully failing to give parole, escaped from Denmark in short order. Only Yeulett remained. He stays there still, his grave tended with care.

6

Peace and Dismissal

Boosting morale by bombing Zeppelins in their sheds was one thing – changing the course of the war was quite another. Destroying monstrous airships did nothing, in 1918, to bring Wilhelm's Empire to its knees. The Western Front decided victors and losers. The German offensive in March 1918 almost succeeded. In the weeks that followed, the Germans hammered a wedge into the Allied lines. Desperate to knock out Britain before the Americans got into the war, they failed to break through.

Scotland had already met the Americans and for many of the civilian population, they were a new and strange breed of people. One American pilot, Lieutenant John MacGavock Grider, having shivered with the cold at Turnberry, where he complained the only food was Brussels sprouts and marrow, went on to the School of Air Fighting at Ayr:

> These Scots may be canny but they are a trusting lot. Any of the banks here will cash checks without asking for any identification. Yet down in England they won't even accept money for a deposit until they got a picture of you and know why your grandfather had to marry the girl . . .
>
> This town is full of statues of Bobby Burns and bars. That's the principal industry. The barmaids are the belles of the town . . . Ayr is really a beautiful spot and I'd like to stay here a while but they kill off pilots too fast for anyone to linger very long.

Ayr hammered home something that every aviator knew – flying killed. The *Ayr Observer* of 4 June 1918, under the terse headline 'Flying Fatalities', reported, with one eye on the censor, grim information from the local aerodrome:

Four airmen were killed at a West of Scotland flying station in the course of last week. Lieutenant Archibald Milburn Makepeace and Second Lieutenant Thomas Albert M'Clure, Royal Air Force, were instantaneously killed through a mishap to their machine in mid-air . . . Lieutenant Howard Rea Smith . . . who belonged to the United States services, was fatally injured through his machine crashing to earth from a height of 1,500 feet. Sergeant John Stabb Tuckett . . . was killed as the result of an accident while flying.

Then, even as some anticipated more death and dying in 1919, the war ended on the eleventh day of the eleventh month at eleven o'clock. Scotland's men had done their duty. Some had created great names for themselves. Gerald Joseph Constable Maxwell first saw conflict in the Lovat Scouts, the regiment his uncle founded during the Boer War. He went to France with 56 Squadron in April 1917, and on his first patrol, he shot down a German Albatross fighter. Six months later, he returned home with twenty victims to his credit. Following a spell at the School of Air Fighting, he went back to France to notch up a further seven successes. He finished the war as a major with a Military Cross and a Distinguished Flying Cross. After the Armistice, he became a stock-broker.

He was not the only Scot in the squadron. For a while, Maxwell flew alongside Ian Henry David Henderson who, with seven victories, returned home to be welcomed by his father, Sir David. Ian joined Turnberry as a flying instructor but in July 1918 he perished in an accident as a passenger. Generals also grieved.

One Scot finished the war as a brigadier-general. A shy, awkward man, born at Moffat, Dumfriesshire in 1882, an early pilot, Hugh Caswall Tremenheere Dowding suffered the nickname of 'Stuffy'. Commander of 16 Squadron in 1915, a squadron member recorded him as 'efficient, strict, calm; he had a sense of duty'. He also added that Dowding was far too reserved and aloof with his juniors, caring too much for his own job and little for theirs. He was wrong. Dowding, like Haig, was a shy man and took every casualty as a personal blow. Dowding and Trenchard did not see eye to eye for Dowding vehemently disagreed with Trenchard's policy of the offensive. He believed it killed too many for too little return. Despite this, Trenchard, who became head of the post-war air force, offered him a permanent commission. Weir, appointed to the peerage as Baron Weir of Eastwood, Renfrewshire, on 26 June 1918, resigned from the Air Council in December 1918.

Production of aeroplanes tapered off as contracts expired. From some factories, the lovingly finished machines went immediately to a stores depot where workers callously reduced them to scrap. Just before Christmas 1918, another airship was ready to leave Beardmore's shed at Inchinnan. His Majesty's Airship R34 had spent a year under construction. Persistent bad weather kept her penned up and it was not until March 1919 that she was carefully taken out into the fresh air. She had cost the taxpayer about £350,000 in 1918 pound notes, the equivalent of some £14 million in 2007 money. She was a monster version of that aeronautical cul-de-sac, the rigid airship, at 643 feet long. Nineteen bags held two million cubic feet of hydrogen while five Sunbeam Maori engines of a reputed 270 horsepower turned her propellers. They were a compromise, although they were specifically designed for airships. The rather better Rolls-Royce powerplants were reserved for aeroplanes. At full power, R34 reached a top speed of 62 miles per hour in still air. With a height of 92 feet, a diameter of 79 feet, she was long enough to accommodate both Glasgow football teams and their Edinburgh opponents on separate pitches and all her bulk, all her power, enabled her to lift a total of 30 tons.

R34 was an Imperial measurement version of the German Zeppelin L33, a victim of anti-aircraft fire that brought her down almost intact at Little Wigborough in Essex on 24 September 1916. Dismembered, inspected, copied, plans went to Beardmore's and Armstrong-Whitworth, each already at work designing an airship for the Admiralty, with instructions to adapt their existing blueprints. The crew nicknamed her 'Tiny'. She began trials at Inchinnan on 14 March 1919. After a peaceful first flight, a modicum of excitement invaded her second trip. On the cold, windy afternoon of 24 March 1919, R34 set out on a longer flight despite the threat of snow, hail and intermittent fog. She flew west along the Clyde, turned south to Newcastle, ventured west to Liverpool, droned across the Irish Sea to Dublin before returning to East Fortune by way of the Isle of Man. At some point, the elevator jammed down, a misfortune that caused the blunt nose to rise but the ship was brought back to level flight and nursed home. At East Fortune, the ground crew made minor harm worse, since during handling, some main girders were damaged along with her propellers.

After repairs, the Royal Air Force accepted the ship. At 1800 hours on 28 May 1919, R34 left Inchinnan for East Fortune but ran into thick fog. To attempt a landing was foolhardy, so R34 headed out over the North Sea to wait and wait for better conditions. At 1530 hours the next day, she finally touched down at East Fortune with a ravenous crew on board who had not eaten for 21 hours. Her first service task, a fortnight after her arrival at her home base, was a six-hour journey around the Firth of Forth and over Berwick in company with R29. She followed this with a 56-hour trip around north Germany's Baltic coast in a not too subtle attempt to persuade the German public they should accept the Versailles Treaty. Zeppelins had bombed London and so British airships could repay the favour. After a sightseeing tour over Denmark, Norway and Sweden, R34 returned to East Fortune.

The Air Ministry decided to send R34 to the United States. The experts chose a northerly coastal route, close to land in case fuel ran short. Two battlecruisers, HMS *Renown*, from the Fairfield's Glasgow yard and HMS *Tiger*, built by John Brown at Clydebank, would patrol the route. They would provide weather reports and be ready to help if R34 got into difficulty. If necessary, they would take the airship in tow. In the very worst case, they would rescue the crew from the cold, grey Atlantic water. Eight men went ahead to New York to instruct the American ground crew in the handling of airships, since no rigid airship had ever been in America. Arrangements also had to be made for a supply of that dangerous airship essential, hydrogen. At East Fortune, food lockers replaced the original bomb racks. Extra hand basins and tables went into the crew quarters. More practically, two dozen extra petrol tanks were fitted along the keel. The airship would take off with 6,000 gallons of petrol for its record attempt.

To keep down the weight, only essentials went on board while the crew was restricted to thirty men including three supernumerary officers. One, Lieutenant Commander Zachary Lansdowne, represented the United States Navy who wanted their own airship branch. The other two 'special duties' passengers were Brigadier General Edward Maitland Maitland and Major John Edward Maddock Pritchard. Maitland was an experienced balloonist and airship expert. A professional soldier, he commanded the airship company of the Air Battalion before it gave way to the RFC. Maitland then took command of the RFC airship squadron. When the Admiralty acquired all British military airships, Maitland transferred to the RNAS. Amongst his minor achievements were parachute jumps from a balloon and an airship. Pritchard, born in England, was the son of a disappointed Confederate who left the United States for other shores when the South lost the American Civil War. An experienced airship pilot, he took the job of official photographer as well, apparently, as acting as an advisory first officer.

Soon after midnight on 2 July 1919 a tractor pulled open the heavy doors of R34's shed. Major George Herbert Scott, her captain, gave the order to 'walk her out', a command repeated by a bugle call, and the ground crew, 700 men, carefully moved R34 into a cold north-east breeze, into a morning of low cloud with a distant dank mist. Take-offs were better in the early hours, since cold air helped the airship get maximum lift from her hydrogen-filled gasbags. At 0148, R34 rose into the air. She turned her nose westward to head for the Atlantic. When she reached 100 feet, she entered cloud. Still climbing she emerged into a star-crusted sky at 1,500 feet. Twenty minutes after take-off, the crew glimpsed the lights of Rosyth below. As dawn crept across the hills of Stirlingshire, R34 was over Glasgow.

She crossed the Irish Sea, and as the crew settled into their routine, the worst job fell to the mechanics and the riggers. The Sunbeam Maori was notoriously temperamental. Greasy hands continually pumped fuel, and repaired and cleaned the five engines. At one stage, the water jacket of one engine cracked and the mechanics had to chew gum to fasten a sheet of copper over the leak. The riggers spent much time outside, on the spine of the airship, inspecting the fabric skin and gas valves. Most scorned the safety ropes and walked, bodies bent, into the wind, checking the surface. The other vital task was to inspect the hydrogen valves themselves, since gas leaks killed.

Across the Irish Sea, beyond Ireland and over the Atlantic she headed. The fog burned away. R34 cruised, not too comfortably, between two cloud layers. To maintain height, Scott kept the ship in a nose-up attitude of 12 degrees. Moisture seeped into R34 and she became cold, clammy and uncomfortable. In the wireless room, electric shocks from the equipment plagued the operators as they chatted to East Fortune and Clifden on the Irish coast.

Between Gasbags Six and Seven, above the crew's quarters, William Ballantyne shivered. Ballantyne was one of the crew who was not picked but he sneaked on board, determined not to miss the trip. However, the cold and a persistent smell of gas beat him and at 1400 hours a chilled and ill Ballantyne turned himself in. To make the stowaway walk the plank was out of the question although Scott, with Maitland by his side, contemplated the thought of giving Ballantyne a parachute and pushing him overboard. Only the fact that it was the Atlantic below and not the green fields of Ireland deterred him. Weight was critical. On board supplies had been carefully calculated. Even water was strictly rationed, and shaving and washing were luxuries – one more man could make a crucial difference.

Spared a soggy grave, Ballantyne was put to work. After a short period of rest to recover from his suffering he spent his days in the galley as cook as well as taking on the hard physical labour of pumping petrol into the tanks. Yet another unauthorised passenger appeared. Leading Aircraftman George Graham, a mechanic, had smuggled a small tabby kitten on board. She answered to the name of Wopsie and joined the special duties list to spend the trip providing entertainment and comfort for the crew.

A buzz of excitement ran through the ship at 1530. The first faint signal from Newfoundland sounded in the headphones of the wireless operators. Still in contact with East Fortune and Clifden, they passed on the news. The weather worsened as the wind grew fiercer. A storm brewed in the distance, and at 3,000 feet the ship plunged in and out of clouds. The temperature dropped. Scott put the engines to full to maintain height, the nose poking up at an uncomfortable angle. The next morning, 3 July 1919 at 0900, R34 reached mid-Atlantic despite the deteriorating weather. Occasional breaks in the cloud gave glimpses of the unfriendly seas below. By evening, the storm had sneaked closer and the airship fought her way against a 50-mph wind that tried to blow her backwards and sideways.

Scott tried to climb clear of the wind but without success, since no matter where R34 went, the wind buffeted her while driving rain hammered against the hull and leaks sprouted. The crew, forced to shout above the incessant noise, worked furiously to patch the fabric. Throughout the storm, R34 maintained a remarkable stability, slowly pitching fore and aft as she headed west. Relief came only with daybreak, when the clouds dispersed. The crew, gazing down, saw icebergs and pack ice in the cold ocean below.

At 1250, on 4 July, the first small islands off the Canadian coast appeared. R34 made landfall at Trinity Bay. Unwashed and unshaven, the grimy crew flew serenely over dark trees and darker lakes – but they still had 1,000 miles to cover. On the south-west course to Nova Scotia, Scott began to worry about his fuel. The petrol tanks had no gauges and dipstick measurement gave an approximate reading of 2,200 gallons remaining. With strong headwinds forecast, it looked unlikely that R34 could reach New York without refuelling. Scott made plans to divert to Rhode Island or Boston to refuel, and on the morning of 5 July, still battling headwinds, he headed for the Bay of Fundy, a long inlet between Nova Scotia and the mainland, in the hope the ship could shelter from the worst of the wind.

Flying along the Bay, a thunderstorm caught up with R34 and she fell several hundred feet. One man, near an open bow hatch, nearly pitched through it as the airship's nose dropped violently but a fortuitous girder saved him. The storm cleared and calm descended. Then a series of bumps in rough air bounced R34 up and down 'like a playful whale'. As if to apologise, the weather relented and the airship picked up a tailwind. Scott, calculating his endurance yet again, decided that it might just be possible to reach New York after all.

At 0900 on 6 July 1919, R34 arrived overhead at Hazlehurst Field, Mineola, New York. A huge grandstand, full of military and civic dignitaries, was surrounded by an enormous crowd. The car parks were jammed full and enterprising citizens sold hot dogs, flags and streamers, though there was confusion below. The eight men sent to New York had trained a ground crew but their commander had dashed off to Boston when it seemed R34 would divert there. An experienced officer was needed on the ground to organise the landing.

Pritchard volunteered to parachute down. Hot water from an engine radiator gave him the luxury of a washed and shaven face. Helped by two others, he clambered out of the control gondola, took a deep breath and jumped. Screams came from the crowd and a shiver ran through the mob until the parachute cracked open. Major John Edward Maddock Pritchard floated serenely down to the land of his father as R34 circled above his head.

At 0950, the 400 men of the landing party grabbed the handling ropes to bring the flight to its official finish at 0954. A band played the National Anthems of both countries and the crowd cheered. Pritchard became the first man to touch American soil after crossing the Atlantic by air. Wopsie took the feline trophy. George Graham subsequently turned down the chance of a smart profit, refusing an offer of $1,000 for the first aviator cat across the Atlantic. At the end of 108 hours and 12 minutes flying time, with 140 gallons of petrol left in her tanks, Scotland's airship had set the world endurance record for time aloft. Her average speed across the Atlantic was a fraction over 33 miles per hour.

R34 stayed in the USA for three days and the crew enjoyed the rest and the unlimited hot showers. Hospitality was everywhere despite Prohibition. The crew grew used to drinking 'lemonade' from anonymous bottles. Visitors thronged around the ship every day. Hugeness impresses, although one observer noted that 'close up one was astounded to see how the frame squeaked, bent and shivered with the cloth covering almost flapping in windy gusts'.

The mechanics overhauled the ship, cleaning and testing the Maoris that had belied their reputation for the most part with a reliable performance over the five-day flight. Engine oil, though, covered the propellers. A local company cleaned it off, free of charge, and took the opportunity to tell the American public so. Brigadier General Maitland visited the dentist while he was in New York – where the cost of his treatment came to a single autograph.

Warned of high winds for the next few days, Scott decided, at dinner on 9 July, to head homeward without delay. With the ship already restocked with food and water, and filled with hydrogen from thousands of cylinders, it became a matter of waiting until the coldest part of the day to get the most lift. At 2354, with a last minute gift of a wooden box of bootleg rum from a well-wisher, HMA R34 left the ground. A mighty cheer came from the waiting crowd as she rose into the air. In a gusting wind of some 30 knots, R34 climbed and headed east. As an appreciative gesture for New York's hospitality, Scott steered his way towards the city's bright lights. At 2,000 feet, carefully chosen to avoid even the highest skyscraper, at 0100 on the morning of 10 July 1919, R34 flew over crowded streets and rooftops. New Yorkers cheered, waved. Searchlights picked out the great silver shape against the summer night sky. After ten minutes, the drone of her engines started to fade as she turned towards the Atlantic.

A strong tailwind pushed the airship along at a spanking ninety miles per hour. As dawn lightened the eastern horizon, New York was already 400 miles behind the airship. The rear starboard engine failed but it made no difference to the speed. Even as the mechanics worked to restart it, R34 continued to race for home. Clouds rolled in to surround the ship, and once again the crew endured the miseries of damp and rain. Scott climbed to 3,000 feet, still taking advantage of the tailwind. Another engine blew and it took two hours to replace the broken valve springs. One mechanic fell against an engine clutch as the ship lifted her skirts to run in front of the wind. Set free from the gears, the engine raced to destruction as the connecting rods fractured. In-flight repair was impossible. The mechanics closed down the Maori but R34 continued to rack up the miles. However, the loss of the engine meant that the airship no longer had spare power for an emergency and so a tentative idea to fly over London was abandoned.

An Air Ministry signal arrived at 1000 hours on 12 July. The airship was not to return to East Fortune but to dock at Pulham in Norfolk. Scott queried the order but confirmation of its correctness came at 2330 with no explanation. Dark thoughts later surfaced that the change was a plot by the aeroplane faction within the RAF to deprive R34 of publicity. Airships had been the province of the old RNAS. The men who flew them were former Navy men and they suspected the worst.

As the clouds lifted, Scott climbed higher to smooth air. At 5,000 feet, the Atlantic below them was cold, grey and empty. Hours went by. Finally, the Irish coast passed underneath. The engines gave more trouble as the ship flew over Liverpool and the Mersey and headed towards Norfolk. When she arrived at Pulham, where a crowd of some 400 waited, most of them the landing party, only two of the five Maori engines worked. The crew let the propellers of the other three windmill in the airstream to give an impression that all was under control. Scott circled the airfield. It was Sunday 12 July 1919 at about 0640 and a small RAF band began to play. Scott approached the landing party, into wind, with all engines shut down. At the last moment, he realised the ship was down by the nose, so to bring it up, he dumped water ballast. It rained down on the musicians as they broke into *See The Conquering Hero Comes*. They played on, banging and blowing, undaunted. R34 docked at 0657, Greenwich Mean Time. She had taken 75 hours and 3 minutes to fly home, much aided by the wind at her back, at a mean speed of almost 51 miles per hour. In all, she had covered 7,420 miles at close to 43 miles per hour – airships were not speedy creatures.

After a stay at Pulham, R34 returned in triumph to East Fortune for a refit. She then went back to Pulham. Six weeks she left for a new home at Howden in East Yorkshire. On 21 June 1921, after another refit, R34 left on a trial flight that also incorporated an exercise for eight trainee navigators. In bad weather, she became lost and smacked into a hill on Guisborough Moor. The control car suffered minor damage but the fore and aft propellers were smashed. With just her two wing engines in use, she laboured back to Howden. The landing party, 400 strong, struggled in a rising cross-wind to move her into her shed but failed. Moored outside, the strong overnight winds pounded her into the ground. Early morning daylight revealed the wreckage: there was no choice but to break her up for scrap. In all, she had flown 400 hours.

Beardmore's had one final fling with airships, and the last to emerge from the great Inchinnan shed was R36. She too was designed using Zeppelin knowledge, not only from a study of L49 brought down in France, but from picking the brains of German designers once the war finished. Although construction began on a military airship, the end of the fighting brought extensive modifications to fit her for civilian use. Another monster at 675 feet long, using 2 million cubic feet of hydrogen, the behemoth lifted 16 tons, requiring a crew of 4 officers and 24 men. She made her trial flight to Pulham on 1 April 1921 and three days later, with journalists and Air Ministry officials on board, she took off on a demonstration flight. When she met some turbulence, the upper fin and rudder collapsed, but fortunately she landed without loss of life.

Swiftly repaired, R36 took on the role of a flying policeman when she flew over Ascot on 14 June 1921 to help with traffic control. On 17 June, 49 Members of Parliament enjoyed a luxurious trip, enhanced by expensive refreshments, over much of East Anglia. One week later, on 21 June 1921, approaching the mooring mast at Pulham, R36 dropped her mooring rope which was swiftly fastened to the landing mast by an attentive ground crew. Unfortunately, she approached too quickly and the rope fouled the foot of the mast. Instead of paying out, it snagged. R36 stopped with a jerk and two forward ballast bags released their contents. The nose shot upwards until halted by the cable and the sudden strain collapsed the bow.

One of the fatal enemies of moored airships approached: a rising wind. To move her into a mooring shed became more difficult as much space was taken by the L64 – a German airship seized as part of war reparations. She became the sacrifice to save R36 who would not survive in the open in a fierce wind. The ground crews collapsed the Zeppelin and set to work with hacksaws and hammers to make room for the Beardmore airship. On 22 June 1921, at around 0230, a handling party delicately moved R36 to the shed. A capricious gust of wind slammed her port side against the hangar doors to cause more damage. Further repairs made her airworthy, but she never flew again and in 1926 she was scrapped, her total flying life being about 80 hours.

When rejoicing maroons sounded and triumphant flags waved in November 1918 to celebrate the Armistice, the Royal Air Force had 22,647 aeroplanes and 103 airships. Some 27,333 officers, 263,837 men and 25,400 members of the WRAF filled 200 operational squadrons and 199 reserve or training squadrons. Scottish firms had produced over 2,000 aircraft during the war, ranging from the basic BE2c to the Handley Page V/1500 four-engined biplane bomber. They had even turned out flying boat hulls for big Felixstowe-class flying boats. They went down to England to the factory where the wings were made. As hulls were more easily damaged and more difficult to repair and transport than wings, it remains an eternal mystery as to why the process was not reversed.

With the defeat of Germany and its allies came change. Lloyd George swept to victory in the General Election of December 1918. The future of military flying, of the Royal Air Force itself, came under scrutiny. As part of the Prime Minister's shuffling for a new administration, Winston Churchill moved from the Ministry of Munitions and Lloyd George offered him either the War Office or the Admiralty and demanded a decision within twenty-four hours. As an afterthought, Lloyd George added that, whatever he chose, Churchill would also be Air Minister. 'I am not,' Lloyd George remarked firmly, 'going to keep it as a separate department.'

Churchill decided to become First Lord of the Admiralty but events intervened. The demobilisation programme, poorly thought out, had infuriated many soldiers and the arcane system resulted in men who had served since the start of the war in the trenches being kept back while others with only months, or even weeks, of service in England received their discharge. The temper of the rebellious troops did not improve when ministers and officers stressed that the penalty for mutiny was death. Insubordination and discontent spread. By January 1919 the situation was critical.

Lloyd George asked Churchill to become Secretary of State for War instead as 'the best man to confront the emergency', and he took up the challenge on 15 January 1919. It was not until the following month that Churchill looked at the second part of his job as Minister for Air. Sensibly, he took the advice of his Glaswegian predecessor. The forthright Weir expressed himself as 'scandalised and horrified' at

Lloyd George's casual decision. The Prime Minister's desire to economise on the fighting services now the war was done outraged the Scot. Admittedly, the air service had cost nearly one million pounds every single day in the last months of combat but destruction of the Royal Air Force was a fearsome remedy. Weir's carefully crafted advice to Churchill saved the day. Aware that the army was being reduced from 3½ million men to 900,000 soldiers as fast as the forms could be signed, Weir believed it was madness to jettison the wartime air force with no thought to the future.

Fortunately for the shape of things to come, Churchill, for once, listened and chose Hugh Trenchard to head a shrivelled air service. Sir David Henderson, who had done so much to create the RAF did not enter into consideration. Weir, though, had done his duty. The Royal Air Force survived. Months, even years of political in-fighting followed 'Boom' Trenchard's appointment. Politicians, admirals, generals and bureaucrats closed in, stilettos in hand, on the upstart, since the Treasury did not wish to spend the money. The other service chiefs resented a loss of power as they wanted aeroplanes for their own services. A third service, they believed, trespassed on their traditional preserves. The shenanigans were in Whitehall. Scotland simply endured their effects.

7

Not Cash But Courage

Lloyd George and Winston Churchill, anxious to scissor military spending, invented the 'Ten Year Rule' in 1919. This decreed 'the British Empire would not be engaged in any great war during the next ten years'. As the rule extended annually, the Treasury anticipated a long period of limited defence budgets. In 1928 Winston Churchill suggested that the rule could be self-perpetuating, to remain in force unless specifically countermanded.

Spending on the Royal Air Force fell to a meagre £15 million in 1920, which meant savage cutbacks. Aerodromes closed, aircraft and spares were sold or scrapped and by March 1920 the RAF had dwindled to 3,280 officers and 25,000 airmen with 3,260 aircraft in 33 squadrons, 8 of which were in the process of formation. The 'third service' barely survived. The War Office and the Admiralty were both anxious to smother the infant but it was saved by a radical proposal. Britain administered, under a League of Nations mandate, Mesopotamia, the former Ottoman Empire territory called Iraq, 'the distant province', by the Turks. The army had a hard time of it, keeping order, since the local population, promised independence, had no wish to change one colonial overlord for another. Trenchard pointed out that a handful of aeroplanes were far less expensive than a clutch of army battalions and that recalcitrant tribesmen could economically be kept in check by tactically placed bombs from above rather than an expensive and bitter ground campaign. When one side has no aircraft at all, air supremacy is not in doubt. Churchill welcomed the plan, since anything that saved Government money appealed to him.

Of the thirty or more airfields in Scotland, hardly any survived. Most of the few that hung on faced an imminent threat of closure. Some went into a state of hibernation known as 'Care and Maintenance' while others reverted completely to their pre-war use. By the end of the decade, Scotland had a mere three military airfields at Leuchars, Renfrew and Turnhouse.

Trenchard re-vamped the organisation of the Royal Air Force, itself an uneasy amalgam of the RFC and RNAS. When the RAF came into being, the home organisation divided within weeks into geographical areas responsible for all air service activity within them. North-western HQ at Glasgow took care of Scotland. By the end of 1920, Scotland's units had progressed from North-Western Area to Northern Area. They finally became 29 (Fleet) Group of the excitingly named Coastal Area in July 1920. Their sole purpose was to support the Fleet. The meagre list consisted of a grass airfield at Leuchars that was home to 203 and 205 Squadrons, Donibristle which served as the Coastal Area Aircraft Depot and a wireless station, RAF Units Afloat on HMS *Argus* and HMS *Furious*, and practice camps at Smoogro and at Houton Bay, which also doubled as a wireless station. Donibristle had kept itself busy overhauling aircraft destined for the two carriers and Leuchars. It also rebuilt war-weary two-seater de Havilland 9A bombers as three-seater fleet spotters with a busy line in scrapping surplus airframes and engines from all over Scotland. Thus military aviation in Scotland had almost ended.

At Newstead, close by Melrose in the Scottish Border country, one man decided to return with his family to his native land. Herman Hansen, a German, had been the town barber in Melrose before the war, and had married a local girl, Jessie Wilson. They had two children and were well liked. His popularity failed to save him from internment after the fighting began. When he reappeared in Melrose after confinement on the Isle of Man, the muttering began and his wife and children endured catcalls and insults. Eventually, 'Herman the German' called it a day in 1920. With Jessie and the boys, Wilhelm and Friedrich, he returned to Germany.

Trenchard had plans for the Royal Air Force. A major aim was to ensure that when war came again, the truncated air force expanded quickly. He instituted an apprentice scheme to supply skilled ground tradesmen and an RAF Cadet College at Cranwell to rival Dartmouth and Sandhurst. The first officer cadets graduated in September 1922. The winner of the Sword of Honour as best all round cadet was a Scot, Douglas Macfadyen, who eventually reached air marshal rank. In time, his son also graduated from Cranwell and also won the Sword of Honour, becoming an air marshal, a unique family achievement.

Trenchard formed the aerial equivalent of the 'Weekend Warriors' of the Territorial Army, and four squadrons founded the initial Auxiliary Air Force. The very first was 602 (City of Glasgow) Squadron, formed on 12 September 1925. It pipped three others to the honour. Two London area squadrons and 603 (City of Edinburgh) began one month later, the first of twenty-one auxiliary squadrons. One more Scottish squadron, 612 (County of Aberdeen) joined them in 1937.

The early squadrons, limited by a parsimonious budget, had 23 officers and 158 men. Trenchard himself chose the commanding officers, adjutants and flying instructors from the scramble of wartime fliers forced out of the savagely pruned post-war service. The frenzied demolition of 1919 tossed many fine officers into civilian life and the Auxiliary Air Force gave them the chance to serve again. The commanding officers, in turn, vetted the other applicants of all ranks with varying degrees of severity. Potential pilots often had to display their skill on a trial flight, and those who treated the control column as a crowbar failed.

Number 602 Squadron formed at Renfrew, handily placed adjacent to Arkleston Cemetery. Its first commanding officer was Squadron Leader Cyril Nelson Lowe, a regular soon succeeded by an Auxiliary officer, James Douglas Latta MC on 1 February 1926. At Edinburgh, 603 Squadron occupied Turnhouse. Major James McKelvie, AFC, took the commanding officer's hat, neatly transferring his rank to squadron leader as a member of the Auxiliary Air Force. Both squadrons were designated to fly bombers. They acquired the DH9A with some Avro 504K aircraft for training.

On 18 October 1929 the *London Gazette* carried the citation for the award of the Empire Gallantry Medal to a Scottish flight cadet at the RAF College. William Neil McKechnie, from Musselburgh, Midlothian, was twenty-one years old when he won the rarely bestowed medal. The citation was clear and precise:

On 20 June 1929, an aeroplane piloted by Flight Cadet C. J. Giles crashed on landing at Cranwell aerodrome and burst into flames. The pilot was stunned, but managed to release his safety belt and fall out of the machine in a dazed condition. Flight Cadet McKechnie, who had landed in another aeroplane about the same time some two hundred yards away, left his machine and ran at full speed towards the scene of the accident. The petrol had spread over an area about ten yards in diameter, in full blaze, with Giles lying in it semi-conscious. McKechnie, without hesitation, ran into the flames and pulled out Giles, who was badly burned. McKechnie, who was himself scorched and superficially burned, then proceeded to extinguish Giles's burning clothing. There is no doubt that without McKechnie's assistance Giles would have been burned to death, as he was quite incapable of moving himself. His machine was entirely destroyed, and the ground for some distance around was burned up by the spread of the ignited petrol.

A few years later, another hero, another Scot, won the Empire Gallantry Medal in May 1932. Edinburgh-born Flight Sergeant Eric Watt Bonar, of the RAF Reserve, was chief pilot of Northern Air Transport Ltd. On 24 May 1932 he was at 5 Flying Training School at Sealand when he rescued the pilot of an aircraft that burst into flames after a crash, grabbing an asbestos blanket, unfastening the safety straps and parachute harness and, with help, dragging the pilot clear of the blazing wreckage. Although he gave the airman first aid, the pilot later died in hospital from his injuries.

In September 1930 Hugh Dowding, the man from Moffat, now an air vice marshal, joined the Air Council as the member for Supply and Research. Funds were limited, and in the middle of an economic depression no politician wanted to spend money on soldiers, sailors or airmen and their expensive toys. Dowding knew well that developments in manufacturing, in airframe design and in engines would revolutionise aerial warfare. When a seaplane, substantially faster than the RAF's frontline fighters, won the Schneider Trophy contest, Dowding issued a specification for a new fighter aircraft. Aircraft makers, scratching a meagre living, submitted plans and began building prototypes. Dowding kept hopes alive.

In 1932, an Indian Army officer, Colonel Stuart Blacker, decided to organise an attempt to fly over Mount Everest, since he wanted to thwart Germany and France, who planned to make the flight themselves. The gloomy National Government, a devil's brew of the National Labour Party, the Conservative Party, the Liberal Party and the National Liberal Party, beset by economic woes, declined to offer financial support. Blacker looked for private sponsorship, and Lady Houston, a patriotic adventuress, obliged. Born in 1857, Fanny Lucy Radmall went on the stage, changing her name to Poppy. Aged sixteen, she eloped with a rich brewer, Frederick Gretton, who abandoned his wife for her. He died but bequeathed her £6,000 a year. In 1883, she married Theodore Brinckman, who succeeded to a baronetcy. After a divorce, twelve years later, she met her third husband, the bankrupt George Frederick William Byron, the 9th Baron Byron. He died in 1917. Fanny already displayed an interesting mixture of eccentricity, determination and patriotism. A determined suffragette, she founded a rest home during the war for nurses back from the fighting fronts, an enterprise that brought her a damehood in 1917.

As Lady Byron, DBE, she began a turbulent relationship in 1921 with Sir Robert Paterson Houston, an extremely wealthy Liverpool shipowner and narrow-minded Conservative MP. Fanny loathed Prussians, communists and socialists in roughly equal measures, considered Mussolini a hero and hated Woodrow Wilson, the US President – all beliefs that attracted Houston. They married in December 1924. Sir Robert died suddenly on his yacht in 1926, after which Fanny inherited more than £5 million. Anxious to see Britain supreme throughout the world, she donated £100,000 for a team to compete in the Schneider Trophy. They won with Mitchell's S6 design, and when she learned of the Everest Expedition, she funded the whole affair.

Two 602 Squadron officers, the commanding officer, Squadron Leader Douglas Douglas-Hamilton, Marquess of Douglas and Clydesdale, and his adjutant, Flight Lieutenant David McIntyre, were selected as the main pilots. Britain had a secret ingredient, the supercharged Bristol Pegasus engine. This had taken an aircraft to nearly 44,000 feet. The Pegasus now went into an aeroplane called the Westland PV3, subsequently renamed the Houston-Westland. Lord Clydesdale was chosen as pilot. A back-up aircraft, the roughly similar Westland PV6, later known as the Wallace, also with the special engine, was assigned to McIntyre. Both machines carried a photographer since vertical survey photographs were an important part of the objective. Each aircraft also had heated cockpits and an oxygen supply.

Under the command of Air Commodore Peregrine Forbes Morant Fellowes, DSO, the expedition arrived at Lalbalu airfield, 160 miles southeast of Everest, towards the end of March 1933. The heavy equipment went by sea. Fellowes, his wife, and some of the other team members flew three de Havilland Moths from England to the base camp, an adventure in itself. On 3 April the summit of Everest was free from cloud. The expedition's meteorologist forecast a wind speed at 28,000 feet of 67 mph and of 58 mph at 30,000 feet. This was high but acceptable, and the pilots decided to go. Both aircraft bore civil registrations as well as RAF markings. McIntyre's Wallace had the registration G-ACBR. Clydesdale flew the PV3 labelled G-ACAZ. Sidney Bonnett, a Gaumont-British cameraman, was McIntyre's observer and photographer. Colonel Stuart Blacker personally did the same for Clydesdale.

At 31,000 feet, the aircraft headed for the summit of Everest but the wind, fierce; and unhindered, drove them off course so that they approached the mountain from the leeward side. Although Clydesdale climbed as hard as possible, a down draught grabbed his aircraft. The cockpit floor fell away from underneath his feet for seconds as the aeroplane dropped 2,000 feet before it escaped the air current. The summit of Everest towered on the left while downwind to the right, 14 miles away, the fifth-highest mountain in the world, Makalu, beckoned. A connecting ridge knifed its way from Makalu to Everest and its sharp summit rose in front of Clydesdale. The wind pushed him towards Makalu and he could not turn back. If he went to the left, he would be back into the down current which could take him straight into the lesser ridges. A turn to the right would take him perilously close to Makalu, aided and abetted by the ever-increasing wind.

Clydesdale climbed and hoped. After agonising minutes, the Houston-Westland missed the ridge by feet. He later admitted it was 'cleared by a more minute margin than he cared to think about, now or ever'. In the rear cockpit, Blacker fought the fierce cold that chilled every metal part. He operated two heavy cameras, one still and one cinema. The still camera had to be loaded for each shot with a glass plate. Fighting for breath with the effort of continually lifting each camera in turn, Blacker watched through the floor hatch as the PV3 scraped over the summit. For one moment, he thought the tail skid would hit the snow below.

McIntyre was also in dire straits, since his Wallace had slightly less performance than Clydesdale's aircraft. Full power didn't take him higher, but luck was with him and an up-current of air caught the aircraft as they approached a certain crash and G-ACAZ scraped over. McIntyre's photographer, Bonnett, trod on his oxygen hose and it split. He had just enough time to tie a handkerchief round it before he fell unconscious. McIntyre looked round and lost the feed to his mask but he managed to clasp the mask to his face before he too passed out. He held it in place with one hand while he lost height as fast as he dared. At 8,000 feet, safe from oxygen starvation, McIntyre let go of his own mask and looked round. Sidney Bonnett, struggling to his feet, was a 'nasty dark green shade but obviously alive and that was enough for the moment'. Clydesdale and Blacker flew around Everest for another 15 minutes. The colonel crammed plate after plate into the camera before they finally turned for Lalbalu.

Press and public alike acclaimed the expedition a success – Everest, unconquered by any mountaineer, had fallen to the aeroplane. Unfortunately, the roses in the garden were withered. Sid Bonnett had spent much of the flight senseless on the cockpit floor while Blacker's survey photographs were ruined by a dust haze. In addition, Gaumont-British wanted more cinema footage. Fellowes decided to make a test flight to check machines and equipment before a second attempt. He flew the Wallace himself, with another observer, over Kanchenjunga, 90 miles to the east of Lalbalu. One of the Moth pilots took charge of the Houston-Westland with Sid Bonnett in the rear cockpit. Both aircraft met severe turbulence over the towering Himalayas and the aircraft lost sight of each other in a welter of cloud. Fellowes suffered oxygen problems. The insidious effects of hypoxia snagged into his brain, although he stayed alert enough to turn the Wallace round and head south out of the peaks.

The Houston-Westland arrived at Lalbalu without further incident. Fellowes did not appear. All the Houston-Westland crew knew was that their last sight of him had been as he headed for Kanchenjunga. While the party at the airfield fretted, Fellowes determinedly followed a railway line with no idea of his position. Finally sighting a station, he landed and a large and enthusiastic audience arrived. Fellowes did not want to switch off the engine, despite the risk of some of the throng walking into the airscrew, since the starting handle was back at base.

The providential railway station was at Shampur, well east of Lalbalu. Now sure of their whereabouts, Fellowes and Bonnett, after some energetic crowd control, produced enough room for the take-off run and became airborne again. Soon afterwards, the needle on the fuel gauge pointed uncompromisingly towards zero. Another convenient village swam into view and the Westland landed neatly at a promising settlement with a telegraph wire. From Dinjapur, Fellowes sent a reassuring telegram to Lalbalu. One of the Moths arrived the next day with cans of fuel and the invaluable starting handle. The Wallace droned happily back to base. The close call of the Kanchenjunga flight put a second Everest attempt into doubt. The expedition's insurers, fearful of a raid on their coffers, hastily advised they covered only two flights over the Himalayas. A third attempt was outside their remit unless, naturally, an extra premium appeared.

Lady Houston, whose eccentricities included a fanatical belief in the healing properties of fresh air and wandering around unclothed, fancied herself also as a prophetess. She sent an ominous telegram as soon as she heard the news: 'The good spirit of the mountain,' she cabled, 'has been kind to you and brought you success. Be content. Do not tempt the evil spirits of the mountain to bring disaster. Intuition tells me to warn you there is danger if you linger.' Whether the spirits heard her is debatable, but what is not in doubt is that Fellowes immediately succumbed to a fever. The meteorologist and an assistant received serious burns when one of their hydrogen balloons exploded. As a final hint, the weather clamped and Mount Everest, the highest peak in the world, vanished under cloud.

Lesser men would have shrugged and gone home, since there was no disgrace in packing in. Clydesdale and McIntyre thought differently, as they had enough oxygen for a final uninsured attempt. When the weather cleared on 19 April, with the firm support of Stuart Blacker and Sid Bonnett, they decided to make their last try. They planned the flight without telling Fellowes because they believed he would forbid the enterprise. The forecast wind was higher than on the first flight and the two 602 Squadron pilots decided to fly down wind at a relatively low level before they turned and climbed to 34,000 feet to approach the mountain in the teeth of the wind.

Their ground speed was close to abysmal as they closed on the mountain. Clydesdale turned east towards Makalu. McIntyre, who felt he and Bonner had missed out the first time round, pressed on. In bright sunshine and clear air, he spent fifteen minutes edging towards the summit with its plume of ice. At last, the top of the mountain disappeared from view beneath the thundering Pegasus engine. McIntyre was not sure if he had passed over the summit. The Wallace seemed to be flying in a vacuum when, without warning, a tremendous bump shook the aircraft. The Wallace was pushed upwards. McIntyre felt relief wash over him. That was the sure sign that he was above the pinnacle. With infinite care, he banked gently to the right. The compass needle swung until it pointed at Lalbalu and an elated McIntyre set course for home.

Two Scottish pilots had been the first to fly over the highest point on earth.

Fellowes was not pleased. Without permission, without insurance, the flight flirted with disaster. But he calmed down eventually, since they had all returned safely and the vertical survey photographs touched perfection. Any residual fury died away when *The Times* neatly referred to the exploit, 'made in uninsured aeroplanes and without authority . . . yielded results of the highest scientific value'. To wipe the slate clean, Sir John Salmond, who had succeeded Trenchard as Chief of the Air Staff, telegraphed his personal congratulations. Lord Clydesdale and David McIntyre were off the hook and they returned to Britain and adulation.

Three months earlier, one Adolf Hitler became Chancellor of Germany. Although Ramsay MacDonald tried to dump the Ten Year Rule in 1931, his Cabinet, led by an obstinate Foreign Secretary, kept it in force. Saving money on the military was essential in the middle of economic depression. The total defence budget in 1932 came to a miserly £102 million. By 1933 the Cabinet, led by the Chancellor Neville Chamberlain, decided such parsimony endangered the nation. In March, they scrapped the rule although they emphasised the decision was no carte blanche to spend money.

By 1934 the most cursory assessment showed Britain's defences were in a parlous state. The RAF had a mere 30,000 personnel. They looked after 732 aircraft, spread over 76 squadrons on 34 aerodromes spread across the whole of the United Kingdom. Government plans called for an increase in frontline squadrons from 41 to 128. More squadrons meant more airfields and a lot more training. Scotland, with its empty airspace became an obvious choice. Training schools, in particular, needed long stretches of flat, well-drained land and, in an ideal world, a fog-free climate. To spread the available money as far as could be, the Air Ministry came up with a wheeze that offered training contracts to private companies. Successful applicants provided and paid for suitable landing fields, aeroplanes and instruction to an agreed standard. In the days when even airliners operated perfectly well from grass fields, when basic aeroplanes cost no more than a large car and plenty of former RAF pilots were around to instruct, there was a modest stampede to collect one of the new contracts. Amongst the applicants was a specially formed company, Scottish Aviation Limited.

The pilots of 602 Squadron had discovered that when their own field clamped in, the Ayrshire coast was usually clear. The Marquess of Clydesdale and David McIntyre, still surrounded by their Everest fame, recommended the site to the de Havilland Company, makers of the renowned Tiger Moth, an aeroplane widely recognised as a perfect training aircraft. The company already operated some of the new schools. One on the Scottish west coast fitted in neatly.

Scottish Aviation received a contract. Their school would have eight instructors and sixteen aircraft for thirty-two pupils. Airfield construction began in September 1935. A pasture on the Ayrshire coast became a proper aerodrome, the ubiquitous 2 Squadron claiming credit for being the first to use the field in July 1913, when three aircraft operated from Monkton Meadow, now covered by concrete as part of Prestwick Airport.

New fighter aircraft appeared – the Gladiator, designed to the 1930 specification, entered service in 1934 while Supermarine and Hawker had new designs on the drawing board. Dowding, aware of what was going on, issued two specifications for fighter aeroplanes, F36/34 to Hawker and F37/34 to Supermarine. They were for monoplane fighters equipped with eight machine guns. His intervention meant that most of the cost of the two designs was borne by the Government. Hawker, who produced a long series of fighter and bomber biplanes for the RAF, used proven methods for their aeroplane. Fabric covered wooden formers. Supermarine broke ranks and went for a metal monocoque construction.

Montrose, which had been sold off like so many other airfields at the end of the First World War, was bought back from its owners for the princely sum of £18,600. Aeroplanes, airfields and men were all needed. The pace quickened and in July 1936 the Government announced the introduction of the Royal Air Force Volunteer Reserve – for men only. The Reserve would embrace all categories of air and ground crew although pilot training took precedence. Initially concentrated, as always, in London and the south of Britain, the scheme slowly spread throughout the United Kingdom.

The Chief of Air Staff was Sir Edward Leonard Ellington, a prime contender for the title of the most misjudged and underrated service chief in history. Ellington brought about the biggest single organisational change in the whole history of the Royal Air Force when, during 1936, he oversaw the scrapping of geographical chains of command for a new system based entirely on function. All fighters were placed under a new body, Fighter Command, which had subordinate area groups. The responsibility for the defence of Scotland went to 13 Group.

Ellington returned the Naval Air Branch to the Admiralty in 1937, giving their Lordships responsibility for flying at sea, a settlement that upset Trenchard and many others. In fact, it was a far-sighted decision. In wartime, carrier operations are a Navy affair. The RAF kept control of land-based maritime patrol aircraft, which came under the newly formed Coastal Command. The new system failed to attract universal joy, since critics claimed that all air fighting, defensive or offensive, should be under the control of a single commander. Ellington stuck to his guns and, in July 1936, he appointed the first head of Fighter Command – Hugh Caswall Tremenheere Dowding.

On 1 January 1937, Dowding received his final promotion to air chief marshal. From his new headquarters, he started to build an effective air defence system. He had three cherished assets: two were the results of the 1934 monoplane fighter specifications. Hawker's called their aircraft the Hurricane. Supermarine named their machine the Spitfire, a title that infuriated the designer, Mitchell, who called it 'a bloody silly name'.

The third precious pearl was the work of another Scot, Robert Alexander Watson-Watt. Inventing ran in his family, one ancestor being James Watt whose observation of a rumbustious lid on a boiling kettle ushered in the era of the steam engine. Born in Brechin in 1892, the seventh child and fifth son of a carpenter, Robert won bursaries, scholarships, prizes and medals with astounding ease. He devoured applied mathematics, electrical engineering and natural philosophy, more familiarly now known as physics, and when he graduated from Dundee, then part of St Andrews, in 1912, he was at once offered an assistant's post by the professor of natural philosophy, William Peddie. Peddie, an Orcadian, inspired Robert to investigate the phenomenon of wireless telegraphy or radio waves.

In September 1915 Watson-Watt arrived at the Royal Aircraft Factory at Farnborough as a member of the Meteorological Office. They had expressed interest in his theory that radio waves could identify thunderstorms. Lightning gives a radio signal when it ionises the air and Watson-Watt believed that if this were detected, pilots could be warned of approaching storms. He soon proved long-range detection was practicable and with the use of a hand-turned antenna, he developed the procedure to decide the signal's direction by its volume. It was not until 1923, with the invention of the cathode ray tube, that he acquired a visual representation on a screen. Watson-Watt had proposed the method in 1916 but it took a while for manufacturing to catch up. With the tube, Robert Watson-Watt detected and located thunderstorms several hundred miles distant. By 1927 two 'Cathode Ray Tube Direction Finders' operated from Slough and Cupar. The system not only found thunderstorms but also pinpointed the source of radio signals.

After the war, Watson-Watt continued his work at the Radio Research Station. This amalgamated in December 1927 with the radio section of the National Physical Laboratory. Watson-Watt became Superintendent of the new body. In 1933 another re-organisation sent him to Teddington as superintendent of the Radio Department of the National Physical Laboratory.

Early Nazi propaganda claimed that Germany possessed that staple of pulp fiction, a death-ray. This remarkable invention would bring down aircraft high in the sky by stopping their engines or even exploding them. The Air Ministry asked Watson-Watt whether beams of high frequency radio energy could do the same. He passed the problem to his assistant, Arnold Wilkins, with the purposeful suggestion that he ascertain how much radio energy was needed to heat a gallon of water from three miles away.

Wilkins took little time to prove the scheme was ludicrous. He showed his workings to Watson-Watt. Asked if anything could be done for air defence, the assistant mentioned that post office engineers who worked on VHF communications noticed a flutter in the signal when an aircraft passed over. Wilkins quickly established how much energy was reflected from an aircraft that passed across a radio beam. A transmitter of reasonable strength could do the job.

A report to the Air Ministry on 12 February 1935 produced a practical experiment fourteen days later. Using a BBC shortwave transmitter at Daventry and an RAF Heyford bomber, a lumbering biplane with a fixed undercarriage, Robert Watson-Watt and Arnold Wilkins tested their theory in some secrecy and showed that the system worked. Known as RDF, or radio direction finding, Watson-Watt led a team of engineers and physicists at a new and secret establishment at Bawdsey in Suffolk. They overcame the inevitable setbacks to produce a reliable defence system and by 1938 the first chain of detection stations operated along the east coast. To supplement the modern science was an organisation that relied on eyesight and binoculars. The largely volunteer Observer

Corps was linked to Dowding's operations rooms as an integral part of the defence system. RDF could find aeroplanes but it could not identify them. Even when a system arrived to distinguish enemy aircraft from friendly ones, the Observer Corps continued to prove its worth time and time again.

Montrose re-opened in January 1936 as 8 Flying Training School. At Prestwick, the Marquess of Clydesdale officially opened a grass aerodrome for 12 Elementary and Reserve Flying Training School. At the earnest request of nearby householders, each Tiger Moth had a silencer fitted to cut down the noise from the single Gipsy III engine. The third of Scotland's Auxiliary Air Force units formed in June 1937. Number 612 (County of Aberdeen) Squadron came into existence as an army co-operation unit at Dyce, then a civil aerodrome. In due course, the RAF took over the complete airfield.

As the international situation worsened, service preparations increased. In 1937 a compulsory purchase order acquired 375 acres of fine farm land on the eastern side of Findhorn Bay on the Moray Firth. The site was ideal for a flying training base although the *Northern Scot* for 29 January 1938 claimed that the new station, Kinloss, would be home to three fighter squadrons. Work began on clearing the site in March 1938. Not too far away, the expansion scheme also saw the development of Lossiemouth as an airfield.

Squadrons based in England used Scotland for training, away from interested eyes. West Freugh, on the Mull of Galloway, opened in 1937 as an Armament Training Camp. But not everything always went to plan as the then Sergeant Pilot Joe Northrop remembered:

The Squadron moved after Hogmanay, flying in formation with a ground party going by train. Few of us had expected to do much flying so far north at that time of the year but we were to be proved wrong. For much of the next three weeks the weather conditions stayed good and we were able to keep to the daily programme on the ranges. Generally speaking the gunnery details against the ground targets and the drogues towed by Westland Wallaces went off without much trouble, and firing live at these targets was much enjoyed by the crews. Our problems started on the bombing ranges when, after initial low level practices at around 250 feet, we attempted bombing at heights above the freezing level.

89

The aircraft were picketed out in the open. When the temperature dropped at night any moisture in the air was condensed on the electrical selector switches inside the cockpit and on the external electro-magnetic releases on the bomb carriers inside the pods on the wings. As soon as the aircraft climbed above the freezing level (and at this time of the year it was usually near the ground) everything froze up and it proved impossible to operate the bombing panel switches in the air. We tried every trick we could think of, e.g. taking off with bombs already selected and master switch on. It made no difference. And when a few switches did work the bomb casings of the practice bombs froze in the air, then fell away on landing. Eventually we abandoned attempts to drop bombs and concentrated on gunnery, carrying out up to four or five daily sorties each on the ground screens and the sleeve targets.

Half-way through our stay at West Freugh we were joined by 101 Squadron who were still equipped with old twin engined biplanes, Boulton and Paul Overstrands.

During our last week there Scotland was hit by line squalls sweeping in from the Atlantic and gales of over 100 miles an hour were forecast moving across the country from west to east. Under such abnormal conditions it would be impossible to ensure the safety of our aircraft if they were picketed facing into the wind because of the large angle of attack presented by the mainplanes in this position. We therefore clamped all the control surfaces and turned the aircraft tail into winds hoping that the wind pressure would push down on the upper surfaces of the mainplanes and hold the aircraft firmly in contact with the ground.

All that night we stood by on emergency and were rewarded by seeing that the plan worked, for when the high winds stuck, the Wellesleys stayed firmly rooted to the ground and rode out the storm without any damage. The other squadron was not so lucky and sustained damage to several aircraft despite the use of treble screw pickets. It was the only occasion on which I ever saw a twin-engined aircraft tethered to screw pickets with its wheels off the ground and both airscrews windmilling from the force of the wind. In the paper the following day we read that a complete squadron of twin-engined Heyfords at an aerodrome on the east coast of Scotland had been blown into the sea and lost without trace.

In February 1938 Turnhouse hit the news headlines when one of Dowding's new fighters, a Hurricane, piloted by the commanding officer of 111 Squadron, Squadron Leader John Woodburn Gillan, flew from Edinburgh to London in 48 minutes. The aeroplane covered the 327 miles at an average speed of 408.75 miles per hour to claim an unofficial world airspeed record, previously held by a specially adapted German Messerschmitt Bf109. Exultant press stories emphasised that the aeroplane was standard-issue and, in addition, had flown the distance at night in a triumph of pilot navigation. They unaccountably overlooked the near 100-knot tail wind that scurried the Hurricane from Turnhouse to Northolt, since propaganda does not wait for the firing to begin. Gillan, from Edinburgh died over France in 1941, having twice won the Distinguished Flying Cross as well as the Air Force Cross.

Scotland, short of airfields and squadrons to call its own, enjoyed plenty of visitors from further south. Number 62 Squadron, normally based at Cranfield, sent B Flight with its Bristol Blenheims for a spell at Abbotsinch. They had a purpose in life for Glasgow hosted the 1938 Empire Exhibition. Each day, the Blenheims would take off to fly in smart formation above the heads of the crowd. The Blenheim owed much of its design to Frank Barnwell, brought up in Stirling with his brother Harold, and educated at Fettes. Jack Cornelius of 62 Squadron recalled:

> Returning to Abbotsinch one day, on landing, Blenheim L1108 overshot the landing strip. The brakes of the aircraft failed to stop it crashing into the Duty Pilot's Office that was, fortunately, a wooden building.
>
> The duty pilot would have normally been sat at his desk, watching the incoming aircraft. He would certainly have been killed. Fortunately, he had just gone to the toilet and, although very embarrassed when he ran out, was amazingly unhurt.
>
> None of the aircraft crew were injured and blessed the fact that the building was made of wood not brick, or the crash would have resulted in a far more serious incident.

In flying, tears and laughter live perilously close to one another. At Kinloss and Lossiemouth, work progressed at full speed. Both were designed to have permanent buildings although tarmac runways were not on the plans. Construction work was scheduled for August 1938 with an opening date for the new flying school pencilled in as April 1939. The Munich Crisis changed that. Even as Neville Chamberlain brandished Hitler's worthless promise in front of film cameras and a cheering crowd, the Air Ministry made decisions. Brick buildings must wait. Kinloss and Lossiemouth made do with wooden huts.

HMS *Furious*, still going strong, put to sea while the politicians debated. The Admiralty dreamed of a pre-emptive strike. Auxiliary Air Force squadrons learned that they were now classed as frontline units. Number 602 and 603 Squadrons, recently equipped with Gladiators, made ready to meet the enemy. At Dyce, 612 Squadron, designated as an army co-operation unit, and flying old-fashioned Hawker Hector biplanes, discovered they were to change their role and receive new machines. The Avro Anson would come their way for their new tasks as a general reconnaissance squadron. At the end of 1938, if sheer numbers were the guide, the Royal Air Force was outnumbered by the Luftwaffe. They had two fighters and two medium bombers for every one of the British. It could have meant disaster in the coming war if Trenchard, now well retired, and Baron Weir, the man from Glasgow, had not created a final, war-winning plan.

In 1936 Trenchard recalled how production shortages, especially with aero-engines, severely handicapped the Royal Flying Corps in the last two years of the First World War. Aware that enemy bombing could cause industrial havoc, Trenchard proposed a scheme of 'Shadow Factories' as satellites to existing plants. The manufacturers agreed to the scheme. Rolls-Royce established a plant at Hillington near Glasgow, which opened in 1939. 'If Hillington had not been in existence,' later recalled the managing director of Rolls-Royce, Arthur Frederick Sidgreaves, 'there would not have been sufficient Merlins to fight the Battle of Britain'.

Weir himself took on the job of organising sub-contractors and he insisted on the highest production standards, an approach that cost money but gave both aircrew and ground staff boosted morale. Quantity is not always better than quality, although Weir managed both with his painstaking approach, in particular, with the Spitfire. Weir himself called it 'a sheer delight to fly but an engineer's nightmare to build'. He had the aeroplane stripped down into every detachable part. Some components were amalgamated while others vanished under Weir's ruthless investigation. With the Hurricane more amenable to mass production, Britain entered the run-up to the conflict with two monoplane fighters largely free from faults. They had eight machine-guns each, a variable pitch propeller, a new retractable undercarriage and a VHF radio link between the pilot and a ground controller.

Without Weir's groundwork, often overlooked, neither Spitfire nor Hurricane would have been around in large enough numbers to fight Nazi Germany. If one man made up for political dithering about aircraft production in the run-up to the war, it was the first Viscount Weir.

8

In Business Again

Chamberlain had little choice at Munich, since Britain had no capacity to fight a war. The deal with Hitler bought time, a priceless asset to a relatively prosperous but poorly armed democracy. In September 1938 Fighter Command had a mere 93 Hurricanes amongst its 666 frontline aircraft and no Spitfires were in service. Even the Hurricanes did not fight above 15,000 feet as they had no heating for their guns. The air defence of Great Britain largely rested with a collection of obsolescent biplanes and against this motley force, the Luftwaffe could send 1,200 modern bombers. One year later, Dowding had more than 500 monoplane fighters, Hurricanes and Spitfires, complete with heating systems for their eight Browning machine-guns.

Most military thinkers recognised that war was just a matter of time, since too many knew of Göring's boast that the day would come when the world trembled before German might. In truth, no policy other than abject surrender would have satisfied Hitler. Chamberlain, an honourable man, had no choice but to sacrifice Czechoslovakia. Although accused of appeasement, his actions saved Britain.

For most voters, the Prime Minister had done the right thing, and even in December 1939 some 60 per cent of those questioned agreed the one-time iron-foundry boss was right to make the deal. Whatever the public belief, the RAF prepared for war. The men with theodolites and maps who tramped through Scotland to find suitable airfield sites did their bit, since construction was the order of the day, along with more men and more aircraft. Newspapers, amongst them the *Falkirk Herald* of 29 April 1939 carried official notices in an almost unbroken stream:

It is announced by the Air Ministry that arrangements have now been completed for the entry of personnel for training at a new Royal Air Force Volunteer Training Centre situated at Edinburgh Airport, Grangemouth.

Applications for entry as pilots, air observers or wireless operators/air gunners are invited immediately from candidates resident in the district.

The Royal Air Force Volunteer Reserve has been created to ensure the maintenance of adequate reserves for the reinforcement of the Royal Air Force in times of national emergency and an increase in the strength of the Volunteer Reserve is an important part of the latest expansion scheme.

At Crail, in Fifeshire, the disused aerodrome from the First World War became the scene of strenuous naval activity. In October the following year, it would come into use as HMS *Jackdaw*. Like many Scottish airfields, it trained aircrew and by the end of 1940, Swordfish and Albacores buzzed busily over the Firth of Forth as they dropped practice torpedoes. The Fleet Air Arm gave the Admiralty a lever to claim back Donibristle as HMS *Merlin*. The Navy commissioned it on 24 May 1939 as a major aircraft repair yard for Rosyth. It also served as a temporary base for carrier squadrons as their home ships were fitted out or repaired.

On the Moray Firth, two new stations opened. An Airspeed Oxford, serial N4584, flown by Flight Lieutenant Reuben Pears Widdowson on 9 May 1939 became the first aircraft to arrive at 14 Service Flying Training School, Kinloss. Across the way, 15 FTS took its first pupils at Lossiemouth, like its neighbour a grass airfield with no hard runways. At Wick, the small grass aerodrome developed by Highland Airways fell into RAF hands. This received hard runways with a collection of permanent buildings. Wick became a major station in Coastal Command, administered from 18 Group Headquarters at Pitreavie Castle in Fife.

Pitreavie Castle itself only passed to the RAF in 1938 for the sum of £12,306. Although enjoying the title of castle, it had been extensively remodelled as a family home. The estate had once belonged to Lady Christina Bruce, sister of King Robert, in the fourteenth century but had passed through a succession of owners until 1884 when Henry Beveridge, a wealthy mill owner, bought the property. When he died in

1922, his widow and children moved into a smaller home on the estate. Pitreavie Castle fell into decay and the gardens ran wild. Desolate, forbidding, gloomy, eventual demolition seemed inevitable.

However, the re-organisation of the Royal Air Force saved it. Although the Navy had a Fleet Air Arm, searching for enemy ships, providing air support to naval forces at sea and acting as long-range reconnaissance for the Navy remained an Air Force task. Close liaison with Royal Navy planners and the need for a joint headquarters was obvious. In 1938, two RAF officers had the chore of finding a suitable site for the proposed Maritime Headquarters and HQ 18 Group. They stumbled across Pitreavie Castle, covered in ivy, with colonies of bats enjoying life in the upper rooms while the unloved gardens merely added to the sense of despair. Underneath the ivy, though, the building was sound – built to last by Victorian workmen. The extensive grounds allowed for extra buildings while the proximity to Rosyth was a considerable bonus.

Work on an underground bunker for the Maritime Headquarters began in 1938 and was completed in 1941. Amongst other commotions, the bunker saw the hunt for the *Tirpitz* as well as the planning of raids against enemy shipping off the coast of Norway. Above all, the Maritime Headquarters was a prime player in the Battle of the Atlantic.

Pitreavie Castle almost outshone Montrose for hauntings. As the site of an ancient castle that had seen its share of blood-letting, it boasted three ghosts to the single one at Montrose, all three dating to the time of the Battle of Pitreavie in 1651 during what yon southern nation calls the Civil Wars but which Scotland knows as the Covenanters' War. Pitreavie supplied a Lady in Green and a Lady in Grey to haunt the castle itself. A headless Highlander provided the third spectre. He roamed the area outside the castle in search of his dead and dying companions whose moans and shrieks were clearly heard. Fortunately all three phantoms seem to have supported the war against Germany. They restricted their activities to placing a ghostly hand on a shoulder from behind or gliding silently through walls.

Montrose itself received the Ansons of 269 Squadron on 25 August 1939. The vice-free 'faithful Annie' had one major defect in the eyes of those who flew it, since the undercarriage manually retracted and lowered. Former crew claim it took 140 turns of the handle to move the wheels up or down. It was a duty much beloved by second pilots who could, allegedly, be distinguished by a bulging bicep on one arm. Not surprisingly, the wheels often stayed down on short flights. The

Ansons had an important, if mind-numbing, job to do. They patrolled out to sea from the east coast to report and ideally prevent an enemy surface raider breaking out undetected into the wide sweep of the Atlantic.

In September 1939 the Royal Air Force had a grand total of 118,000 personnel. This included the first 8,000 members of the newly formed Women's Auxiliary Air Force, an offshoot of the Auxiliary Territorial Service formed in 1938 to help the army. There were 9,343 aeroplanes, of which 1,191 were designated as first-line machines.

Scotland wasted no time in meeting the enemy. A Glaswegian, Flying Officer Andrew McPherson of 139 Squadron, became the first British pilot to enter German airspace in the war when he captained a Blenheim IV, N6125, on a photographic sortie over the German fleet, north of Wilhelmshaven, on 4 September 1939. Later awarded the Distinguished Flying Cross, he was killed on 12 May 1940. On the second day of hostilities, a Lockheed Hudson from 224 Squadron of Coastal Command, based at Leuchars, attacked a German flying boat, a Dornier 18, over the North Sea. The Hudson, a twin-engined monoplane maritime patrol bomber, was a recent addition to the RAF inventory. It comfortably out-gunned the obsolescent enemy aircraft. Powered by a pair of diesel engines, mounted in line so that one pulled and the other pushed, the two-gun Dornier was no great combat machine. This particular one escaped. A similar machine enjoyed the melancholy distinction of being the first German aircraft shot down when it succumbed to a Fleet Air Arm Blackburn Skua over the North Sea on 26 September 1940. The Skuas came from HMS *Ark Royal*, on patrol between Scotland and Norway. Two weeks later, on 9 October 1939, a 224 Squadron Hudson shot down yet another Dornier 18 off Jutland.

The men who flew Hudsons enjoyed better amenities than those of the Coastal Patrol Flights based at Dyce and Abbotsinch. Their fine identity disguised the perilous fact that they flew the ever-willing single-engined DH82a Tiger Moth biplane trainer. Generally known as 'Scare-crow Patrols', their existence owed much to the theory that a U-boat skipper would dive at the sight and sound of an aircraft. Each Tiger Moth carried emergency gear in the form of an inflated inner tube and two carrier pigeons in specially designed containers.

Scotland's two Auxiliary Air Force squadrons served as the region's air defence. Both squadrons began to receive Spitfires during September

1939. Nearly all fighter stations were in the south of England, a remnant of military thinking that assumed two things. First, the capital had to be protected, come what may. Second, as France had long been the enemy, commonsense demanded deployment to meet that threat.

The two major naval bases of Scapa Flow and Rosyth were the main military targets in Scotland. Defending Rosyth was simple enough: the two auxiliary squadrons waited with keen anticipation for an attack. Scapa Flow presented a bigger problem. Curiously, the Admiralty neglected to mention to the Air Ministry until March 1939 that the remote island haven would become the base for the Home Fleet when war came.

The Orkneys were well outside any air force defence scheme, since without the Fleet, their military significance was trifling. By July 1939 the two services had agreed on a plan designed to take effect in 1941. Once the war started, the planners proposed to install two fighter squadrons at Wick with a Sector Operations Room set up at the local primary school. Five more squadrons would be on hand together with an enormous collection of barrage balloons. This scheme had a few drawbacks, since the airfield at Wick was still under construction. No barrage balloons were to be had. Finally, some London balloons, accompanied by their disbelieving operators, were packed off to the Orkney Islands. As an emergency measure, the Admiralty put two Fleet Air Arm squadrons into the newly acquired airfield at Hatston.

Captain Ernest Edmund Fresson, the pioneer of civil flying in the Highlands and founder of Highland Airways in 1933, suggested the site. He also pointed out that modern aircraft in wet weather, not unknown in the area, rapidly turned grass runways into miniature bogs. The Admiralty took his advice and Hatston became probably the first airfield built in the British Isles to have hard tarmac runways, a claim disputed with some vehemence by Stornoway. In due course, throughout the war, more than 200 Fleet Air Arm squadrons spent time at Hatston, renamed in naval fashion HMS *Sparrowhawk*. It was not, though, an air attack that drove the fleet from Scapa. On 14 October Kapitänleutnant Günter Prien and U47 inched into the Flow. Two torpedoes did for HMS *Royal Oak*. With belated recognition that the Scapa Flow defences were not quite perfected, orders came for the Home Fleet to move to Rosyth within seven days.

At 0920 on 16 October 1939 the RDF screens at Drone Hill in Berwickshire painted the first contacts of two aircraft approaching from the North Sea. Fifteen minutes later, a faulty valve shut down the RDF station and other stations in the chain picked up the slack. At 0945 hours, the first report came from the Observer Corps which identified the two enemy aircraft, flying well apart from each other, as Heinkel 111s. They came from Kampfgeschwader 26, on an armed reconnaissance sortie, target Rosyth. The previous day, a KG26 Heinkel had spotted a large British battleship off the east coast. German intelligence identified her as HMS *Hood* although she was actually HMS *Repulse*, a near-identical sister ship, and an early morning flight had shown her about to enter the Forth. Her sinking would be an admirable Luftwaffe triumph to set off against the Kriegsmarine's destruction of *Royal Oak* as Hermann Göring demanded. A Luftwaffe strike against HMS *Ark Royal* had failed. Nonetheless, if the Luftwaffe disabled the handful of big ships in British waters, the German *Scharnhorst, Gneisenau, Bismarck* and *Tirpitz* would dominate the Atlantic Ocean.

At 1008, the lookouts on HMS *Edinburgh* saw the German high above them. After a few minutes, the Heinkel turned around to head for its home base of Westerland on the island of Sylt, just off the German coast. At 0948, Blue Section of 602 (City of Glasgow) Squadron took to the air from their base at Drem to hunt down the interloper. Drem, in East Lothian, was active in the First World War under the names of West Fenton and, later, Gullane. Reactivated under the Expansion Scheme, Drem became the home of 13 Flying Training School. With the war, 602 Squadron took up residence. Their rivals, 603 Squadron, moved to Turnhouse. Each squadron had received reinforcements and more would arrive as casualties mounted, both from the regulars and the Volunteer Reserve. Like many Auxiliary squadrons, 602, 603 and 612 tried to maintain their pre-war élan but not every new arrival found this congenial. 'Auxiliaries,' said one sharp-tongued observer, 'are gentlemen trying to be officers. Regulars are officers trying to be gentlemen. VRs are neither, trying to be both.' To the Air Ministry, numbers and operational efficiency took a clear priority over lingering tribal loyalties.

The Spitfires caught the Heinkel near Dunbar and the German crew swiftly headed for cloud. Two of the three Spitfires fired from long range but the Heinkel escaped. The second German avoided interception completely, and its pursuers, Green Section of 602 Squadron, short on fuel, landed at Leuchars instead of returning to Drem. Lunch and more fuel were their main requirements.

Stammering morse messages from the returning Heinkels brought another unit at Sylt to readiness. Number One Wing of Kampfgeschwader 30, abbreviated to 1/KG30, prepared to fly to Scotland with orders to sink the *Hood* but only if she were in open water. Bombs were not to fall on land with the consequent chance of killing civilians by order of the Führer. KG30 had the very latest aeroplanes in the German armoury, the Junkers Ju88 A-1. Its great advantage, the more optimistic crews believed, was its superior speed that allowed it to show a clean set of elevators to any enemy fighter. At 1155, on Monday 16 October 1939, the first of twelve Junkers lumbered down the runway and into the air and Hauptmann Helmut Pohle, commander of KG30, led the way to strike a devastating blow against the Tommies.

Throughout the morning, flying carried on as normal over Scotland. Naval Skuas, single-winged dive bombers, assiduously practised formation flying around Edinburgh and over Dunbar. Some army anti-aircraft batteries identified them as enemy aircraft. Fortunately for the Navy, the batteries only opened fire on receipt of specific instructions from higher authority. Tiger Moths, with dry-mouthed pupils at the controls and occasional ashen-faced instructors in the front cockpit buzzed over fields and hedges. Ansons, Oxfords, Blenheims, a sporadic Navy Swordfish and Fleet Air Arm Skuas roamed the skies with no apparent pattern to their lawful wanderings.

Out to sea, at 23,000 feet, the Junkers ground towards Scotland, their Jumo 211 engines pushing them on at an indicated 400 kilometres per hour. There were 12 aircraft and 48 men. Each Ju 88 had a pilot, a co-pilot, a radio operator and a gunner. The formation was loose, the 4 sections, each of 3 aircraft, spread over a wide area. Puffs of cumulus cloud dotted the sky. Minutes dragged by. Eyes searched for the coastline, and just before 1400 hours, Pohle's co-pilot nudged his captain: enemy coast ahead, twenty miles distant. The first section headed directly for the Forth rail bridge, gently dropping off height as they approached and the three Junkers, about 400 metres apart, flew steadily up the Forth. Pohle's original plan was to attack from the west with the sun behind him but he changed his mind. The three bombers hurtled out of the east at 10,000 feet and Rosyth dockyard was immediately below.

The large cruiser, *Repulse*, that German intelligence believed was HMS *Hood*, stood out clearly in the bright afternoon sunlight, in dock. Orders were specific: she had to be in open water. But it mattered little, since two cruisers lay at anchor close to the Forth Bridge. HMS *Jervis* and the carrier HMS *Furious* were under way in the Firth, heading towards Rosyth. The pilots picked their targets and the blunt noses of the Ju 88s dipped into a dive. Pohle concentrated on the *Southampton*, the grey shape growing larger by the second as he hurtled down at an angle of 80 degrees. The speed climbed in the near-vertical dive. The aircraft shuddered briefly and a clap of sound smashed through the cockpit as the top of the canopy flew into space. The rear Model M15 machine-gun went with it. The design fault had not been corrected during trials. Pohle held his dive as the altimeter needle unwound: 600 metres. *Southampton* filled the Lotfe bombsight and Pohle pressed the release. Two 500-kilogram bombs fell away towards the cruiser below. The Junkers continued to scream down until Pohle pulled it out at 300 metres. He hauled his aircraft round to the right to watch the rest of the group attack.

Leutnant Hans Sigmund Storp led the second section out of the west as planned, the sun behind them. A veteran of the Condor Legion, Germany's volunteers in the Spanish Civil War, Storp had plenty of experience. He had taken part in the abortive effort against *Ark Royal*. This time there would be no mistakes as everything had gone well on a perfect flying day. He had hit his landfall at Berwick-on-Tweed absolutely on the nose. The run-in to the Forth was perfect and all he needed now was to sink a British ship.

At 1438, Storp and his section began their dive. The leutnant saw the pseudo-*Hood* in dry dock, off limits by order of Hitler and switched his attention to the unfortunate *Southampton*. At 1438, messages reached the frustrated gunners of the anti-aircraft batteries scattered around Edinburgh that they had permission to open fire. At the same time, HMS *Repulse* brought her guns into action. On *Southampton* and *Edinburgh*, the gun crews added their quota of shrapnel. White smoke puffs burst far behind the Luftwaffe's bombers.

Like Pohle's section before them, the three Junkers of KG30 hurtled downwards in near-vertical dives. At 750 metres, Storp freed his bombs. He held his aircraft in the dive to watch them tumble earthward. As with Pohle, he was sure he had placed them straight into the target. Surrounded by water spouts as the explosives smacked into the Forth, *Southampton* took one hit. A single bomb from one attacker cut its way through three decks before leaving the ship at the bow, close to the waterline. Once it was in the open air, 500 kilograms of German bomb exploded, wrecking the Admiral's barge and a pinnace moored alongside.

Three men on the ship received injuries while on *Edinburgh*, seven men were injured but, remarkably, nobody died.

The third wave of attackers reached the scene. As they went into the attack, the Spitfires of 603 (City of Edinburgh) Squadron arrived. A gaggle of British fighters chased nine Junkers aircraft. Storp, heading back to the coast, found Spitfires on his tail as he climbed. A burst of fire stopped his port engine and the rear gunner died. Storp's chances of survival faded rapidly and four miles off the coast at Port Seton, at a mere 700 feet, the elevators collapsed. The Junkers headed down to the water with all the grace of a falling brick. Just before it hit, Storp jettisoned the canopy and the impact tossed him, still strapped in his seat, some seventy yards. Revived as he sank under the sea, Storp made it to the surface as did the remainder of his crew. The Junkers stayed afloat for a few minutes before it slipped under the waves at 1445 hours. After a numbing half hour in the cold waters, a fishing boat pulled them aboard and headed for shore.

The three Spitfires of Red Section, their job done, headed back to base. The leader, Flight Lieutenant Patrick Gifford, had shot down the first enemy aircraft over Britain during the Second World War. They beat 602 Squadron to the honour by ten minutes. Blue Section of the Glasgow unit, scrambled from Turnhouse with the news of a raid on Rosyth, experienced a few moments of confusion. They ignored a twin-engined aircraft on its own about three miles distant to concentrate on three unknown shapes which proved to be a trio of Navy Skuas from Donibristle. The mistake recognised, Blue Section hurried after the aeroplane they had rejected, flown by Helmut Pohle.

In the climb through scattered cloud, one aircraft of Blue Section lost contact while the other two, flown by Flight Lieutenant George Pinkerton and Flying Officer Archie McKellar, rapidly overhauled the fleeing German. Climbing above and behind Pohle, the two Spitfires dived, opening fire at 1443 hours. Bullets smashed into the port wing of the Junkers which quickly scurried for cloud cover. Broken cloud is no great hiding place, and each time Pohle dodged out of the sporadic clumps of cumulus, the two Spitfires fired. Finally, as the coast came closer, the Junkers put down its nose and bolted for safety. The optimists were wrong: the Junkers could not out-run fighters. Pohle learned exceedingly swiftly that the Ju88 A-1, flying flat out, was 60 miles per hour slower than a Spitfire.

Pinkerton sat on the right hand rear of the German. McKellar took up station on the left and both weaved a course 50 yards behind the Junkers. With half its canopy and the rear gun somewhere in Scotland, the Junkers was no threat. In clear skies, Pohle chose a desperate measure as he decided to try and outclimb his opponents believing the Junkers might be able to fly higher than the enemy fighters. He yanked back hard on the control column. The Junkers pointed upwards to present the perfect shot for both Spitfires. Pinkerton's swift burst shattered the remaining canopy and severely damaged the cockpit. The co-pilot and the gunner died at once while the radio operator escaped with wounds. Archie McKellar sprayed the port wing, rupturing the fuel tanks, before destroying the engine. Pinkerton's second burst hit the starboard engine and although it kept turning the Junkers was mortally crippled.

Pohle's war was over, and in a last attempt at retaining freedom, he aimed the Junkers at a trawler. At 500 feet, the remaining engine straining frantically, he headed towards the fishing vessel. If his luck was in, she would prove to be a neutral. If his luck was really in, the ship would be the *Hornum*, a trawler that the Kriegsmarine positioned off the east coast of Scotland for the exact purpose of saving aircrew. The commander of KG30 ditched. Dragged from the water, Pohle collapsed on deck. The ship was British. The radio operator did not survive while the Observer Corps, vigilant as ever, recorded the splash-down at 1455 hours.

The fourth wave of the assault was well behind the others. On the Forth, one of the escorts to an incoming convoy, HMS *Mohawk* came under fire. The destroyer, neatly positioned between Kincraig Point on the northern bank and Gullane on the southern shore, narrowly escaped direct hits from two 500-kilogram bombs. They burst within 50 feet of the ship. Shrapnel scythed through the air bringing down men on deck, and to add to the disaster, the Junkers sprayed the ship with machine-gun fire before heading east. Two officers and thirteen men died in the attack. Others were wounded, amongst them the *Mohawk's* captain, Commander Richard Frank Jolly, who was hit in the stomach by shards of shrapnel that penetrated the bridge. Jolly's wound was serious but he refused to leave his post, meeting all requests and suggestions that he should go below for treatment with the terse reply: 'Leave me. Go and look after the others.' Rosyth, with all its facilities, was 35 miles away. With so many casualties, Jolly pressed on as fast as he could. It took *Mohawk* 80 minutes to reach home. Weakened by loss of blood, fighting intense pain, Jolly whispered his orders to his wounded Navigating Officer who repeated them. The destroyer finally reached 'Y' Berth at Rosyth. Jolly personally rang off the main engines then collapsed while shore staff swarmed onto the ship. He died five hours later.

The Second Supplement to the *London Gazette* dated 23 December 1939 carried the announcement that King George VI was graciously pleased to approve the posthumous award of the Medal of the Military Division of the Most Excellent Order of the British Empire for Gallantry to Commander Richard Frank Jolly of the Royal Navy. Less than one year later, on 24 September 1940, the Empire Gallantry Medal ceased to exist. Its holders, or surviving next-of-kin, were obliged to exchange it for the newly instituted George Cross, a decoration with the same status as the VC.

As Jolly took *Mohawk* up the Forth, Spitfires from 602 and 603 Squadrons intercepted the Kampfgeschwader. Most of the German aircraft dropped height and contour chased to escape. Several headed out to sea, apparently trailing smoke. The mauled KG30 limped back to Sylt without their commander or his deputy. Confused British accounts later alleged that one badly damaged Ju88-1 headed for the neutral Netherlands, where it crashed near Breda. All four crew were, the stories claimed, found dead in the wreckage and buried by the Dutch at Ijsselstein. The pilot was allegedly Friedrich Gustav Hansen, son of Herman Hansen and the former Jessie Wilson of Melrose. Hansen is indeed buried there. He was the radio operator, not the pilot, of a Junkers 88 that was based at Eindhoven. He died on 9 January 1941, a casualty from an encounter with RAF Blenheims. The reasonably accurate official account of the *Mohawk* raid, released to the world's press, gently eulogised the part-time fighter pilots:

> Victory over the first German bombers to raid Great Britain since the war began has been largely shared in by men who, a few weeks ago, were Scottish stockbrokers, lawyers, and sheep farmers. At least two of the four enemy raiders accounted for during Monday's raid on the Forth were shot down by British fighter aircraft. They beat off the raiders in such a way that not more than half the German aircraft are believed to have returned home. About twelve or fourteen bombers took part in the raid. Apart from four which were brought down by British fighters, and anti-aircraft, and naval gunfire, several are thought to have been too crippled to complete the passage of the North Sea. No pilot claims to have brought down one of Monday's

raiders single-handed. Their defeat was a team job. One running fight began over the Pentland Hills. British fighters chased a German bomber away from the Pentlands, and it crashed into the sea off Port Seton. Shots from several aircraft helped to cripple it, but the 'coup de grace' was delivered by an auxiliary pilot who, before the war, practised as a lawyer. He had taken a bet that he would be the first member of his squadron to bring down a German plane. Swooping low over Edinburgh, a Squadron Leader, who was a stock-broker in civil life, chased another enemy raider out to sea. Two other members of his squadron, a sheep farmer and the manager of a firm of plasterers, shot down a bomber off Crail.

In London, C. G. Grey, still the single-minded editor of *The Aeroplane*, added his own spiral twist to the authorised account. One captured German pilot, 'a fervent Nazi', burst into tears, Grey assured his readers, when he learned that his conqueror was not only an auxiliary but a lawyer as well. The disgrace and dishonour was too much to bear.

The sight and sound of enemy aircraft hurtling above Edinburgh streets, even though there was usually a Spitfire in close attendance, infuriated many of the citizens because no air raid warning sounded. Shrapnel from anti-aircraft fire, bullets from both attackers and attacked, had fallen in the streets, broken windows, smashed occasional pieces of furniture and destroyed the odd antique. The row reached the House of Commons. Neville Chamberlain did his best to downplay the furore. The raid, he explained, 'was local and appeared to be developing only on a small scale, and as our defences were fully ready, it was not consid-ered appropriate . . . to issue an air raid warning, which would have caused dislocation and inconvenience over a wide area'. This sedative statement calmed neither ire nor nerves. But with assurances that lessons had been learned, Britain got on with the war. In all, throughout the war, Edinburgh would endure fourteen raids from the Luftwaffe. Twenty civilians died. A further 210 received injuries.

Scotland had not waited any time for its second, and far less dramatic, attack. On the very next day, 17 October 1939, the Luftwaffe visited Scapa Flow when, shortly after 1100, a handful of German aircraft roared in from the sea. Unfortunately for them, most of the fleet were at sea. Not only that, the anti-aircraft guncrews welcomed the relief from their monotonous life. One raider went down, a claim made by several gunners, including those of HMS *Sharpshooter*, a Halcyon-class minesweeper. The Junkers 88 crashed in the water at the mouth of Pegal Burn on Hoy. The others concentrated their attention on the Battle of Jutland veteran HMS *Iron Duke*, serving as a depot ship. She suffered and, although not directly hit, was holed and beached with one rating losing his life. Later refloated, she continued to serve as a base ship and port defence vessel until the end of the war.

The first bombs to hit British soil as opposed to land in Scottish water fell on Hoy during the raid. Whether *Sharpshooter* or a land-based gun shot down the enemy, it became a footnote in the history books as the first raider officially brought down over Britain by anti-aircraft fire in the Second World War.

On 22 October 1939, 603 Squadron shot down a Heinkel He111, the first enemy aircraft to crash on real British earth. Six days later, the two squadrons of 'weekend flyers' shared the destruction of another He111 from KG26 on a reconnaissance mission over the Forth and the Clyde. The Heinkel went down at Kidlaw, six miles south of Haddington. The Auxiliaries previously mistook an Anson for the target and a stream of bullets hit the Coastal Command aircraft. The pilot, wounded in the jaw, landed safely although irate. On 13 November 1939 a bomb dropped on the Shetland Islands, blowing a large hole in the ground and apparently killing a rabbit whose body was found in the crater. Despite dark allegations that the rabbit came from a local butcher, the news brightened Britain and the unfortunate bunny supposedly inspired the song 'Run, Rabbit, Run'.

Following the German invasion of Poland, an ill-prepared, meanly equipped, poorly trained British Expeditionary Force embarked for France. Contrary to most expectations, little immediately happened as the Germans sat solidly behind their frontier as the French clung to the concrete defences of the Maginot Line.

For Britain and France it was *La Drôle de Guerre*, the Phoney War. It was all to change.

9

Dauntless in War

Scotland's war effort gathered speed. Unlike the panicky days of 1914, when contracts to make complete aeroplanes fluttered onto the desks of companies of all sizes, Scottish industry from 1939 onward made components or assembled parts from other factories.

After Beardmore's died as an independent aircraft maker, the Scottish aviation industry all but vanished. But a few signs of life appeared in 1938 when a group of Clyde shipbuilders wanted to build flying boats at Greenock. The Air Ministry objected for reasons about which the files are silent. Good ideas, though, are hard to keep down and in due course, Scottish Aviation Ltd serviced Coastal Command's flying boats at the same spot. They also modified dozens of Consolidated PBY Catalina flying boats from the United States to meet Royal Air Force specifications.

The same company enjoyed a contract from de Havilland for an unusual Tiger Moth. They made a pilotless gunnery drone aircraft, controlled from the ground by radio. Designated the 'Queen Bee', some fifty of these came off a Prestwick production line. A good many fell to over-enthusiastic gunners while others suffered from equipment failure. The radio controlled autopilot operated compressed air valves to move the flying controls. Transmission faults sent 'Queen Bee' droning away into the far distance until the fuel tanks ran dry.

Scottish Aviation had a further healthy trade reconditioning and upgrading damaged Spitfires throughout the war. About 1,200 returned to service by 1945 after a Prestwick makeover. In time, Kelvin Hall, Glasgow, became the centre for the production of convoy and barrage balloons. The product undoubtedly enhanced morale although the results were not always those anticipated. During the whole of the war, the balloon barrage ensnared nearly one hundred aircraft of which twenty-four were German. However, they did account for 278 V1 flying bombs so Kelvin Hall more than earned its keep in that alone.

Like many other weapons, the balloons attracted their fair share of rumours. One school of thought claimed that the cables were really enormous magnets that attracted falling bombs and that once they reached the cable, they slid harmlessly to the ground. A more blood-thirsty group alleged the mooring cables carried a fearsome electric current which meant that any aircraft that touched a cable was imme-diately fried into oblivion along with its occupants. But the men and women who operated the balloon barrage did not need magnetic or electrified cables to add to their problems as the Operations Diary of B Flight of 948 Squadron, based at Rosyth, makes clear:

15 May 1940

Sudden thunderstorm caused N15 SLZC 479 (500 ft of cable) and N16 SLZF104 to burst into flames at 21.45 hours. No previous warning. Cable of N15 fell across train going towards Nth Queens-ferry which, by its forward movement, caused burning balloon to be dragged on to roof of rear carriage. Roof burnt, no casualties, Forth Bridge undamaged. N16 (90 ft cable) fell across High Tension cables. New balloons issued; N15 SLZF240 N16 SLZF 234.

At Renfrew, the American Lockheed Aircraft Corporation eventually took on hundreds of workers to assemble aircraft shipped across the Atlantic in sections, and by the end of the war they had turned out several thousand aeroplanes.

Blackburn Aircraft, a company that began life in Yorkshire before the First World War, produced 250 Short Sunderland flying boats at their Dumbarton factory. They also made some of their own design Botha, a twin-engined high-wing torpedo bomber that was grievously underpowered compared to its rival, the Bristol Beaufort, and an unsentimental RAF soon relegated it to training units.

If the newsreels were true, the British troops in France spent the Phoney War filling sandbags, singing about their washing on the Siegfried Line and wildly applauding innumerable personal appearances by George Formby and his ukelele. In Scotland, matters were different and Coastal Command's war began immediately. The 'Kipper Fleet' was the least well equipped of the three operational commands. Fighter and

Bomber Command, with some justification, took the greater portion of the air budget. Coastal Command's task was to help the Admiralty in its traditional duty of maintaining British maritime communications and destroying the enemy's. Given the considerable superiority of the Royal Navy's resources compared to those of Hitler's Kriegsmarine, the slower refurbishing of Coastal Command was no surprise.

In September 1939, although new aircraft were on order, the maritime resources of the RAF were generally obsolescent when not positively ancient. With the single exception of the Hudsons of 224 Squadron at Leuchars, the rest of the general reconnaissance squadrons flew the Anson, complete with its undercarriage handle. Aside from this minor drawback, they suffered from a lack of range, limited speed and little armament. The Ansons at Montrose, with a range of 250 miles, could only reach a point some 50 miles from the south-west tip of Norway before they turned for home. The 500-mile sortie over water took about three hours flying time.

With long-range flying boats, the situation was even worse. Coastal Command had six squadrons, two of which had the Sunderland, an exceedingly fine aeroplane that ranged over 850 miles with a 2,000-lb bomb load. The remaining squadrons soldiered on with aged Saro Londons and Stranraers, both twin-engined biplanes, generally outclassed by any well-armed enemy that they met. Moreover, Coastal Command's strike aircraft, two squadrons of Wildebeest torpedo-bombers, were even more antiquated. Roughly equivalent to the Fairey Swordfish, they were swiftly withdrawn to flying convoy patrols and other mundane tasks.

The Admiralty considered, in the early months of the war, that Coastal Command had one prime task – to patrol the North Sea to look for surface raiders. The Navy believed that ships, such as *Graf Spee*, *Deutschland*, *Gneisenau* and *Scharnhorst* were the prime danger to British ocean trade. Any raider breaking into Atlantic waters from a German port was almost bound to pass between Scotland and Norway so Coastal Command created an endless chain of air patrols. The Ansons flew as close to Norway as they could manage. As Hudsons became available, they relieved British submarines of the duty of patrolling further north of the Ansons' range. In addition, Hudsons from Leuchars held the south of the patrol line at dusk. North of it, the flying boats from Sullom Voe and Invergordon ensured there were no dawn surprises.

Sullom Voe came into operation before the war began to cover the gap between Norway and Iceland. On 9 August 1939 the Sunderlands of 201 Squadron arrived, only to be replaced in a straight swap by the Saro Londons of 240 Squadron in November from Invergordon. A posting to Sullom Voe was like a journey to a foreign land for many English personnel, as the outer islands, the Orkneys, the Shetlands and the Hebrides, were simply unknown territory. Even the journey to the RAF station was an epic event. Derek Gilpin Barnes, posted to Sullom Voe as an intelligence officer, recalled:

At some pale, cold hour we put to sea in a grey, workmanlike steamer which proved to have a turn of speed that was out of keeping with her matronly beam and modest size . . . She had been a popular pleasure steamer, plying to and from a holiday island at the other end of Britain. But she was no pleasure steamer now! She was stripped and she was darkened, and she was as cold as the North Pole. Those decks, upon which tourists once gaily strolled or drowsed in canvas chairs, shrieked now with Arctic gales and were packed solid with life-jacketed soldiery. The select saloons were gutted, and our breath made clouds upon their frosted air . . .

She was, to be ungratefully frank, a pig of a vessel. She had five hundred men sick within fifteen minutes. She froze us all to the marrow. She clanged and boomed, as though a mine had got us, every time one of those tremendous seas hit her staunch side. And, rolled up in a greatcoat, gloved, and with Balaclava helmet, I had my first lesson in contract bridge in her derelict dining-saloon with the cards sliding off the dirty table at every wicked heave and plunge and roll.

We came in the fullness of a most unpleasant time, to the Shetland Islands. And, here again, my childhood dreams had long ago endowed those lonely crofts and peat bogs with imagined romance. I went ashore prepared for archaic, fur-clad figures and, had our transport been sleds and husky dog-teams, I would have felt no atom of surprise.

For the shivering new arrivals from England in the first winter of the war, matters were made worse by the weather and meagre facilities. After a miserable journey from railway stations in the south to strange-tongued destinations of which they had never heard, life seemed as if it could never get worse. At freshly completed stations, finished in a hurry with sparse wooden huts as opposed to substantial brick barracks, newcomers enjoyed a donkey's breakfast. Straw-filled mattresses, with three monotonously grey or brown blankets spread on the bare floor, were the sleeping arrangements. Every other facility seemed miles away, usually reached through feet-deep snow.

On 18 January 1940 a snowstorm swept across Glasgow. An aircraft with two crew on board crashed close to 18 Balloon Centre, manned by Auxiliary Air Force staff, at Bishopbriggs. It burned, the flames scorching though the falling snowflakes. Several airmen from the centre rushed to the scene, amongst whom was Corporal John McIntosh McClymont from Prestwick. With several others, he pulled one man from the cockpit. Ammunition and signal flares exploded in the intense heat and a shouted order told everybody to stay well back. McClymont heard the order but also ignored it on the grounds that it did not stop a solo attempt to save the other crew member. Instead of pulling back, he decided to enter the inferno. An officer soon joined him, and between them they pulled out the other man moments before the petrol tanks exploded. During the second operation, McClymont held back part of the cabin. Although his hands burned, he carried on with the rescue despite the imminent danger of his own death. Both of the crew had died on impact but McClymont's action would have saved them both if they had survived the initial crash. McClymont received the Empire Gallantry Medal.

Coastal Command's long patrols over the cold waters of the North Sea and the Atlantic were a dreary business. The aircrew had nothing in the way of equipment other than their own eyes and a pair of binoculars. The Kriegsmarine, in an unsporting but eminently sensible fashion, took full advantage of bad weather to send out their surface ships. When the Ansons and the Hudsons, the Sunderlands, the Londons and even the Tiger Moths were stuck on the ground because of fog, heavy rain, low clouds, or gales, German raiders put to sea. Sometimes, the eyes in the air got lucky, and on 16 February 1940 a Lockheed Hudson spotted the German tanker *Altmark*. Originally a supply ship for the *Graf Spee*, she was returning to Germany with nearly 300 prisoners, British merchant seamen taken from vessels sunk by the *Graf Spee*, on board. As an auxiliary vessel rather than a combatant ship, she could claim exemption from search by foreign forces.

The Hudson's wireless message sent the Royal Navy into action. HMS

Arethusa, a cruiser, supported by a drove of destroyers, set off to intercept. *Altmark* took refuge in Jössingfjord, firmly in neutral waters, escorted by two Norwegian torpedo boats, and the Norwegians warned the British not to interfere. Signals flashed between *Arethusa* and Whitehall Wireless. Winston Churchill, First Lord of the Admiralty, ordered the Royal Navy to board the German after a British suggestion that *Altmark* dock at Bergen to allow a search was stiffly rejected. The destroyer HMS *Cossack* tried to get alongside *Altmark*, a much larger ship. The German captain attempted to ram the destroyer. In the manoeuvring in the shallow coastal waters, *Altmark* ran aground.

British sailors boarded the German vessel. After some hand-to-hand fighting and flourishing of bayonets, they freed the prisoners, an action that was greeted with newspaper headlines across Britain. Norwegian protests about the blatantly illegal breach of her neutrality received no consideration. The familiar law of unintended consequences neatly kicked in. Hitler decided that the Allies would not respect Scandinavian neutrality so ordered German planning for the invasion of Norway and Denmark to be intensified, a decision that brought Scotland firmly into the front line.

On the night of 8 April Hitler launched his assault of Denmark and Norway. The following morning, German forces entered Bergen harbour, led by two cruisers, the 6,650-ton *Königsberg* and her sister ship *Köln*. Aided by fog and the use of the White Ensign to confuse the defenders, the German naval force quickly occupied the town. The Norwegian battery guarding the harbour damaged *Königsberg*, putting her engines out of action. An RAF reconnaissance flight that day, with a Royal Navy observer on board, led to a hastily arranged raid by Bomber Command. One squadron of Hampdens and one of Wellingtons attacked the same evening. All thirty 500-lb bombs dropped by the raiders missed although one fell close enough to slightly injure some German sailors.

The RN observer was Lieutenant Commander Geoffrey Hare of 800 Squadron of the Fleet Air Arm. Along with 803 Squadron, 800 normally lived on board HMS *Ark Royal*. Both squadrons had disembarked to form part of the air defences of Scapa Flow. Their Blackburn Skua dive bombers, the first monoplanes in RN service, doubled as fighters when necessary and they carried four Browning machine-guns in their wings as well as a rearward-facing Lewis gun.

Hare learned of Bomber Command's dismal performance and begged, bartered, stole and demanded a flight to Hatston, finally arriving by courtesy of RAF Lossiemouth. The decision was quickly made to send the Skuas to Bergen for a dawn attack. Although the crews had not recently practised dive-bombing, some things stay locked in the memory. The two squadrons mustered sixteen Skuas for the raid, five from 800 Squadron and eleven from 803. Seven crews, each of a pilot and a gunner/wireless operator came from 800 Squadron while 803 provided nine crews.

Well before dawn, on a chilly night, the first of sixteen Bristol Perseus engines coughed into life. The pilots almost felt their way to the end of the dimly lit runway where each aeroplane, trembling in time to the engine, waddled under the weight of 163 gallons of fuel and a 500-lb semi-armour-piercing bomb, partially recessed under the fuselage. One after another, throttle levers went forward. The Skuas gathered speed, lifted off the dark ground. Undercarriages retracted. The aircraft climbed painfully slowly into the star-sprinkled sky where they found formation, two attacking waves heading east, on course for Bergen, 300 miles away. One aircraft lost contact with the others. The pilot, Lieutenant Edward Winchester Tollemache Taylour, and the gunner, Petty Officer Howard Gresley Cunningham, carried on. To return did not enter their minds. The Skuas flew for something over four hours at normal cruising speed with brimming fuel tanks. Flying time to Bergen came out at a fraction over two hours. Landing back at Hatston might be a matter of dry tanks and dry lips.

Accurate navigation was essential. Luckily, the sun always rises in the east so dawn was a sufficiently good pointer to guide the assault to a landfall a mere twenty miles south of their target. They turned north, maintaining their height of 12,000 feet, safely hidden above a thin layer of cloud – and they needed to be, since the alarm had already sounded. At 0720, British time, the Skuas arrived over Bergen where they dropped cautiously through the cloud to look down on the harbour. *Köln* had gone, having slipped away during the night. But *Königsberg* waited for them, her stern pointed out to sea so that two gun turrets and the port torpedo tubes dominated the harbour entrance.

The Skuas circled before they attacked out of the bright sun. They dived towards the bow, pulling out over the stern. A smattering of anti-aircraft fire from the cruiser's 2-centimetre flak guns greeted the first raider as it passed through 8,000 feet. To the north of the harbour, more 2-centimetre guns joined in. Their Kriegsmarine gunners, like those on *Königsberg*, squinted blindly into the bright sunshine, desperately trying to pick out the Skuas as they gobbled down from the pale sky. The Skuas released their bombs at between 1,500 and 2,000 feet. One pilot, Lieutenant William Coutney Antwiss Church, unhappy with his first approach, went round again with his gunner, Petty Officer Bryan Maurice Seymour and this time, he released at a mere 200 feet.

The first bomb to hit the *Königsberg* apparently killed all electrical power on the ship. The 88-mm flak guns at the stern which had flung shells in pursuit of departing Skuas fell silent, as power-operated turrets need electricity. The cruiser took at least four direct hits, one on the bow and three amidships. Two other bombs bounced off the dockside and on to the vessel, causing as much damage as a direct strike.

When Lieutenant Taylour and Petty Officer Cunningham arrived, ten minutes behind the main body, they found the German cruiser burning readily at the bow. She looked finished but the pair attacked nonetheless. With no power, the *Königsberg*'s crews could barely fight the flames. Nor could they pump out the water that flooded in when bombs tore open her side. After 2 hours and 45 minutes, the German cruiser turned on her side and sank, part of her stern remaining above the water. For the first time in warfare, a major warship had been sunk by air attack. And it was Scottish-based aircraft that had done the job.

All the Skuas, bar one, returned safely to Orkney although a number brought back a collection of holes caused by German flak. The sole casualties perished when good luck blinked. As the Skua of Lieutenant Bryan John Smeeton climbed through cloud, he became disorientated. The Skua spun and, since it was not an aeroplane that recovered swiftly from a spin, Smeeton and his gunner, Midshipman Frederick Watkinson, perished. One month later, a clutch of awards went to some of the men who took part in the raid. The Hatston Skuas continued to guard the Flow and to take the fight to the enemy.

The Nazi invasion of Denmark and Norway thrust the airfields in the north and north-east of Scotland into major operational roles in addition to their training commitments. Kinloss came, for a while, under the control of 4 Group of Bomber Command. Whitley bombers from 77 and 109 Squadrons arrived to operate against German-held airfields at Stavanger, Oslo and Trondheim.

The RAF collected some useful aircraft as Norwegian pilots escaped from their own country to fight another day. Sullom Voe acquired a US-made Northrop floatplane at an early stage. Of more immediate

Dunne's D1 Glider, Glen Tilt, 1907. The inclined ramp was designed to produce flying speed. Sometimes it worked. Any resemblance to Dunne's inspiration, the *zanonia microcarpa* seed, is entirely in the eye of the beholder. © *Courtesy of the Bruce/Leslie Collection. Licensor www.scran.ac.uk*

The cutting edge of the Royal Flying Corps. A contemporary postcard that shows 2 Squadron's BE2 aircraft at Montrose in 1913. In the foreground is a Farman. *Courtesy of the Montrose Air Station Heritage Trust*

Aeroplane Disaster at Montrose.
Funeral of Lieut. Arthur.

Above. Isaac's Tribute. The flying services always strive to send off the departed in some style. Desmond Arthur's funeral was not, however, the end of him. *Courtesy of the Montrose Air Station Heritage Trust*

Right. Sir David Henderson, architect of the Royal Flying Corps and, at one time, the oldest active pilot in the world. *Courtesy of the Imperial War Museum, Q069460*

Four BE2 biplanes of Number 2 Squadron at Stranraer, 1913 just before they flew to Ireland – the first time that the RFC left mainland Britain. *Courtesy of the Montrose Air Station Heritage Trust*

Scottish Industry found itself swamped with contracts. Although few companies had any experience of building aeroplanes, overwhelming need produced a swift response. Shown is the first BE2C biplane completed by Beardmore's at Dalmuir. © *Courtesy of the Bruce/Leslie Collection. Licensor www.scran.ac.uk*

Left. A Sopwith 2F1, 'Ship's Camel', is pulled out of the Firth of Forth in 1918. The Beardmore trademark stripes are clearly shown on the elevators. © *Courtesy of the Bruce/Leslie Collection. Licensor www.scran.ac.uk*

Below. By the end of the war Beardmore's, in common with every other maker, turned out the most advanced aeroplanes in service. This Handley Page V/1500 heavy bomber at Inchinnan in 1918, was one of them. Parked under a wing is a Sopwith Camel from the same factory. © *Museum of Flight, National Museums of Scotland. Licensor www.scran.ac.uk*

Scottish-built aeroplanes served across the world during the First World War. This one found itself in India in 1918. © *Courtesy of the Bruce/Leslie Collection. Licensor www.scran.ac.uk*

An aeronautical blind alley – the R34 at the time of her Atlantic Flight in 1919. Large airships needed monstrous numbers of ground handlers. Ponderous creatures, increasing their miserly payload meant making the airship bigger. *Courtesy of the Museum of Flight, National Museums of Scotland*

Left. Wopsie, the first cat to fly the Atlantic. Smuggled on board the R34 by LAC George Graham (pictured), an admirer offered $1000 for the tabby kitten. Graham refused. *Courtesy of the Museum of Flight, National Museums of Scotland*

Below. Annual Camp was the highlight of the year for the Auxiliary Air Force. The officers of 602 (City of Glasgow) Squadron prove, according to taste, that the kilt does not enhance Officers' No. 5 mess dress or, alternatively, that it substantially improves the uniform. The photograph was taken at the Palace Hotel, Southend in 1937. The tartan is the Grey Douglas of their CO, the Marquess of Douglas and Clydesdale. *Courtesy of the Royal Air Force Museum London, www.rafmuseum.org*

The Marquess of Clydesdale (2nd from left), later the Duke of Hamilton, and David McIntyre (second from right) before the Everest Flight in 1933. © *The Scotsman Publications Ltd. Licensor www.scran.ac.uk*

The Houston Westland PV3 G-ACAZ approaches the Kangchenjunga Range during the 1933 Everest Flight Expedition. *Courtesy of the David F. McIntyre Collection, RAF Museum, PC96-261*

Blenheim L1108 of 62 Squadron comes to grief at Abbotsinch during the 1938 Empire Exhibition. *Courtesy Jack Cornelius*

An Avro Tutor trainer of 612 Squadron, Auxiliary Air Force, flying from Dyce in 1938. Just one year away from the Second World War, the squadron was equipped with obsolete Hawker Hector biplanes. © *Courtesy of the Dugald Cameron Collection. Licensor www.scran.ac.uk*

Nobody doubted that the Second World War would see massive aerial attacks on British cities. The barrage balloon had proved its value in the 1914–18 conflict. Glasgow's first balloon duly rose above the city in 1939. © *Museum of Flight, National Museums of Scotland. Licensor www.scran.ac.uk*

During the first months of the war, much of Scotland's aerial defence came from her own Auxiliary squadrons. 'A' Flight of 602 Squadron are pictured on 3 September 1939. *Courtesy of the Royal Air Force Museum London, P009450, www.rafmuseum.org*

Scottish airfields were major operational bases during the Second World War. Aircraft from Scotland patrolled far out over the Atlantic and North Sea, attacked U-boats and flak ships, bombed battleships and enemy bases. Here a Lockheed Hudson of 320 (Netherlands) Squadron takes off from Leuchars in 1941. *Courtesy of the Royal Air Force Museum London, P 008143, www.rafmuseum.org*

The Air Transport Auxiliary ferried factory-fresh aircraft to operational and training units. To the dismay of traditionalists, the ATA recruited women pilots as well as men. The first eight 'aviatrixes' reported for duty in January 1940. This photograph shows seven of them preparing for their first delivery flight – the basic but cold open-cockpit Tiger Moth. As the war ground on, several remarkably fine female pilots single-handedly delivered four-engined heavy bombers to front-line squadrons. *Courtesy of the Royal Air Force Museum London, PC 93-2ATA, www.rafmuseum.org*

John Hannah VC. *Courtesy of the Royal Air Force Museum London, PC 76-23-21, www.rafmuseum.org*

Kenneth Campbell VC. *Courtesy of the Royal Air Force Museum London, PC 76-23-44, www.rafmuseum.org*

Hugh Gordon Malcolm VC. *Courtesy of the Royal Air Force Museum London, PC 76-23-24, www.rafmuseum.org*

William Reid VC. *Courtesy of the Royal Air Force Museum London, PC 76-23-27, www.rafmuseum.org*

John Alexander Cruickshank VC. *Courtesy of the Royal Air Force Museum London, PC 76-23-33, www.rafmuseum.org*

George Thompson VC. *Courtesy of the Royal Air Force Museum London, PC 76-23-36, www.rafmuseum.org*

William Neil McKechnie GC. *Courtesy of the Royal Air Force Museum London, PC 76-24-31, www.rafmuseum.org*

Eric Watt Bonar GC. *Courtesy of the Royal Air Force Museum London, PC 76-24-4, www.rafmuseum.org*

John McIntosh McClymont GC. *Courtesy of the Royal Air Force Museum London, PC 76-24-33, www.rafmuseum.org*

The first winner of the PDSA Dickin Medal for bravery – the 'Animal VC' – was Winkie, a carrier pigeon with the RAF. Winkie collected her award from Maria Dickin herself in 1943. *Courtesy of the People's Dispensary for Sick Animals*

Above. A line-up at Peterhead of Spitfires Mark Vc of 350 (Belgian) Squadron in 1944. After a period of night training, the squadron moved back to England for the invasion of Europe. *Courtesy Alf Allsop*

Opposite. A busy day at the office. A Mosquito of the Banff Strike Wing in action shortly before the war's end. *Courtesy of the Imperial War Museum, C 005117*

A myriad of mechanics, clerks, fitters, riggers and a multitude of other tradesmen and women were needed to keep aircraft flying. In 1944, Sergeant Cynthia Routh at Brackla negotiated a concession for her airwomen during the remarkably hot summer of that year – they could take off their jackets. The men sweltered on as this photograph shows. *Courtesy Cynthia Routh*

The shooting war of 1939–1945 turned into the Cold War as the Iron Curtain descended across Europe. One early manifestation was the Soviet blockade of West Berlin. The RAF, and many Scottish airmen who had bombed that city, found themselves flying in food and essential supplies in Avro Yorks (here pictured), direct developments of the Lancaster.
Courtesy of the Royal Air Force Museum London, R1818, www.rafmuseum.org

The Auxiliary Air Force, honoured for its wartime achievements with the prefix 'Royal' disbanded again on 10 March 1957 despite the fact that they could hold their own against the regular Service. Here, a de Havilland Vampire of 603 Squadron is re-armed for a training flight in 1956. © *Courtesy of the Dugald Cameron Collection. Licensor www.scran.ac.uk*

From the glamorous world of the fast jet to the underground caverns of radar sites, thousands of men and women served in Scotland during more than four decades of the Cold War. In this picture, Flight Lieutenant Ian 'Beery' Weir of 8 Squadron at Lossiemouth celebrates his achievement at reaching 10,000 flying hours, many of them on the Shackleton.
Courtesy of Flight Lieutenant Chris Dean

Hanging on in there. For much of the Cold War, Soviet aircraft spent many long hours probing Britain's air defences. The RAF in Scotland spent many long hours proving that they were ready to meet any threat from the skies. A 43 Squadron Phantom FG1 Leuchars escorts a Soviet Air Force Bear D away from the British coast. *Courtesy of the Royal Air Force Museum London, tn6716-34, www.rafmuseum.org*

From simple crosses in country churchyards to a fully fledged museum such as Montrose or East Fortune, memories remain of the men and women who served the Tartan Air Force. Shown are a memorial at St Fergus Church, Dyce and part of the present-day Montrose Heritage Centre. © *Aberdeen City Council. Licensor www.scran.ac.uk; and Courtesy of the Montrose Air Station Heritage Trust*

benefit was a German Arado 196 and a gaggle of Heinkel 115A float-planes. In time, they proved extremely useful for covert operations over occupied Europe.

With Scotland firmly in the fighting line, any relatively flat ground in the entire country had the chance of becoming an airfield. Operations and training were both vitally important. In May 1940 Castletown opened as a satellite landing ground for Wick. It also served as another base for the defence of Scapa Flow. On the west coast, Campbeltown, a small airfield used by Scottish Airways from 1934, was requisitioned by the Royal Navy on 12 February 1940. It was not ideal and one pilot, later in the war, described it with feeling:

> The field was really quite primitive. Ground-to-air signals were still in the Stone Age and there was only one small hangar, supplemented by a Bessoneau with a tendency to fly off on its own. The control tower consisted of Mr McGeachy, the Scottish Airways agent, a stove, ample supplies of tea, and a telephone. During night flying, one of the observers was laid on – with an Aldis lamp . . .
>
> It was an unmistakeable Admiralty selection between two sharp ranges of hills and up and down in all directions like the ocean wave in six cross-winds. It was ninety miles from the nearest rail station so engines came by sea.

Scottish airfields were ideally suited to a new development. Before the war began, pilots, after initial training, learned the nuts and bolts of their business on their squadron. Gunners and observers did on-the-job training. In wartime, it became impossible to clutter up operational squadrons with aircrew who were not efficient on the frontline aeroplane. In its simplest terms, the fliers had to join their squadron with much of the knowledge and experience they would have learned at squadron level in the days of piping peace. The answer was the Operational Training Unit. Number 14 Flying Training School left Kinloss for the south while the station took on the role of 19 OTU to train crews for Bomber Command. It was one unit amongst many that would make Scotland familiar to thousands of men and women from around the world.

May was not a good month for the British cause as the German army efficiently bundled British troops out of Norway. The Norwegians surrendered the day before the meaning of blitzkrieg became painfully clear to the Dutch, the Belgians, the Luxembourgers, the French and the

British. The Allied divisions offered little resistance to the Germans, and by the end of the month, the larger portion of the British Expeditionary Force crouched behind a thinly held defence line at Dunkirk and hoped for rescue.

The Fleet Air Arm, often with limited success, continued to fly from Hatston against German shipping off Norway. Six Swordfish aircraft made the first torpedo strike against a capital ship when they tried to sink the *Scharnhorst*. Enthusiasm outweighed familiarity and knowledge, since the Swordfish crews, working at their maximum range, did not have enough experience. *Scharnhorst* demolished two attackers and went on her way, unscathed.

With the collapse of France, 15 Group of Coastal Command moved house, settling in Stranraer to provide support and convoy escort in the Western and South Western approaches of the Atlantic. Number 18 Group took responsibility for the northern part of the North Sea and the area to the west of Scotland, north of an imaginary line running north-west from the Mull of Kintyre.

At Montrose, 8 SFTS carried on as normal. Irrespective of any spectral airmen, it was a dangerous place, as one trainee pilot, Sergeant Jack Charles Wood, wrote to a friend:

I've gone solo – had two flights of dual and went off again last Saturday – it's damned dangerous here flying – they have a beautiful large landing field but as there are so many aircraft flying it's like a bee-hive – you get about 6–7 machines all landing together – all coming in at different heights and some of the pilots haven't done much yet and it's really dangerous.

I had a horrible experience this morning – I was coming in behind another machine with a third machine on my port side. The damned fool in front suddenly swung around to the right and kept his height and I had to suddenly turn away from him and a damned great tree loomed up. I sweated blood for about 1½ seconds and had to suddenly open the throttle to try and clear it. I pulled the control column back and braced myself in my straps and hoped for the best. I just cleared it by about 10 feet. Sounds a lot but at 80 mph it's pretty terrifying. Some blokes are a positive menace.

A few days later, on 23 May 1940, Wood's luck ran out and he perished in a head-on mid-air collision.

Night flying at Montrose tested the strongest nerves, for the aircraft had no radios. The airfield, black as a witch's hat in the Scottish night, used gooseneck flares, flames fed by paraffin, to mark the runway. Once airborne, the apprentice pilot was totally on his own. In the absolute darkness to the west lay the Grampians. It was enough to cause the bravest to flinch, and one trainee, who made it all the way to a frontline squadron, confessed that he found discretion was by far the better part of valour. On one particularly hairy night, he carefully taxied to a far corner of the aerodrome, and waited. After a decent interval, he trundled back to the hangars.

Apart from the usual hazards that flying offered, Luftflotte 5 did their best to inconvenience the war effort from their Norwegian bases. Small raids by handfuls of determined intruders throughout the summer and autumn of 1940 spiced up the daily routine. Every airfield on the east coast was a target. Scapa Flow was also a target and, not surprisingly, the war home of the Fleet was jam for German wasps. On 24 July 1940 a stray bomb from one raider fell near the Bridge of Waith. James Isbister, a 27-year-old Orcadian, died, the first British civilian to do so in an enemy bombing attack. Two people in England were killed three months earlier when a Heinkel 111 crashed onto their home in Essex.

Organised defence came slowly, since the specialist Royal Air Force Regiment had not been formed. The more fortunate units had an army battalion close by. Usually the job fell to the ground personnel and any available trainee aircrew who dug slit trenches and foxholes. Contractors occasionally arrived to construct pill-boxes and coils of barbed wire appeared, although these failed to deter the Junkers and the Heinkels. Various weapons, often Lewis guns of First World War vintage, appeared along with Vickers guns. Mounted on a hangar roof, these often surprised unwary enemy pilots as one German crew discovered in a raid on Lossiemouth on 26 October 1940. Three He 111s swept in at low level, killing three people on the ground and shooting up some conveniently parked Blenheims from 21 Squadron, detached from the south to attack German shipping. A determined RAF machine-gunner brought down one of the raiders.

Both the RAF and the RN opened new bases with the Fleet Air Arm settling in at Arbroath with a training station, HMS *Condor*. On the Shetland Isles, Scatsa, 24 miles north of Lerwick, took the crown as the most northerly airfield in the British Isles, serving as a satellite of Sumburgh and a support base for the Sullom Voe flying boats.

By August 1940 the Battle of Britain was in full swing. In essence, it was fought by 11 and 12 Groups of Fighter Command. Scotland formed part of 13 Group, with its headquarters at Newcastle-upon-Tyne and a sector station at Turnhouse. During August, with the fight trembling in the balance, the Spitfires of Scotland's two Auxiliary fighter squadrons went south. On 15 September 1940 the air fighting over England saw more than 1,000 sorties by the Luftwaffe beaten off by Fighter Command. Fifty-six raiders went down against a British loss of twenty-six. Adolf Hitler ordered the indefinite postponement of *Fall Seelöwe*, Operation Sealion, the invasion of Britain.

That night, Bomber Command made another raid against the occupied Channel ports. The Hampdens, the Battles, the Whitleys, the Wellingtons, the Blenheims had spent the previous ten nights attacking German ships, port communications and defences and, above all, the hundreds of invasion barges that were ready to cross the narrow straits of Dover.

Amongst the attackers were fifteen Hampdens of 83 Squadron, an original Scottish squadron, formed at Montrose in 1917. Disbanded at the end of 1919, the squadron had reformed in 1936 at Scampton in Lincolnshire. The Hampdens took off soon after 2200 hours to attack Antwerp where several hundred barges waited up river, ready for the invasion of Britain.

Cold searchlight beams lanced across the sky and German flak guns spattered furious shells as the Hampdens ran towards the target. Pilot Officer Clare Arthur Hovendon Connor, unhappy with his first approach, decided to go round again. He sat alone on the high central flight deck and at 2,000 feet, his Hampden, P1355, bored in once more. Shrapnel sprayed the Hampden as Connor held it steady for the attack.

'Bombs gone!'

Sergeant Douglas Hayhurst, the navigator and bomb-aimer, in the perspex nose cone, yelled the report. The aircraft lifted as the bombs fell away, and almost immediately, the Hampden shook violently as shells exploded in the bomb bay and tail boom. One punctured the wings, piercing the fuel tanks on both sides, while inside the aircraft, flames licked along the rear fuselage.

Behind Connor, two manual fire extinguishers and the aircraft dinghy sat in a floor well. Then came a three-feet-wide aluminium door with a small central window, that effectively separated the pilot and navigator from the other two crewmen. The door, the full width of the fuselage, opened onto an upper cabin with a perspex cupola. Here sat Sergeant

John Hannah the wireless operator air gunner, facing towards the tail. To keep him company, a brace of homing pigeons nestled in a special carrier. Two Vickers machine-guns poked out into the sky through the Perspex while spare ammunition cans sat in racks alongside. Below Hannah, a step led down to the belly gun position, the province of Sergeant George James. He also nursed two Vickers machine guns with spare ammunition all around him.

In the Hampden's slender fuselage, just one yard wide, moving from front to rear and back again in cumbersome flying kit was a difficult, clumsy business. The first rush of flame was a fireball. James had little choice but to bale out as the floor melted beneath his feet. Hannah could have made his own exit through an escape hatch, but as his own cabin began to burn, he decided to stay and fight the blaze.

Hannah, born in Paisley, had joined the Royal Air Force in 1939. After his wireless operator/air gunner course, with spanking new sergeant's stripes on his arm, he joined 83 Squadron at only eighteen years old. Connor sent Hayhurst to learn what had happened. Unable to open the dividing door, he peered through the window to see only that the rear-gunner had vanished while John Hannah was apparently on fire. Assuming that Connor would follow, Hayhurst left the aircraft through the forward hatch. Hannah was alight. He smothered the flames that licked at his bulky flying suit before he struggled to the aluminium door, forcing it open to grab a fire extinguisher. The flames hardly noticed and continued to consume the aircraft fuselage. They melted the floor and left only the cross-members while Hannah's parachute pack burned. The pigeons had died in the first rush of heat. Close to suffocation with the heat and fumes, Hannah switched on his oxygen and gasped it in through his face mask. This revived him enough to open the perspex in his compartment to gulp lungfuls of cool air.

In the searing heat, the cased ammunition, thousands of rounds, started to explode and Hannah kicked and heaved the boxes out through a gaping hole in the fuselage. The second extinguisher did rather better although the flames continued. John Hannah beat at them with his logbook, and when that charred into oblivion, he used his hands. The last flickers of fire died at last. Burned hands, scorched, blackened face, eyebrows and lashes shrivelled, Hannah crawled forward in his charred flying suit to Connor. With Hayhurst gone, Hannah wriggled forward to collect the charts and navigation logs, wedging himself behind the pilot. Between them, they found their way home to Scampton.

On 10 October 1940 Sergeant John Hannah from Paisley went to Buckingham Palace to collect the Victoria Cross from King George VI. His nineteenth birthday was still seventeen weeks away. At eighteen years old, he became the youngest airman ever to wear the decoration. Pilot Officer Connor received the Distinguished Flying Cross while the Distinguished Flying Medal went to Sergeant Douglas Hayhurst. Now a prisoner-of-war, the Antwerp raid was his thirty-ninth operation.

In July 1940 the Minister of Aircraft Production, Lord Beaverbrook, had turned his attention to shipping aircraft across the Atlantic Ocean. US and Canadian companies already had orders for machines with a delivery rate of one thousand every month. Strict observance of the Neutrality Laws saw aircraft made in the United States taken to airfields that bordered Canada. There they were carefully wheeled across the international boundary.

That accomplished, the aircraft were taken apart, put into crates and shipped to Britain by sea. The chance of U-boat attacks as well as the huge amount of shipping space needed made the process increasingly uncertain and a major problem. Beaverbrook was air-minded. The obvious solution, as he saw it, was to fly the larger aircraft across the Atlantic. In 1940 though, this was easier proposed than executed, since navigation needed to be precise. Radio aids hardly existed. The long distance, often allied with foul weather, made the risk too high – except to Beaverbrook, himself a Canadian by birth with many friends. He approached Sir Edward Beatty, the chairman of the Canadian Pacific Railway, and on 16 August 1940 they signed an agreement. Ground personnel, supplies and administration would come from the CPR. The Ministry of Aircraft Production would provide crews, manage the operation and pay all expenses other than wages. The whole operation would be a strictly civilian enterprise, thus staying firmly on the right side of international law.

The first route ran from Saint Hubert airport, near Montreal, to Gander, Newfoundland, where the aircraft would refuel. After that, they would head out across the ocean for Aldergrove in Northern Ireland, the nearest UK airfield to North America. The project seemed feasible even if danger attended the enterprise. The programme began on 10 November 1940 when seven Lockheed Hudson aircraft left Gander under the command of an Australian, Donald Clifford Tyndall Bennett, a former RAF officer and airline pilot.

The Hudsons flew in formation, within sight of each other, mustering only one navigator between them. As they reached the end of the flight, the weather worsened and three aircraft got lost. The remaining four landed at Aldergrove after eleven hours in the air. The experiment was repeated on 28 November 1940. One Hudson lost touch with the formation. The crew used the radio direction-finding equipment at Prestwick to land there on 29 November after ten hours non-stop across the Atlantic. The same thing happened on 18 December when another crew found Prestwick in place of Aldergrove.

Bennett himself led the last formation of Hudsons to Aldergrove, landing on 29 December 1940. After that, Hudsons made the journey singly, since formation flying across the Atlantic, no matter how loose, was nerve-jangling. Bennett also changed the destination airfield. Aldergrove was dumped in favour of Prestwick, whicht meant more miles to fly and longer in the air for the ferry crews. On the plus side, however, Prestwick enjoyed better weather than most of the British Isles and, more importantly, was one end of the Great Circle between Canada and Britain. The classic definition of a great circle is an imaginary circle on the surface of a sphere (such as the Earth) that has a radius equal to the radius of that sphere and whose centre is also the sphere's centre. Talk like this is meat and drink to old-fashioned celestial navigators. Normal people need only know that a great circle is the shortest distance between two points on a sphere. For this reason, aircraft bound for New York from London, head out over Prestwick and fly over Canada before they reach their destination.

Navigators guided aircraft across vast distances by means of sextants and star-sights, drift calculations and allowances for magnetic variation and deviation. Sensible pilots prized good navigators higher than several bags of Burmese rubies. In bad weather, it comforted the soul to know that the aircraft was on a course well clear of any granite centres in the cloud ahead. Modern pilots punch in co-ordinates to a computer and satellite navigation systems do the rest. Proper navigators, like flesh-eating dinosaurs, have vanished from the earth. The first direct flight from Canada landed at Prestwick on 11 February 1941 – the first of many.

As the days shortened and December loomed, Coastal Command prepared a special Christmas present for the enemy in Norway. Responsibility for a successful delivery went to the squadrons at Wick. The target was a smart hotel, some chalets and the railway station at Finse, a popular sport and skiing resort in Norway. A large number of German officers and Norwegian collaborators visited Finse for a luxurious break. A flying visit from the RAF would, it was hoped, kill enemy officers and their treacherous friends. Destruction of the links between Finse and the rest of Norway would be an added bonus.

The crews watched a pre-war travelogue that usefully displayed their target and on 18 December 1940 the Hudsons of 269 Squadron attacked, despite heavy cloud both en route and over the target. Squadron Leader Richard McMurtrie led the raid and in a cool display of courage, McMurtrie successfully attacked the target before circling it with his navigation lights on to lead the rest of the Hudsons to it. Unfortunately, several had lost their way and returned home without dropping their bombs. Two days later, Bristol Beaufort torpedo-bombers from 42 Squadron had another try. The Beaufort, a powerful development of the Blenheim, carried a crew of four and a collection of machine guns in the nose, the wings and a dorsal turret. Again, McMurtrie led the raid and the Bristols gleefully knocked down the snow sheds and damaged the railway line.

Two days later, when the Germans possibly hoped that everything had stopped for Christmas, McMurtrie returned with more Beauforts. This time, they hit the hotel and, as a farewell gesture, demolished two of the railway's snow-ploughs. The line remained blocked for many, many days. The faltering German daylight bombing offensive led the Luftwaffe to night attacks and the first great offensive came on London on the night of 8 September 1940. They continued until the night of 12 November – London, always London. Then plans changed. The war had a long time still to run.

10

A Common Effort

Luftwaffe night bombing had largely ignored Scotland. After London, Southampton, Birmingham, Liverpool, Bristol, Plymouth, Manchester, Sheffield, Cardiff, Portsmouth and Avonmouth all found themselves on the receiving end of Göring's bombs. The enemy adopted the unsocial habit of bombing the same target two or three times at short intervals to impede recovery. Neither production nor British morale appeared shaken, a result that produced mounting discontent within the German High Command. Carefully voiced criticism reached the Führer, whose plans to conquer Russia were well advanced. This led to an extra emphasis on certain targets.

Britain's weakness, the generals reminded Hitler, was her reliance on imports and a shortage of hulls in which to ship them. The Wehrmacht, preparing for the land assault to the east, could do nothing about either factor but the Kriegsmarine and Luftwaffe could. Hitler listened and on 6 February 1942 he issued a Führerbefehl. The U-boats were to destroy shipping as never before. The bomber force was to lay waste ship-yards and docks. To keep the RAF within bounds, Göring's men had also to make sporadic raids against aircraft factories and munitions workshops. This was all with immediate effect.

However, the immediate effect needed to wait upon the weather. At Rosyth, B Flight of 968 Balloon Squadron recorded:

7 Feb. 1941
Gale gusting to 85 mph
0930 – IB2706 broke away
1015 4389 broke away at 2,300 ft

1154 KB2243 broke away
1520 KB2382 broke away
1520 KB2700 broke away at 2,000 feet
1525 KB2397 broke away while flying at 2,000 feet after lifting
Winch No. 570 and depositing or dropping same down cliffs, a
drop of 75 feet. Winch retrieved and towed to Sqdn . . . First
known instance of winch being flown from Balloon.
1600 KB2395 broke away.

On 19 February the new-style offensive began, and during the next
three months, sixty-one major raids smashed London, Birmingham,
Coventry, Nottingham, Portsmouth, Plymouth, Bristol, Avonmouth,
Swansea, Merseyside, Hull, Newcastle, Sunderland – and Clydeside.

On the clear moonlit night of 13 March 1941 the Luftwaffe made
its first visit to Clydeside where the attack, although long anticipated,
still came as a shock to some. Particularly surprised were the optimists
who had convinced themselves that a raid was unlikely as the Germans
were not antagonistic to the Scots. An equally deluded group assured
credulous listeners that magnetic fields in the surrounding mountains
disrupted enemy compasses.

The sirens wailed over a frosty Clydeside at about 2100. The first
wave were Heinkel 111s of a special targeting group, Kampfgeschwader
100. Their navigators used one of Germany's technical aids, 'X'-Gerät,
a radio navigation system that guided the bombers to their aiming
point without the use of a magnetic compass. The lead aircraft
approached at 3,000 metres, near enough to 10,000 feet to Scottish
observers, well above the height of any lurking barrage balloons. In
the headphones, the German navigators heard the sound of the
X-Gerät change. First came a general indication that they approached
the target. It changed when they got closer. A third and final tone told
the navigators that they were in the right place; bomb-aimers
immediately pressed an automatic release that calculated the final
dropping point. To be doubly sure, the navigators map-read their way
to the final specific targets. This was not difficult. The full moon
silvered the river below, picking out the canal and docks. The first
bombs fell. One witness recalled:

It began with dozens of flares, some incendiaries, and a few high
explosives. One of the high explosives got the distillery. Nothing

could be done to stop that blaze. Then they were on us like wasps, and everything came down.

Flares and incendiaries filled a grim purpose, since they marked the target for the remainder of the attackers. No navigation was needed when crews saw a burning Clydeside from miles away. The main force, flying from occupied Europe, had little to fear from the defences as the bulk of Britain's radar-equipped fighters patrolled the south and east of Britain. The night was ideal for the Defiants that looked after Scotland. A full moon, a swarm of raiders; fully trained crews could take on the enemy as long as the anti-aircraft guns reduced their fire.

The incendiary bombs came in different-sized containers that weighed anything from 70 to 250 kilograms. As they dropped, the containers opened, spreading their contents in a devastating pattern. When each bomb exploded on impact, their thermite contents burned, reaching temperatures of 5,000 degrees Fahrenheit. Steel and aluminium melted in the ferocious heat.

An early hit started a fire at a distillery to the east of Clydebank. Bombs fell into a timber yard, a 40-acre site crammed with lumber. A second distillery, to the north-west, also caught fire. Its warehouse dumped the equivalent of one million whisky bottles into a stream close by. Since whisky burns readily, a string of fire added to the night's glare.

Admiralty oil storage tanks at Dalnottar, one of the Luftwaffe's prime targets, also ignited, and in every street of Clydebank, houses collapsed under the onslaught. The Heinkels from their airfields in Denmark, Germany, Belgium and Holland flocked like vultures to a carcass. More incendiaries, more parachute mines, more high explosive, this time in the form of heavy bombs.

The black figures of desperate firefighters silhouetted against the flames that swept through Clydeside. Knightswood, Scotstoun, Lambhill, Kelvingrove, Hutchesontown, Yoker, Kingston, Hyndland, Kelvindale, Partick, and Clydebank all suffered. In all, 250 pumps went to fires in these areas, their task made no easier by German bombs that put five fire stations out of action and wrecked several fire tenders.

Destruction of a major control room as well as broken water mains made it increasingly difficult to deal with the overwhelming blaze. Cratered roads, collapsed buildings and burning streets prevented outside assistance reaching the front line of fires. Communications collapsed. In a desperate attempt to quell the flames, firefighters ran their hoses long distances into the canal. Great heroism became commonplace. And the bombs still fell.

When dawn came, the last bomber left and the dazed and shocked population of Clydeside blinked into the light. They found smashed, smouldering heaps of rubble, streets littered with broken glass and debris in an unrecognisable Clydebank. Crumpled tenements had trapped their occupants and all day, rescue workers, maintenance men, firemen, canteen volunteers, doctors and nurses struggled with the aftermath of the raid. Clydebank continued to burn. The suddenly homeless were moved out of the demolished town. Nearly 50,000 Scots had become refugees, moving to other parts of Scotland and even to England, some never to return.

As night fell, the next fleet of incoming bombers simply pointed their noses towards the glow. Clydeside reeled again under another massive attack. On Saturday 15 March 1941 it was possible to count the cost. The bombing killed 528 people and seriously wounded more than 600. Many hundreds more suffered less severe injuries ranging from cuts from flying glass to broken wrists. The Luftwaffe directly hit or damaged many of its essential targets. Aside from the Admiralty oil tanks, that blazed for two weeks before they were put out, William Beardmore's factory complex, the shipyards and docks as well as the Royal Ordnance Factory all fell victim.

In striking these, the bombers also wiped out Clydebank's housing. The raids destroyed one-third of the town's 12,000 homes. Another 4,500 suffered exceptionally heavy damage whilst 3,500 took mild to serious hits. Only seven houses escaped unscathed. In addition, public buildings, schools, churches and offices disappeared in the onslaught. Luftwaffe records suggest more than 400 aircraft dropped 500,000 kilograms, some 500 tons, of high explosive on Clydeside during the two raids along with nearly 2,500 containers of incendiaries. The bombers returned in far less force on the night of 7 April and on 6 and 7 May 1941. These were the final throes in the major air offensive against Britain. New and vital fronts had opened. By the end of June 1941, two-thirds of the German bomber force had withdrawn to fight elsewhere as Russia, Greece and Yugoslavia beckoned.

In December 1939 the British Government had reached agreement with Canada, Australia, New Zealand, South Africa and Southern Rhodesia to set up the massive Empire Air Training Scheme. With the subsequent addition of the United States, under the Tower Scheme, many fledgeling British aircrew received elementary tuition in Scotland before travelling overseas for further instruction.

On their return, they often came back to Scotland for operational training with the Royal Air Force or the Royal Navy. The FAA base at Arbroath, under the name of HMS *Condor*, became a major naval training unit. It was, in some eyes, positively luxurious as not only did it have hard runways but the buildings, although wooden, were soundly made. The staff and trainees also enjoyed bathrooms with hot and cold running water.

New and strange accents reached Scotland. When Europe fell into Nazi clutches, stubborn, determined, bloody-minded men bent on continuing the fight, found their way to Britain. Scots became accustomed to hearing Polish, Czech, French, Dutch and a myriad of other pronunciations, and misunderstandings occurred. The traffic was not all one way as Lieutenant John Welham, then a naval flying instructor at HMS *Condor* recalled:

> We also sent our pupils out over the sea to find their way back without the aid of an observer. On one occasion a Canadian pupil became hopelessly lost, eventually found land and came to earth, without breaking his aircraft, in a large field. When the locals rushed up to him he assumed from their voices that he had landed in Germany and set his Swordfish on fire with his Very pistol. He had, in fact, landed near Montrose and had failed to recognise the Aberdeenshire accent.

In March 1941, 320 Squadron arrived at Leuchars, displacing 233 Squadron who emigrated to Aldergrove in Northern Ireland. The new squadron was formed from members of the Royal Netherlands Naval Air Service on 1 June 1940. It first flew the Fokker aircraft that it brought to Britain. An increasing spares quandary caused forced retirement for the Fokkers, which were replaced by Ansons and Hudsons. The squadron patrolled the North Sea on Rover missions, reporting and attacking enemy shipping. On 30 August 1941 they made their offensive sweep with four aircraft. Only one returned. The Dutch, like other exiles in RAF and RN uniforms, knew how to die.

No matter what plans Hitler had for Russia, Admiral Ernst Raeder made it clear to the Kriegsmarine their task had not changed. 'The main target for the Navy during the Eastern campaign,' he wrote in March

1941, 'still remains Britain.' The exploits of *Scharnhorst* and *Gneisenau* in the North Atlantic encouraged the German Naval Command to contemplate more striking successes. The two battle-cruisers had sunk or captured 22 merchant ships with a total tonnage of more than 116,000 tons. They could have sunk more if it had not been for the battleships that escorted the convoys. The German Navy had the answer.

Two further powerful pieces were about to enter play. *Bismarck* and *Tirpitz*. The four together, formed into a battle group, would wreck enemy commerce. They were a match for any enemy warships that got in their way. Annoyingly for the Germans *Scharnhorst* and *Gneisenau* were in port at Brest. *Scharnhorst*, indeed, was in dry dock for boiler repairs. At the best estimate, she would not take to the seas again until June. *Bismarck*, the 50,000 ton battleship, was in the Baltic, finishing her acceptance trials. *Tirpitz*, her sister ship, was only commissioned in February. With her trials outstanding, she would not be ready in the spring.

Nevertheless, the Kriegsmarine went ahead, and on 2 April Raeder decided to send *Bismarck* and the heavy cruiser *Prinz Eugen* to war. They were to break into the North Atlantic to attack Allied convoys sailing north of the Equator. *Gneisenau* would join them when ready. *Bismarck* would see off the convoy escorts while the others tore the unarmed merchant ships to pieces. This rosy scenario suffered brusque discouragement from the joint efforts of Coastal and Bomber Command. Brest docks came under attack by some 200 bombers over the next days. Although they missed both ships, an unexploded 250-lb bomb close by *Gneisenau* persuaded the Germans to move her to the inner harbour on 5 April until the bomb disposal men had done their job. A camera in a high-flying photo-reconnaissance Spitfire captured the battle-cruiser's non-smiling image soon after. *Gneisenau* lay wide open to an aerial torpedo strike.

Coastal Command arranged an immediate strike by the Beauforts of 22 Squadron, temporarily based at St Eval in Cornwall. The aeroplanes could carry a torpedo or bombs, but not both, and the squadron had a mere six aircraft available. Three were tasked with the torpedo attack while the other three would carry bombs. The bombers would drop their load to take out any torpedo nets that might guard *Gneisenau* while the torpedo pilots were to circle the harbour until they heard, or saw, the explosions.

The next morning, as dawn crept across the dockyard at Brest, a single Bristol Beaufort roared through the haze towards *Gneisenau*. The pilot, Flying Officer Kenneth Campbell from Saltcoats in Ayrshire, was the only one of four to find the target in the misty morning. As he approached, the alarms sounded an urgent warning around the harbour.

Gneisenau lay alongside a quay, protected to the seaward by a long curving concrete mole or breakwater some 500 yards distant. Behind her, anti-aircraft guns bristled on rising ground. Around the ship, more flak guns dominated the area from two spits of land. Between the guns behind and to left and right, a devastating barrage would meet any attacker. To add to this curtain of cross-fire, three flakships in the outer harbour seethed with armament. On the *Gneisenau* itself, the ugly snouts of the ship's own anti-aircraft guns swung to meet the danger. In all, some one thousand gun barrels trained on the Beaufort.

The whole mission began badly, as two bombers bogged down on the airfield. The third got airborne. The three torpedo-carriers had already left, all heading for Brest independently through rain, fog and darkness. The only bomber lost its way and never reached Brest. It dropped the bombload on a ship miles away before heading back to Cornwall. Campbell attacked alone. Having circled the harbour to find no waiting Beauforts, he put his aircraft into a shallow dive and headed for the target. He had to cross the mole before he could drop his torpedo in the clear patch of water and at release point, the distance to the high ground behind *Gneisenau* was painfully short. The chances of climbing clear diminished the closer he approached the target.

A torpedo run requires a steady course and an unhurried attack. Evasive action when a trenchant enemy plasters the sky with metal is not possible. At 50 feet, with the needle hovering somewhere around 140 knots, on a rock-steady approach, the Beaufort swept past the flakships, below mast height. Campbell skimmed over the protecting mole. As the concrete flashed beneath him, he dropped the torpedo into the calm waters of the harbour.

It ran true. *Gneisenau* rocked as the torpedo crashed into her stern, cutting into her below the waterline before it exploded. Her propeller shafts buckled. Campbell started a hard, climbing turn to the left. There is always a chance of escaping the inevitable. The Beaufort might just clear the slopes behind the German ship. The aeroplane shivered as it ran into a ravaging storm of shellfire. Steel and shrapnel smashed into the Beaufort – into wings, fuselage and tail as it plummeted into the water at full speed.

The Kriegsmarine recovered the bodies from the wreckage, submerged in the chill water of Brest Harbour: Flying Officer Kenneth Campbell, Flight Sergeant Ralph Walter Hillman, Sergeant William Cecil Mullis, Sergeant James Philip Scott, from the Royal Canadian Air Force. They buried the crew, side by side as befits a gallant band, with full military honours. Campbell's fearlessness did not receive immediate recognition. The last official sight came from another Beaufort whose pilot saw the attack begin. Reports from the French Resistance finally reached Whitehall, and nearly one year later, the *London Gazette* of 13 March 1942 announced the award of the Victoria Cross to Flying Officer Kenneth Campbell. Four days later, another raid on Brest further damaged *Gneisenau* and the Kriegsmarine's dream of a powerful battle group became a sweaty nightmare.

Bismarck and *Prinz Eugen* remained but caution suggested that the foray into the Atlantic be delayed for six months. Longer days and shorter nights approached which made it more difficult for the ships to break out without detection. Further, a delay until the autumn would see the two Brest casualties ready for action once more. In addition, *Tirpitz*, as puissant as *Bismarck*, capable of taking on the best of the English navy, could join the expedition. Ernst Raeder scorned prudence, since the longer the wait, the more powerful Britain became. As it was, her situation was critical as attacks on her convoys might produce a death rattle. To push England out of the war would mightily assist the Führer's plans for Russia. Planning continued.

Events conspired against the German scheme, now named *Rheinübung* – Rhine Exercise – to mislead unauthorised ears. During a passage to Kiel from the Baltic, *Prinz Eugen* struck a wandering mine which meant another delay. Raeder again dismissed a suggestion to postpone the operation, believing the hold-up would be short. *Rheinübung* would continue, and once the two ships were in the wide Atlantic waters they would massacre the enemy merchantmen. *Bismarck* took on board a U-boat liaison officer. If the chance arose, the wolves of the Kriegsmarine would join the big ships in the slaughter.

After some more irritating minor delays, both ships sailed from the Bay of Danzig where, joined by three destroyers, they reached the Kattegat on the morning of 20 May 1941 to become the subject of many eyes as Danish and Swedish fishing boats dotted the area. The Swedish cruiser *Gotland* spotted the battle group and wirelessed Stockholm. That afternoon, the British Embassy flashed the news to London. At dusk, the Norwegian resistance saw the cluster of ships as they passed into the Skagerrak, nearing open water. Another message bleeped across the air waves to London.

The German battle group turned north towards Norway, and at 0900 on 21 May, they entered the Korsfjord, south of Bergen. In the clear weather, their chances of escaping detection were slender. *Bismarck* entered Grimstadfjord for the day. *Prinz Eugen* steamed a little further on to Kalvanes Bay. They would wait out the daylight hours before sailing once more in the dark. Two hours later, at 1100, Flying Officer Michael Frank Suckling of the Photo Reconnaissance Unit left Wick in his Spitfire to look for the German ships. He found them. From 26,000 feet, his cameras clicked busily. One hour later, he landed back at Wick with the evidence.

The weather clamped which was good news for the Kriegsmarine but disastrous for the Royal Air Force. The next morning, Lieutenant Commander Noel Ernest Goddard and his crew volunteered to take their Martin Maryland reconnaissance aircraft to the fjord. They made it to Norway as the navigator Commander Geoffrey Alexander Rotherham, in a triumph of his art, guided the aircraft 300 miles to an accurate landfall despite solid cloud down to 200 feet. The Fleet Air Arm crew hurtled up Korsfjord where they checked each inlet. *Bismarck* and *Prinz Eugen* had gone.

Goddard flew to Bergen where the Maryland came under intensive anti-aircraft fire. Peppered, she escaped into cloud without heavy damage. Attempts by the radio operator to contact Coastal Command met with no response. Finally, in desperation, he transmitted blind on the 771 Squadron frequency. Above Scapa Flow, a bored wireless operator on an aircraft towing a target around for the benefit of the gunners below caught the faint morse transmission. He copied it, repeated it. Within minutes, the hunt for *Bismarck* and *Prinz Eugen* took on new impetus. Scotland's part in the saga of the *Bismarck* had, however, ended. Royal Navy surface ships detected *Bismarck* and her companions. After the Battle of the Denmark Strait, in which the ill-fated HMS *Hood* blew up, the German battleship sank on 27 May 1941 after an epic and gallant fight against numerically superior forces.

On the night of 10 May 1941 London received its last major attack. All was quiet in Scotland until late in the evening. At 2208, a coastal radar station picked up a trace that there were three aircraft approaching from the North Sea, heading for Bamburgh on the Northumberland coast. The news flashed to 13 Group at Ouston that London was under attack. This could be a diversionary raid and radar gave it the identification of 'Raid 42'. After some minutes, two Spitfires Mk II, already on patrol near the Farne Islands, received the order to intercept. Based at Acklington, the Spitfires came from 72 Squadron. The pilots depended on the ground controller for vectors, or the course to steer, and the controller vectored the two fighters on to their own tracks, a simple but not uncommon mistake. At the same time, the radar station amended its report. Only one aircraft approached. This was no massive diversion raid.

Another Spitfire scrambled, the radar smudge indicating the incomer was at 15,000 feet. At 2020 hours, Sergeant Maurice Pocock in his Spitfire rattled off the ground, and as he climbed, the stranger slipped off height, down to low level, vanishing against the dark sea. Radar lost contact when it crossed the shoreline. Coastal radar stations could not see inland – that was a job for the Royal Observer Corps. The organisation had received the regal addition to its title just one month previously.

The Embleton post reported the engine sound at 2223 hours. Two minutes later, the Chatton observer saw the aircraft and reported it as an Me Bf110. As minutes ticked away, the ROC monitored the interloper over the Cheviots, and across the border into Scotland. At 2234 hours, the Messerschmitt entered Ayr Sector.

At the Monkton operations room, Squadron Leader Charles Hector MacLean, who lost a leg flying with 602 Squadron in the Battle of Britain, dismissed the identification. The Bf110 did not have enough fuel to reach the centre of Scotland and return to the Continent. Even so, the stranger needed investigation. Hector MacLean told a Defiant night fighter from 141 Squadron at Prestwick, already on routine patrol, to catch the stranger. Pilot Officer William Cuddie and his gunner had no airborne interception radar and relied on the controller for a course to steer.

The interloper reached the west coast then, inexplicably to those on the ground, it turned round and went back the way it had come. The Defiant, not the speediest of aircraft, followed the calm instructions from control and vectored after the intruder. The Messerschmitt climbed, and minutes passed before anybody realised what had happened. At 2,000 metres, near enough 6,000 feet, the German pilot took to his parachute. The Bf110, with no hand at the controls, crashed at 2309 hours.

At Floors Farm, near Eaglesham, just south of Glasgow, the head ploughman, Donald MacLean, heard the sound of a low-flying aircraft. He looked out of the cottage he shared with his mother to see a man dangling on the end of a parachute, slowly dropping to earth. MacLean grabbed a pitchfork and went outside. He asked the new arrival if he was German or British. The pilot spoke good English and confirmed he was German. After which, MacLean helped him into the tiny cottage, where Mrs MacLean offered him a cup of tea. He refused: a glass of water was sufficient. Mrs MacLean later recorded that he was a true gentleman and, German or not, was some mother's son. When the local policeman and a Home Guard arrived, the pilot identified himself. 'I am Hauptmann Alfred Horn. I have an urgent message for the Duke of Hamilton. Please take me to him at once.'

Hector MacLean's dismissal of the ROC identification severely annoyed Assistant Observer Group Officer Major Graham Donald whose imposing title partially concealed the fact that he was himself a former RFC and RAF pilot. Determined to vindicate his men, Donald set out for the crash site. Once there, he quickly confirmed the aircraft type. He then went on to the local Home Guard headquarters to where the pilot had been taken under guard. Graham Donald recognised the man in the elegant, expensively tailored Luftwaffe uniform. This was no mere captain in the German Air Force – the parachutist was rather more important than that. Rudolf Hess, Deputy Führer, had arrived in Britain.

The Hess Flight has generated acres of print with reams of crack-brained theories as to the purpose of Hess's mission. They range from the Duke of Hamilton being a secret homosexual lover to a coup to overthrow Churchill. They include delights such as a British Intelligence 'sting' operation, the use of SS-trained doubles, astrologers, substitute aircraft, conspiracy and shenanigans at every level of British society. Fortunately, they are all outside the scope of this book. The curious or desperate can check the shelves of their local library or browse the Internet. Nearly every theory, however, makes assumptions that either cannot be proved or are simply untrue.

Prestwick now boasted a 6,600-feet-long runway. The Atlantic Ferry Command had taken over the original Canadian Pacific and Ministry of Aircraft Production Operation in March 1941. Whitehall believed that the international situation required the original operation to be the responsibility of the British Government. The Ministry of Aircraft Production took over the whole organisation, but, to outside eyes, little changed. The aircrew remained much the same, largely civilians from Canada, Britain and the USA. A sprinkling of Australians, New Zealanders, Dutch and French pilots added spice to the mix. They included, Ernest Gann observed, 'some of the most colourful aeronautical soldiers of fortune ever to find themselves engaged in a common effort'.

The system changed rapidly in the middle of the year. The US Lease-Lend law of 11 March 1941 authorised the sale, loan or leasing of war material to 'any country whose defense the President deems vital for the defense of the United States'. Franklin Delano Roosevelt informed Winston Churchill that aircraft destined for Great Britain could fly direct from the factory to their Canadian departure airfield. The ferry flights would be handled by the US Army. This proposal allowed the civilian pilots who flew the aircraft from western Canada to be redeployed on the Atlantic route. The offer came with the proviso that the US military pilots could hand over their charges only to another military body, not a civilian organisation.

Within a remarkably short time, the Royal Air Force gained a new command. Ferry Command began work on 20 July 1941. The new operation employed the same aircrew, ground crew and administration. To outside eyes, it continued to look like an air operation largely run by a railway with a sprinkling of military assistance.

The former CPR, ex-Atlantic Ferry Organisation, now Ferry Command pilots were not the only civilians flying aeroplanes from Prestwick. The Air Transport Auxiliary Number 4 Ferry Pool arrived in September 1940. The ATA itself began in 1938 with the aim of transporting mail, personnel and casualties in the event of war. The organisation had, in a manner of speaking, hardly got off the ground when the conflict came and in a very short time it took on the job of ferrying RAF aircraft from factories and storage depots to airfields. It used pilots unable to serve in the RAF for various reasons. Some had lost a limb while others were too old, so the proposal came that some should be women.

Charles Grey Grey used *The Aeroplane* for another rant. After the usual preamble along the lines that women had their uses, he launched into his standard vituperative mode:

the trouble is so many of them insisting on wanting to do jobs which they are quite incapable of doing. The menace is the woman who thinks that she ought to be flying in a high-speed bomber when she really has not the intelligence to scrub the floor of a hospital properly, or who wants to nose around as an Air Raid Warden and yet can't cook her husband's dinner. There are men like that so there is no need to charge us with anti-feminism. One of the most difficult types of man with whom one has to deal is that which has a certain amount of ability, too much self-confidence, an overload of conceit, a dislike of taking orders and not enough experience to balance one against the other by his own will. The combination is perhaps more common amongst women than men. And it is one of the commonest causes of crashes, in aeroplanes and other ways.

Grey was not alone, since much of the RAF agreed with him.

On 1 January 1940 the first eight women pilots joined the ATA, their initial role being to fly Tiger Moth trainers from the de Havilland factory at Hatfield to training airfields that, strangely, were always in the north of England or Scotland. Two reasons apparently made women suitable for the job. Firstly, nobody else wanted it, since the Tiger Moth, with its open cockpit, was a very cold aeroplane. Secondly, Tigers were cheap and easy to replace, and the doubters all knew it was inevitable that a woman would break one.

In May 1940 a famous name joined the ATA when Amy Johnson, who had flown solo to both Australia and South Africa, joined the organisation. She was glad, she said, of the chance to do some everyday flying as war work along the lines that Grey deemed suitable, of scrubbing hospital floors, did not appeal. On 3 January 1941 at 1045, Amy Johnson delivered an Airspeed Oxford to Prestwick and then had the job of returning a similar aircraft to Kidlington. Thick cloud loomed over the airfield and along her return route. Amy called her base and was told not to try to return at once. She decided to fly to Squires Gate at Blackpool to spend the night with her sister and brother-in-law.

The next day she left for the south. The weather remained grim, but Amy, who had flown many, many miles on her own with nothing more than a map and compass did not worry since she would go over the top, above the clouds, she assured onlookers. At 1515 hours that afternoon, an Oxford crashed into the Thames Estuary. Onlookers saw a parachutist drifting down into the water. HMS *Haslemere*, a cross-channel steamer, hurried to the rescue. Lieutenant Commander Walter

Fletcher, the ship's captain, dived into the ice-cold water to rescue her but she and her parachute slid under the stern of the ship before he reached her. Her body was never found and Fletcher, pulled out of the water by some of his crew, who had also dived in to help, died of hypothermia in hospital at Sheerness. As with Rudolf Hess, conspiracy theories began almost at once and bizarre rumours of secret missions circulated. But once again, they are, happily, outside the scope of this book.

The ATA began as neither flesh nor good fresh fish at Prestwick. Although in a dashing uniform, they operated initially from a derelict single-decker bus, tucked away on the northern side of the airfield – and the commanding officer operated from the driver's cab. The ATA later moved to a proper building. In 1943 the ATA became the first organisation in Britain to pay its employees the same salary according to status, irrespective of gender. Women pilots drew the same money as the men, an innovation bold enough to shatter C. G. Grey's monocle.

On 13 June 1941 nine Beauforts of 42 Squadron, flying from Leuchars, gave the Kriegsmarine another headache. Following a sighting by a Leuchars-based Blenheim IV of 114 Squadron, the Beauforts pounced upon the pocket battleship, the 10,000-ton *Lutzow*. Flight Sergeant Raymond Herbert Loveitt, in L9939, surprised the ship, surrounded by a protective destroyer screen. His torpedo, dropped at 0218, crippled *Lutzow* and she had to limp to Kiel for repair work that lasted until January 1942. Another surface raider had failed to make it to the Atlantic.

More airfields, more depots spread across Scotland. In the Western Isles, Benbecula opened in August 1941 as an emergency landing ground for Coastal Command aircraft coming back from Atlantic patrols. At Dalcross, hard runways allowed air gunner training, at Number 2 School, to begin on 16 August 1941. Dornoch, in the Highlands, became a Satellite Landing Ground. The RAF commandeered the golf course and the Royal Golf Hotel became airmen's billets. The Royal Navy took over Abbotsinch completely on 11 August whilst Twatt, on Orkney, welcomed a new Fleet Air Arm airfield under the name of HMS *Tern*. Macrahanish, rescued from its oblivion after the First World War, became HMS *Landrail* and more than 200 Navy Squadrons used it before the war ended.

At Kinloss, the home of 19 OTU, aircraft brand new to the RAF arrived for another operation against the German Navy. Four Boeing 17-C aircraft, known to the RAF as the Fortress I, of 90 Squadron set off on 5 September 1941 to bomb the *Admiral Scheer*, yet another German pocket battleship. She had made a thorough nuisance of herself in the Atlantic. Now, berthed at Oslo, there came a chance to put her out of the war for good.

The raid was less than distinguished. One aircraft returned early with supercharger problems while the remaining three, unable to see the target through the cloud that covered Oslo harbour, dropped their bombs from 30,000 feet. Three days later, they tried again and once more, one aircraft, finding itself unable to climb above the blanket of cloud, returned to Kinloss. The remainder fell in with some distinctly unfriendly Me Bf109 fighters of Jagdgeschwader 77, based at Stavanger-Sola, close to Oslo. Two spiralled down, flown by Flying Officer David Romans and Squadron Leader Alex Mathieson, while the sole survivor climbed to escape. At about 35,000 feet, two gunners collapsed from oxygen starvation and the pilot dived. At 29,000 feet, a Bf109 buzzed around the Fortress once more. One gunner perished and another was wounded. One engine went out and a single burst of German cannon fire shot away the aileron controls. The navigator's maps and equipment vanished through a hole in the floor, and to add a final touch of excitement, choking smoke from a damaged glycol tank filled the cockpit. Despite the considerable difficulties, the pilot, Flight Sergeant 'Mick' Wood, located Kinloss and without ailerons, in a collapsing aircraft, he landed AN535 downwind. The Fortress crashed in a cloud of dust, never to fly again. The Oslo raid confirmed the worst fears of the RAF about the Flying Fortress and its use in daylight bombing. In fact, the need for aircraft was so great that operating advice from the US Army Air Corps had been ignored. The Fortress I was withdrawn from operational service by the end of the month.

Kinloss was accustomed to crashes, since its Whitley aircraft were past their best. New aeroplanes went to frontline squadrons while cast-offs, often stressed and battered beyond belief, started new careers at training stations. The Whitley, a slab-sided machine that immediately received the grim nickname of the 'Flying Coffin', was the mainstay of 19 OTU. Generally underpowered, but kind, with no vices, it was essentially a gentle creature that could take punishment and cheerfully absorbed the worst of bad bouncing landings without complaint. The OTU pilots racked up around 20,000 flying hours in the first year of operations. Set against this creditable performance were 68 accidents.

Engine failure, bad weather, inexperience all took their toll, and, as always, the amusing incident was only a literal few inches from grim disaster as Ron Waite, then a pilot officer, recalled:

On October 4th 1941, I was flying the two-engined old Whitley bomber and I was making my first solo night flight.

It was a dark night and the flares, with their flickering yellow flames and black smoke, looked eerie. The perimeter of the airfield had a high hedge, on the other side of which was the public road between Findhorn and Forres.

At about 90 mph, I had just become airborne. As I flew over the trees I felt a slight jolt in the aircraft. My co-pilot and I looked at each other, raised our eyebrows in surprise but said nothing.

The next night we were off duty and decided to celebrate our previous night's flying success with a drink in the Station Hotel in Forres.

As we entered the bar, a group of local men paused briefly in their drinking to glance at us, then returned to their glasses.

We talked quietly, supping our pints, when I heard the word 'aeroplane' crop up. We listened. A man with thinning hair and sallow, hollow cheeks, asked:

'Did you hear aboot the bus from Findhorn last neet?' Savouring the moment, he went on. 'My missus, Moira, was coming back to Forres. Along the stretch of road wheer it bends and runs alongside the airfield, an aeroplane roared overhead, making a terrible din.'

'There's nothing unusual in that,' objected one of his fellow drinkers.

'Maybe not, but the driver said there was a bang on the roof and he almost lost control. When they got out at Forres, the driver took a look and theer was a great dent in the roof.'

We remembered the bump we had felt the previous night. The undercarriage must have grazed the bus as it passed below. If the Whitley had been a few inches lower . . .

We tried to affect an appearance of nonchalance as we drank up and left before we were asked any awkward questions.

At Woodhaven, on the southern side of the Tay opposite Dundee, the Heinkel 115 seaplanes flown to Britain by escaping Norwegians went back to war. They landed resistance workers, weapons and wireless sets. The ether soon crackled with news about German garrisons, merchant shipping and enemy movements.

The Luftwaffe did not ignore Scotland, however, even if the Eastern Front loomed ever larger in their operations. Hit-and-run raids occurred all down the eastern coast. One of the last in 1941 happened at Peterhead on 30 November when a single Junkers 88 swept low across the airfield in a surprise attack. Two bombs crashed down along with sprays of machine-gun fire that killed an unlucky officer, wounded three airmen and damaged a Spitfire of Canada's 416 Squadron, formed only days earlier.

Peterhead at least had a few comforts. In the Western Isles, Tiree, bereft of many facilities, nonetheless became operational in November 1941 to help safeguard Atlantic convoys routed north of Iceland. The station had no water and no electricity. As 1941 ended, the highlight of the Hogmanay celebrations at the unit was provided by a pilot officer who played in the New Year on his saxophone.

Life had to get better.

11

Blizzards and Battleships

In the second half of 1941, Adolf Hitler enjoyed a flashing insight into Allied strategy. Sometimes right, sometimes wildly inaccurate, his infamous instincts kept his commanders on the hop. Britain, he declared, intended to invade Norway to deprive Germany of the Scandinavian iron ore and nickel she needed for her munitions industry while also protecting the Allied convoys to Russia. When, on 17 September 1941, Admiral Raeder outlined the Kriegsmarine's plans to disrupt the Atlantic convoys, Hitler countered with his own ideas.

Brest must send *Gneisenau*, *Scharnhorst* and *Prinz Eugen* to Norway, since they would be much safer there from air attack. Positioned along the coast, they could defend Norway from invasion and their very presence would also tie up British battleships. The English would not dare move from Scapa Flow for fear of an offensive behind their backs. Raeder would have much preferred to operate his big ships from the French Atlantic coast. Opposition to Hitler's sudden fancies, however, tended to bring dismissal and disgrace. Worse, the Führer's flashes of insight had the disconcerting habit of becoming strict orders.

By 13 November 1941 the Admiral had yielded to Hitler's suggestion that *Tirpitz* move to Norway when ready. Pushed into a corner, he warily admitted that it might be possible for *Prinz Eugen*, then at Brest, to make a dash through the Channel. Hitler immediately asked why *Scharnhorst* and *Gneisenau* could not do the same. Raeder cautiously agreed to think about it and then asked for Hitler's approval to send *Admiral Scheer* into the Atlantic or even the Indian Ocean. Hitler, despairing of the stubbornness of his admiral refused permission. 'Any warship not in Norway,' the Führer declared, 'is in the wrong place.' *Scheer* was of more value in the 'vital point', the Norwegian Sea.

140

In apparent confirmation of Adolf's keen insight into matters maritime and military, British commando forces made a raid on Vaagsö Island, mid-way between Bergen and Trondheim. Operation *Archery* included a diversionary attack on the Lofoten Islands to the north. Air cover and bombing support for the raid came from squadrons operating from Wick and Sumburgh.

A bitingly cold blizzard on 26 December nearly wrecked the whole operation, when both airfields disappeared under thick snow, and the commando assault was held back for 24 hours. Throughout the day, the ground crews periodically ran the engines and cleared away the snow. The next morning, before dawn, half-frozen hands cleared engine intakes and control surfaces, swept away snow and cleaned canopies. Finally, the bombed-up Hampdens of 50 Squadron staggered into the air to make the long flight to the target. Blenheim IVF fighters from 254 Squadron and 404 Squadron of the Royal Canadian Air Force followed to tangle, in due time, with Luftwaffe Me Bf109s. From Sumburgh, 250 miles further north, 235 Squadron with newly acquired Beaufighters joined the operation.

Blenheim bombers from 110 and 114 Squadrons left Lossiemouth to patrol the coast and bomb the German airfield at Herdla, the closest enemy base to Vaagsö. The attack succeeded. The raiders destroyed oil and fish processing factories, radio transmitters, a lighthouse, a power station, stores, and 4 merchant ships totalling 15,000 tons. A total of 150 enemy soldiers died, 98 were taken prisoner while 71 Norwegians left the island to join the Allied forces. British casualties came to less than 100 dead and wounded amongst the ground troops. The Royal Air Force lost 2 Hampdens, 7 Blenheims and 2 Beaufighters, along with 31 aircrew. The raid confirmed Hitler's belief in an imminent invasion. He ordered 30,000 troops from the Atlantic Wall garrisons in Normandy to Norway where they would be of much more use.

Tirpitz moved north and on 14 January 1942 she left Germany to berth in the Fættenfjord, 15 miles from Trondheim, 2 days later. The fjord, three-quarters of a mile wide, hid *Tirpitz* well with steep cliffs on three sides. Well camouflaged, protected by torpedo nets and booms, defended by flak guns and searchlights as well as her own substantial weaponry, *Tirpitz* was a particularly tough nut to crack. She waited for action on the edge of the Atlantic battleground, a potent, looming threat.

'The destruction or even crippling of this ship,' wrote Winston Churchill on 25 January 1942 'is the greatest event at sea at the present time. No other target is comparable to it.' Bomber Command responded, and on 28 January 1942 a bevy of four-engined bombers from English bases arrived at Lossiemouth. The station had no hard runways and so the heavy bombers had to land and leave on grass sewn on sand. But it was frozen hard enough to take their weight.

At 0030 on 31 January 5 Stirlings from 15 Squadron and 2 from 149 Squadron left Lossiemouth in poor weather. Ninety minutes later, 4 Halifax bombers from 10 Squadron, with a further 5 from 76 Squadron, followed the Stirlings. The cloud reached 20,000 feet from ground level but the man with the issue seaweed promised clear skies over the target. In the cloud, ice formed on the aircraft and the Stirlings, never the fastest and highest of climbers, suffered, since the de-icing system did little more than keep the aeroplanes controllable. Unable to gain height, the Stirlings laboured on as the ice built up. Two pilots, one with an overheating engine, turned back after they jettisoned their bombs in the freezing waters below.

One Stirling claimed to have seen the topmasts of *Tirpitz* but was too low to bomb, as the armour-piercing bombs needed to drop 8,000 feet to be effective. The remainder saw nothing at all – the seaweed had fibbed. All 4 of the 10 Squadron aircraft returned early as they ran short of fuel. The 76 Squadron aircraft reached the target area but cloud covered the *Tirpitz*. One pilot optimistically dropped his bombs when flak burst around his aircraft. All the aircraft returned safely except for a single Halifax of 76 Squadron. One engine failed. Worse – the fuel ran out. The pilot successfully ditched a mere 3 miles off shore, close to Aberdeen, where the local lifeboat quickly came to the crew's aid.

Snow halted any immediate further raids against the pocket battleship, and after 5 days, Bomber Command prepared to return south. The bitterly cold weather confirmed the beliefs about Scotland of the vast majority of airmen and airwomen, brought up in the towns and villages of southern England. It was isolated, cold, strange. It might even be heathen.

At Lossiemouth, a sudden thaw caused problems and the heavy bombers started to sink into the grass of the airfield. But they left before their wheels vanished under the surface. Snow blanketed their own airfields in the south and so they went to Peterhead and Wick, both of which now boasted hard runways. All the aircraft were grossly over weight limits. Fuelled to the brim, with full bombloads, to take off in the slush and waterlogged grass runway was suicidal. Lossiemouth had only a few bowsers. To take out fuel from the aircraft caused problems, while removing the bombs was even more nerve-wracking. Each weighed a little under one ton and every Stirling or Halifax carried five. The only way to remove them was to set them to safe and jettison them onto the ground below. Fortunately, none exploded.

The Stirlings and the Halifaxes floundered through the myriad of puddles on the runway, engines labouring at full power to overcome the braking effect. Wings and elevators streamed water, and in lingering slow-motion, each aircraft made it safely into the air. All nine Stirlings reached Peterhead, a Fighter Command station, with two hard runways at right angles to each other. The cleared runways had 5-foot high banks of packed snow on each side. Safely down, the Stirlings parked nose-to-tail on the cross-wind runway.

At dawn, on 7 February, the regular reconnaissance Junkers 88 appeared overhead. A Spitfire scrambled with no success. The German retreated in good order with the knowledge that nine heavy bombers occupied Peterhead. The Spitfire returned. Since the Stirlings had parked, the wind had changed and they now faced into it. The returning aircraft approached into a stiff cross-wind. The fighter touched down, swung in a ground loop and careered through the wall of snow at the side of the runway. The undercarriage gave way. The Spitfire sat down firmly on its belly.

With the Junkers hastening back to its base, the order came for the Stirlings to leave before the Luftwaffe returned with some of their bomb collection to give away. As the English bases were open, they could go home. The heavy aircraft, like the Spitfire, had to function with the wind blowing at right angles to the take-off run. Then disaster struck. The Stirling that had turned back from the *Tirpitz* raid with engine trouble thundered down the runway. The airspeed crept towards lift-off when the two port engines lost power. Stirling N6086, 'MacRobert's Reply', went off the runway, found the hole in the snow wall with unerring accuracy, and discovered the stricken Spitfire. The under-carriage collapsed and the bomber sat down heavily on top of the smaller aircraft. Although eventually repaired, N6086 never flew again in action. A second 'MacRobert's Reply' took its place.

Lady MacRobert, widow of Sir Alexander MacRobert of Crawnmore and Cromer, gifted the Stirling to the Royal Air Force in memory of their three sons, Alisdair, Roderic and Iain. All three were enthusiastic flyers. Alisdair, who succeeded to the title in 1922, died in a flying accident in 1938. At the outbreak of war, Roderic joined the RAF and was soon flying Hurricanes. Iain followed him into the service, becoming a bomber pilot. Sir Roderic Alan MacRobert, a flight lieutenant with 94 Squadron, was killed in action in Iraq, ground-strafing the German-held airfield at Mosul, in May 1941. The youngest son, now Pilot Officer Sir Iain Workman MacRobert, flying a Blenheim with 608 Squadron, failed to return from a rescue operation over the North Sea on 30 June 1941.

Lady MacRobert did not go into a decline: she was made of far sterner stuff. An American, the daughter of a renowned geologist, author explorer and Anglophile, she was a former pupil of Cheltenham Ladies College. Astoundingly, in Edwardian England, she also took a degree in geology at Imperial College, London. Undaunted by the loss of her children, she wrote to the Air Ministry to donate the money to pay for a bomber:

> It is my wish to make a mother's immediate reply, in the way that I know would also be my boys' reply – attacking, striking sharply, straight to the mark – the gift of £25,000 – to buy a bomber to carry on their work in the most effective way. This expresses my reaction on receiving the news about my sons . . .
>
> They would be glad that their mother replied for them, and helped to strike a blow at the enemy. So that I feel a suitable name for the bomber would be 'MACROBERT'S REPLY'. Might it carry the MacRobert Crest or simply our badge – a frond of bracken and an Indian Rose crossed?
>
> Let it be used where it is most needed. May good fortune go with those who fly in it! I have no more sons to wear the Badge, or carry it in the fight . . . If I had ten sons I know they would have followed that line of duty.

After the accident to N6086, a new Stirling of 15 Squadron, W7531, bore the name. This lasted until 17 May 1942 when, during a minelaying operation in Norwegian waters, flying at 200 feet, the Stirling met *Prinz Eugen* and two support ships. Hit by flak and machine-gun fire, W7531 flew towards the Jutland peninsula to be met by more flak. The Stirling crashed into a forest, the remaining mines exploded. One man, the wireless operator, survived.

In November 1941 Rachel MacRobert gave a further £20,000 that allowed four new Hurricanes of 94 Squadron to bear the names of her three sons with the inscription on the fourth reading 'MacRobert's Salute to Russia – The Lady'. Her legacy lives on in 'MacRobert's reply', the name of a Tornado of 15 Squadron at Lossiemouth.

Throughout 1942 a fresh breed of aircraftman appeared on RAF stations in Scotland. The ongoing need for ground defence led to the creation of the Royal Air Force Regiment. Largely recruited, at least initially, from the Army, the new arrivals suffered the usual gamut of insults and nicknames – of which 'Rockape' was the mildest. It naturally became a source of pride to regiment members.

Neutral Sweden started to fly through the dangerous skies around Scotland. They instituted a diplomatic service between Stockholm and Dyce on 15 February 1942. The aircraft chosen was the DC3, known to the British as the Dakota. Painted bright orange for easy identification, three were forced down by German aircraft before safe conduct was negotiated. As part of the deal, the aircraft displayed rows of lights that were kept on throughout the flight. Inevitably called the 'flying Christmas trees', the orange aeroplanes kept flying until May 1944.

On the morning of 24 February 1942 an exhausted, wet and oil-streaked homing pigeon fluttered into its loft at RAF Leuchars. Like many thousands of similar birds, NEHU 40 NS 1 was on war service. Both in Coastal Command and Bomber Command, aircraft carried pigeons for emergency use. Radio equipment was often damaged or destroyed during operations. Even when it did work, it was often unreliable, so pigeons provided an essential emergency service for downed aircrew.

Pigeon fanciers and breeders all round Britain offered their prize birds to the Services. Often enough, they ended up far from their original home loft and had to be retrained. NEHU 40 NS 1 came originally from Sunderland but had been trained by Messrs Ross and Norrie at Broughty Ferry. A blue chequered hen, she now went out with the Bristol Beauforts of 42 Squadron.

Her Beaufort had transmitted a garbled distress call ninety minutes before dusk the previous day, giving an approximate radio fix. A search of the position failed to yield results. The pigeon had no tiny message canister attached to her leg. Sergeant Leslie Davidson, a pre-war fancier with a formidable knowledge, ran the Leuchars loft. He knew that pigeons loathed flying at night, and surmised that she must have rested somewhere. At sea, the most likely refuge was a ship. The oil on her feathers suggested it had been a tanker.

The operations room had a suitable ship on their plot. Davidson worked back to her position of the previous evening, then assessed the state of her bedraggled feathers and general exhaustion to calculate how far she probably flew that morning. This information led to a new search area, and after just fifteen minutes, a Lockheed Hudson found the half-frozen crew in their dinghy. Three hours later a high-speed rescue launch arrived to pick up the four airmen and the second pigeon that had refused all inducements to leave.

The men from the Beaufort swiftly organised a dinner at which the successful pigeon was guest of honour. Throughout the celebration, she appeared to be winking so they named her 'Winkie', a title that slipped off the tongue more easily than NEHU 40 NS 1. The reaction of the eyelid was not a human gesture but the after-effect of extreme fatigue. In 1943 Maria Dickin and the Peoples' Dispensary for Sick Animals announced the institution of the Dickin Medal, the 'Animals' VC', with its green, dark brown and pale blue ribbon. Winkie led the list of the first three names.

On 6 March 1942 *Tirpitz* put to sea with a battle group of three destroyers to intercept two British convoys. After two days, having failed to find them, she turned back to Norway. On 9 March, 12 Fairey Albacore biplanes, modernised versions of the Swordfish, attacked from HMS *Victorious*, but the torpedo-bombers, from 817 and 832 Squadrons, failed to score a hit and *Tirpitz* shot down two of her attackers. By late evening, she was anchored in Bogen Bay, near Narvik, and at midnight on 12 March she slipped away in the darkness to sail back to Trondheim. By 2100 the following evening, she had berthed in her secluded spot in Fættenfjord.

Bomber Command tried again to win the coconut, and in late March the heavy bombers came back to Scotland. Halifax aircraft from 10 Squadron arrived at Lossiemouth while Kinloss became the temporary home of more Halifax aircraft from 35 Squadron. At Tain, the Halifax aircraft of 76 Squadron settled in and two Lancasters from 97 Squadron were to join them. One crashed on take-off from its home base. The other went to Lossiemouth instead of Tain. But confusion took over and the Lancaster returned to its base under the impression the raid was cancelled.

On the evening of 30 March 1942 twelve Halifax aircraft from 76

Squadron left Tain to form the first wave of attackers. They were to arrive over *Tirpitz* between 2145 and 2230. Each carried a specially developed high explosive high capacity 4,000-lb blockbuster bomb along with 500-lb or 250-lb general-purpose bombs. An ordinary 500-lb bomb usually had one-third explosive and two-thirds casing by weight. The big bombs, that looked like overgrown dustbins, reversed this proportion. They were little more than metal drums packed with explosive and streamlining was minimal. A 4,000-lb 'cookie' needed only to land in the general area of the target to do immense damage.

The second wave of ten Halifaxes of 10 Squadron and twelve from 35 Squadron was a desperately low attack as they were to fly in at 600 feet. They carried mines and incendiaries, the mines modified from the picture book round mines with horns. They would drop into the water as close as possible to the hull of the ship, and resulting explosions, everybody hoped, causing severe damage. This attack was timed to arrive between 2235 and 2315. The distance to the target and return was about 1,300 miles, which gave a flight duration, allowing for time over the target, of eight hours or more. Both waves, with the exception of one Halifax from 35 Squadron that returned with engine failure, reached the Norwegian coast on time, in clear weather with a bright moon. As they approached Trondheim, the cloud thickened and fog allied with solid cloud at low level thwarted any attempt to see *Tirpitz*. The only guide was the hailstorm of flak that rose up to greet the attackers.

The Halifaxes dropped their bombs and mines wherever they saw anti-aircraft fire or searchlight beams. Two aircraft from 10 Squadron went down, and two 35 Squadron aircraft also fell victim to determined German gunners. One other made it back to Shetland, but at low level, it crashed into cliffs and killed all on board. One aircraft from 76 Squadron passed over Sumburgh and then vanished, the pilot's body being later recovered from the sea.

Sumburgh had its own problems. The Station Medical Officer reported, in confidence, that an unusually high number of ground staff had reported as sick with some form of neurosis. Some had been on the unit for more than the twelve months that a benevolent Air Force thought was reasonable. The doctor suggested that the presence of airwomen would greatly improve morale and, more prosaically, he also felt that a supply of fresh vegetables would help. Inadequate storage meant that provisions quickly went bad. The tale went up the line to higher authority and within a short time, high-winged mono-plane Handley Page Harrows with fixed and welded undercarriages, bombers-turned-transports, flew regular supplies of fresh food to Sumburgh. Sullom Voe, even further north, benefited from the same arrangement.

A song that originated on RAF stations in the south in about 1940 journeyed north with one vital word changed at each unit it reached. By the time it reached Sumburgh, it was in a form that many people know:

> This bloody town's a bloody cuss
> No bloody trains, no bloody bus,
> And no one cares for bloody us
> In bloody Orkney.

After another five verses, the song grinds to an end with a wail of resigned despair:

> Best bloody place is bloody bed
> With bloody ice on bloody head
> You might as well be bloody dead
> In bloody Orkney.

The fresh vegetables had to make up a lot of ground.

Spring pushed tentative fingers northwards and as the bad weather of the previous months passed into memory, Denis Peto-Shepherd, then a flight lieutenant, wrote of his flying from Montrose:

The Moray Firth was a most beautiful place in which to be situated. Dalcross, an almost copybook airfield, was neatly rectangular and as flat as the proverbial billiard table; lying as it did in the narrow strip of plainland between the Firth and the hills. To the south, the Nairnshire hills rose abruptly behind us giving way to the rugged masses of the Monadhliath mountains, the Cairngorms, and the Grampians in the distance. In front of us to the north lay the Firth, across which only four of five miles away was the low-lying hulk of the Black Isle; behind which in turn, lay the great mass of the mountains of Ross and Cromarty. To our west lay Inverness at the head of Loch Ness and the Caledonian Canal; the great gash cleft through some of Scotland's wildest mountain scenery. To the east lay the firth and open sea. Here, I lost my heart completely and irrevocably to Scotland . . .

For the airman, the beauty was fraught with danger and the sudden changes in weather could be murderous. Bad visibility or low cloud is a problem to a pilot, as in it flight must be partially or wholly carried out on instruments. There then comes a point at which it is impossible to know or determine the exact position of the aircraft. Once cut off from the ground reliance has to be placed on dead reckoning, or a mental log of the aircraft's position calculated on a speed and time basis, with corrections for drift caused by wind. This can only be approximate, and the longer such conditions last the more inaccurate it is, as time rapidly increases any error in dead reckoning calculations.

. . . in those days our radio communication was very limited, and navigational aids in Scotland few and far between.

The heavies returned to Scotland on 23 April for another crack at *Tirpitz*. Once again, 10, 35 and 76 Squadrons arrived with their Halifax aircraft. This time, potent assistance came from twelve Lancasters with two squadrons, 44 and 97, supplying six each. The Lancasters went to Lossiemouth to join 10 Squadron. Kinloss welcomed 35 Squadron while 76 Squadron returned to Tain.

As with the March attack, the raid consisted of two waves. The twelve Lancasters, supplemented by the Halifaxes of 76 Squadron, each carried a blockbuster cookie especially for *Tirpitz* with a selection of 500-lb bombs to cow the searchlights and flak. They would approach at a relatively safe 6,000 feet.

The crews of the other two squadrons had a trickier task, since they were to drop the mines. This time, the attack height was set at 150 feet with each aircraft having four 1,000-lb mines. In theory, if they fell along the side of *Tirpitz* in an orderly pattern, the battleship would capsize. If the attackers did not find *Tirpitz*, they had alternative targets. Two miles north of the Fættenfjord, in Lofjord, sat the three heavy cruisers, the 18,000-ton *Admiral Hipper* and her sister ship *Prinz Eugen*, together with *Admiral Scheer*. They too were dangerous and had to be crippled.

At one minute past eight in the evening, British Double Summer Time, the first of the forty-three aircraft took off. One by one, at the three airfields, the others followed. As they headed to Norway, the gathering darkness was held at bay by a Chinese lantern of a moon, suspended in a cloudless sky. Three aircraft, one Lancaster and two Halifaxes, turned back as engine revolutions dropped, but forty aircraft pressed on, a Lancaster from 44 Squadron in the lead.

The bombing force throbbed across Norway. Beneath them, in a near-deserted landscape, curtains twitched at isolated farms and cottages to briefly let out light as the conquered heard the British engines. The short blinks of light were followed by a longer one: dit dit dit dah, the morse code for 'V' and Victory. *Tirpitz* was clear to see in the silvered fjord. The Lancaster headed in. The battleship nudged its way into the sights.

'Bombs gone!'

The 4,000-lb cookie fell away towards the target, followed by a trail of lesser companions, and almost immediately an acrid screen of black drifted across the area as alarms sounded below. Smokeships, smoke barrels cloaked *Tirpitz* from the hunters. Every aircraft in the first wave was under strict instructions to go for the alternates if they had not bombed by 0030. That was the time of the low level attack. Some aircraft headed for *Prinz Eugen*, *Scheer* and *Hipper*.

When the low level attack arrived, with 10 and 35 Squadrons flying up the fjord at 150 feet, *Tirpitz* had vanished beneath the choking chemical cloud. Pilots, navigators, bomb-aimers relied on spotting an outcrop of rock close to the ship to use as an aiming point. Ferocious flak greeted them and five crashed. One was flown by Wing Commander Donald Clifford Tyndall Bennett, the same pilot who had led the first Hudson flights across the Atlantic to Britain. He and his crew baled out. Three fell into the hands of the Germans while the other four, Bennett included, walked to Sweden and freedom.

Pilot Officer Ronald Waite, the man who almost decapitated the Forres omnibus, was in Halifax R9486 as second pilot and flight engineer. Late over target, they attacked *Prinz Eugen*. On the return, they flew over where *Tirpitz* waited:

It was like putting a foot in a hornet's nest. Venomous red jets were flashing from the *Tirpitz's* guns; shells were exploding all around. Kenny threw the Halifax all over the place, but there was no evading all the gunfire. He banked so steeply, I thought I would fall on top of him. At times we were flying so low that searchlights appeared to be pointing down on us! Several shells exploded so close that we could hear the pieces of shrapnel puncturing the fuselage.

The Halifax lost one engine and a holed petrol tank spewed out fuel. The bomb doors jammed open and they decided to try to make it home rather than head for Sweden. After more than nine hours in the air, they reached Tain and the Halifax touched down, the crew giving a collective sigh of relief. The remaining three engines cut, one, two, three as the last petrol sloshed through the fuel lines.

When the light returned, after dawn, a photo reconnaissance Spitfire headed for the Fættenfjord. With twenty 4,000-lb blockbusters going down, together with forty-four mines with a selection of smaller ordnance, there was every chance that *Tirpitz* would have taken enough damage to keep her firmly anchored. But she was unscathed and by noon, every pilot and navigator, bomb-aimer, wireless operator and air gunner heard the news that they were to try again that night. The attack plan changed in one particular. There would be no gap between the end of the first wave attacks and the beginning of the second. The Lancasters and Halifax aircraft in the first assault would have ten minutes, from 0030 to 0040, to drop their bombs. At 0041, the second wave would come in low. Their assault would last until 0050.

The first wave carried a single cookie each. The second wave, to make up for unserviceable aircraft, each carried five 1,000-lb mines. The weather was a replica of the previous night though numbers were down to a total of 34 aircraft despite herculean efforts by the ground crews. Again, the crews saw furtive victory signs from below as they bored across the night sky under a bright moon. The crews had received one simple instruction before they left their briefings. 'Sink the *Tirpitz* whatever the cost.'

The Germans anticipated a new attack, as Ronald Waite recalled. His crew had been given the spare aircraft as their own had 58 shrapnel holes as well as faulty bomb doors:

We were in very good spirits as we took off again for Trondheim, and in the back of our minds was the axiom 'lightning never strikes twice'. This time we . . . arrived over the target on time. As we flew over the snow-capped mountains so close below, the fjord came into view. We flew along the north bank, approaching Aavikaunet where the *Tirpitz* lay, when all the defence opened up. The Germans must have moved in every searchlight and anti-aircraft gun in

Norway to defend their prize battleship. The entire sky was swept by powerful beams, leaving no dark space of safety. The shore batteries were pumping up storms of light flak, their tracer shells appearing like whiplashes. We could not see the battleship, she was hidden by a smoke screen.

With Teutonic guile, the smoke started as soon as the defenders heard the throb of engines. Most aircraft bombed blind while others sought out searchlight and gun batteries or bombed any other ships they could see. Two Halifax bombers of 35 Squadron fell to the flak gunners. The next day's reconnaissance photographs told the familiar glum story. *Tirpitz* had escaped any significant damage. The heavy bombers returned south. With the enemy defenders on the alert, further immediate air attacks had little chance of success.

At Banff, known locally as Boyndie, work began on yet another new airfield. Nobody doubted that the war would last a long time even though the United Kingdom had gained two new allies in 1941 in the form of the Soviet Union and the United States. The need to strike at enemy forces in Scandinavia required advanced bases in north-east Scotland. The new station would not only serve Coastal Command but be able to take up to 24 heavy bombers when required.

One new airfield, Tealing, four miles north of Dundee, saw a positive sign of Russian involvement in the war on 29 April 1942. A Tupolev TB-7 brought the Soviet Foreign Minister and a herd of advisers to Britain for talks. Three weeks later, another TB-7, confusingly also called the Petlyakov Pe-8, arrived. It went on to Prestwick to take the Russians to Washington for talks on the conduct of the war.

At Prestwick, signs of American allied effort showed in the arrival of the first B-17 Flying Fortresses for the US Army Air Corps. By the end of the conflict, 12,357 aircraft for the US 8th Air Force had passed in transit through one of the busiest airfields in the world.

Scottish-based squadrons continued to help the war effort farther south. On 30 May 1942 the Blenheims of 614 (County of Glamorgan) Auxiliary Air Force Squadron moved temporarily from Macmerry in Lothian to West Raynham in Norfolk. They flew intruder missions over German night-fighter airfields to support the 1,000 Bomber raids on Cologne on the night of 30 May, Essen on 1 June and Bremen on 25 June. Like the Scottish Auxiliaries, the Welsh squadron now had pilots from around the globe.

To keep up the numbers for its three big raids, Bomber Command pulled in crews from its operational training units. Kinloss sent twelve Whitleys to Abingdon for the Bremen attack and they formed a tiny part of the 963-strong force. One Whitley was amongst the 49 aircraft lost on the raid itself; another crashed on the return flight to Kinloss.

Wing Commander Donald Bennett had made it back to England after the abortive *Tirpitz* raid. He soon had a new job, with promotion to air commodore, and founded the Pathfinder Force, a specialist unit formed to mark the targets for Bomber Command's assaults. Crews were often misled by the sophisticated diversionary tactics used by the German defences. Bennett's job was to overcome them and he wanted the best crews available. For his right-hand man, his 'horse thief' who would steal the very best crews from the operational squadrons, he chose a regular officer, Hamish Mahaddie from Edinburgh.

Mahaddie had joined the RAF as a Trenchard apprentice in 1928 and became a pilot in 1935, gaining his 'wings' during a tour in the Middle East. He completed two operational tours on Whitleys and Stirlings before he joined Bennett, and created minor history in February 1943. At a single Buckingham Palace investiture, he collected the Distinguished Service Order, the Distinguished Flying Cross, the Air Force Cross and the Czech Military Cross. Mahaddie's skill in finding, selecting and training crews was a major role in the success of the Pathfinder Force.

On the 25 August 1942 Denis Peto-Shepherd found himself flying on a day when, as the old saying had it, even the birds preferred to walk:

In the afternoon of 25th August 1942 I was ordered into the air to search for a crashed Sunderland aircraft, across the Firth in the Langwell Forest area of Caithness. This, we were informed, was of especial importance and every effort was to be made to find it. However the weather was dreadful, with low cloud lying on the mountains, and even the most desperate of low flying failed to penetrate the area. We suspected that the aircraft was carrying highly secret equipment, or the search would never have been pressed so desperately in such poor conditions. I was again ordered into the air the next morning to continue the search, with no greater success.

At Oban, Dorothy Williams of the WAAF, a wireless operator, also followed a changed routine. As she recalled, 'on the station we had a particularly good crew. Their abilities were known to everybody. They were a very, very efficient crew. One day they were sent away and we knew they were flying from another station down the coast'.

When she reported for duty that afternoon of 25 August she entered a tense atmosphere in the wireless cabin where she worked. She was sat down in front of her set with orders to listen out on a frequency she had never previously operated. In no circumstances was she to transmit. The afternoon dragged by with nothing happening. When her shift ended, another operator took up the task. Soon after noon, on 26 August 1942, searchers from 2716 Squadron of the RAF Regiment at Skitten, a base a few miles from Wick, found aircraft wreckage. Denis Peto-Shepherd was released from duty at midday on 26 August:

> That afternoon, when off duty and waiting beside the road at the main gate for a bus to Inverness, I was surprised when a convoy of the special Daimlers used as Royal cars raced past heading north. There was a momentous purposefulness about that convoy, but I did not then connect it with my search. What had occurred was that the Duke of Kent (the King's younger brother) had taken off from Invergordon at about 13.00 hours on 25th August, as a passenger in a Sunderland flying boat bound for Iceland. The aircraft crashed into the hills in the Langwell Forest area some 30 minutes afterwards, but owing to bad weather, the wreckage was only found at about 13.00 hours the next day, some 24 hours later. The only survivor of a crew of ten, and four passengers, was the tail gunner. This grievous loss to the royal family and the nation was the first son of an English sovereign to be killed on active service for more than 500 years.

George Edward Alexander Edmund Windsor, aged 39, an air commodore in the Inspector General's department of the Royal Air Force, left Invergordon at 1310, bound for Reykjavik in Iceland. A specially constructed airfield at Kaldadarnes, near to Reykjavik, was home to Coastal Command squadrons engaged in the weary business of protecting Atlantic convoys.

The weather at Invergordon, if not bad enough to deter eagles, would have disheartened a sparrow. Although visibility was reasonable at about

1,000 yards, the black cloud base came down to 400 feet. There was little wind and the Sunderland, heavily laden with passengers, baggage and freight, needed a long, long run to lift clear of the placid waters at Oban.

The flying boat and crew came from 228 Squadron. The Sunderland Mark III itself, W4026, was meticulously checked before the journey. It sported the new Coastal Command camouflage scheme. The white boat had its top surfaces painted in slate grey and sea green while, strictly against regulations, the nose carried a painted mascot of a kangaroo in boxing gloves, a nod in the direction of its Australian captain, Flight Lieutenant Frank McKenzie Goyen.

Although a pilot qualified to fly heavy aircraft, the Duke was a passenger. Goyen had two other pilots to help with the business of handling the Sunderland. The squadron's boss, Wing Commander Thomas Lawton Moseley, was one while the other came from Goyen's regular crew, Flying Officer Sydney Wood Smith, another Australian. The rest of the crew were selected personally by Moseley and most came from Goyen's regular crew. The navigator, Flying Officer George Saunders, got his place through a game of chance. Like every navigator on the squadron, he was well experienced in long flights over an ocean without landmarks.

Fifteen minutes after take-off, at 1325, the Sunderland entered cloud. Seventeen minutes later, it flew into a ridge in Caithness. It was about 14 degrees off course and had hit the ground in a nose-down attitude. The Sunderland caught fire, the only survivor being the tail gunner complete with turret, who was thrown clear.

The inevitable conspiracy theories began at once with a mixture of fact, fiction and imaginative reconstruction. The most obvious explanation for the disaster is a navigational error, as the Sunderland had been over land instead of the open sea, the normal route from Invergordon. Even the most experienced operators occasionally make elementary mistakes. The Sunderland had recently acquired a new piece of equipment, a distant reading gyro magnetic compass. This mouthful of jargon disguises an instrument whose purpose was to overcome the problems of magnetic field fluctuation. Set incorrectly, the pilot would follow the wrong course. In excellent visibility that would become apparent and, in general, be harmless. But in cloud, the opposite applied. Once again, Isaac claimed his due.

Heavy aircraft needed hard runways, so airfields throughout

Scotland exchanged grass for concrete. Prestwick, increasingly busy, acquired extended aircraft parking areas as well as a new runway, 4,500 feet in length. This new facility had one problem, since aircraft using it found that their flight path clashed with aircraft operating from Ayr. This conflict of interest caused occasional heart-stopping moments as most of the aircraft that used Prestwick were long-range, multi-engined machines, Ayr serving as a fighter base. In general, the fighter pilots took the necessary evasive action.

In November 1942 the RAF base at Skitten was the starting point for the first British glider-borne assault of the war. The target was the Norsk Hydro electrolysis plant at Vemork in the Telemark region, about 80 miles inland and 60 miles south of Oslo.

It was an operation that made history.

12

Grim Days, Valiant Heroes

When it opened in 1911 Vemork was the world's largest power station. A town soon grew up around the hydro-electric plant and cheap power allowed the area to turn out chemical fertiliser at unbeatable prices. In 1934 Vemork started to supply heavy water, first isolated the previous year. Men of science patiently explained that it was no more than ordinary water in which the hydrogen atoms are replaced by deuterium or heavy hydrogen. It looks and tastes like ordinary tap water but has special properties, since it boils, for example, at 101.41 degrees Celsius and freezes at 3.79 degrees Celsius.

Fascinating experiments discovered that it killed worms, tadpoles and fish while plants given a diet of heavy water also died. Seeds did not germinate in it. On the positive side, ice cubes made of heavy water sank to the bottom of the glass, a trick that enabled the boffins to win bets.

Heavy water had several scientific applications. The Norsk Hydro plant began production in 1934 and as the years passed, more uses were found. In early 1939, Norsk alerted both the French and British Governments that Germany was buying large amounts of heavy water. Both countries assumed that Hitler and his cohorts planned a new and deadly biological warfare weapon.

When Germany occupied Norway, an early target was the Norsk plant. It was not long before disturbing reports reached the Allies that the new owners, Nazi Germany, were making great efforts to increase production. All the heavy water went to Germany and the biological weapon might be enormous. Then came a new worry.

The theoretical discovery of nuclear fission, in which a critical mass of uranium would explode violently, suggested a use for heavy water.

Early attempts at creating nuclear fission in uranium had failed. The reaction was too swift and no bangs resulted. Heavy water, though, could be used as a moderator to slow down the process, and it took little time for one thought to emerge. Hitler was developing an atomic bomb.

The Vemork plant at once became a high priority target. No risk was too great if it put the plant out of action. It took little thought to realise two possibilities existed: bombing or sabotage. Bombing Vemork was not easy, since the river valley in which it sat had steep sides, rising 3,000 feet from the river below. Thickly wooded, precipitous, they presented a desperate challenge to air attack. The hydro-electric works themselves sat on a rock shelf some 1,000 feet above the river enclosed by sheer cliffs, surrounded by a nightmare of guns and defensive positions.

If bombing was a long shot, the answer was sabotage. Two choices presented themselves. Either the Norwegian Resistance could attempt this or Britain could send in men trained in demolition work. Airborne troops could go in by parachute or by glider and fortunately, a suitable force was available. In January 1942 the RAF had formed 38 Wing, within Army Co-operation Command, whose brief was to produce a force of paratroopers, glider tugs, glider pilots and target tugs. In early October, the Wing received warning of the newly named Operation *Freshman*. The sooner it happened, the better for all concerned, and the time of the November full moon was the earliest possible date. The same periods in December and January, although feasible, would be when the snow was deep and harsh cold would bite far into the bones. Number 38 Wing decided that parachutists ran too high a risk of separation from each other. To keep them together, they had to be delivered by glider. Tugs would pull Airspeed Horsa troop-carriers instead.

A plateau, optimistically thought to be no more than five hours' stiff march away from Vemork, was chosen as the landing area for the gliders. Whether anybody would be able to pick it out by moonlight, on a snow-covered landscape, was overcome by modern science. An advance party of four Norwegians, local to the area, parachuted down on 19 October 1942. They would use a Eureka radio aid to guide the tugs to the landing site. The operation was scheduled for 19 November 1942.

To make success doubly sure, 38 Wing doubled up on the demolition teams. Twin-engined Whitleys not in the first flush of youth had little power to spare at the best of times. With a tow rope and glider behind them, any engine problem during the 400-mile journey would spell disaster. A snapped tow rope was equally catastrophic. Only pessimists thought that to double the teams doubled the chance of failure.

With just four weeks to go, *Freshman* had a lucky break when the Ministry of Aircraft Production supplied three pristine-new four-engined Halifax aircraft. These greatly enhanced the expedition's chances, since the Halifax could keep flying with one engine out, even with a glider tied on behind. The Whitley pilots took a hasty conversion course to master the new arrivals.

Whether Whitley or Halifax, a tow aircraft needed a lot of runway. Skitten, usefully remote and closer than most to the destination, had 4,500 feet of concrete available. Halifaxes and Horsas duly arrived at Skitten, not without incident, on 17 November 1942. One Halifax fell by the wayside with engine problems. Inside each Halifax was a Rebecca receiving set to pick up the Eureka calls from Norway. On the morning of 19 November, the day of the operation, RAF Wick produced the weather report. Thick cloud would dominate most of the journey. Near the objective, though, the forecasters promised clear skies and bright moonlight. The raid was on.

Despite minor problems with the intercom connection between tug and glider, the first Halifax took off in darkness at 1750. The second followed twenty minutes later. The Horsa gliders each carried sixteen men with one officer. The odds, as everyone knew, were against them, and whether the raid succeeded or not, the only way home was to trek more than one hundred icy miles to neutral Sweden.

At least six Scots took part in the raid. The second pilot of the first Horsa away was Sergeant Peter Doig, a 25-year-old Glaswegian in 1st Glider Pilot Regiment. Sergeant James Falconer, from Edzell in Angus, served as the flight engineer on one Halifax. Within the assault teams were two Stirlingshire men. Lance Corporal Alexander Campbell of 261 (Airborne) Field Company came from Grangemouth. Sapper John Glenn Vernon Hunter, serving with 9 (Airborne) Field Company, was a Lennoxtown lad. One other Angus soldier endured the relentless cold that seeped through the Horsa gliders. Sapper Robert Norman, also of 9 (Airborne) Field Company, was from Brechin. In 9 (Airborne) Company was Corporal James Dobson Cairncross from the Border town of Hawick.

To fly a towed glider at night, in cloud, on basic instruments alone was not the easiest of tasks. The tow rope vanished into the darkness ahead and the Halifax could not be seen. It was a long flight. Five hours after take off, a faint signal was heard from one Halifax at 2351, asking for a course to steer to reach base. Four minutes later, at 2355, the other aircraft called that it had released its glider above the coastline. Rebecca had not worked. Close to the target, short of fuel, in fog, with ice forming on the wings, the Halifax crew had no choice. At 0143 the first Halifax to leave touched down at Skitten after nearly eight hours in the air. The remaining fuel would scarcely have filled an egg-cup. Its crew were the lucky ones.

The other Halifax had crashed, all crew members dying on impact. Its glider had crash-landed as intended, with casualties. Both pilots perished, one soldier receiving fatal injuries and dying soon after while fourteen men were unscathed. Captured, they met the consequence of a particularly infamous Führerbefehl of 18 October 1942:

> all enemies on so-called commando missions in Europe and Africa,
> even if they are in uniform, whether armed or unarmed, in battle
> or flight, are to be slaughtered to the last man.

Taken to a nearby army camp, one by one, the survivors, in uniform and clearly prisoners-of-war walked out to meet an eight-man firing squad.

'Hoch! Legt an! Feuer frei!'

The German soldiers, men of the Wehrmacht, not the SS, made ready, aimed and fired, since orders were orders. The survivors of the other Horsa, released over the coast, fared even worse. Eight men died when it landed, including both pilots. Of the nine survivors, the four injured men were taken to the nearest jail and became prisoners of the Gestapo, each one dying after a great deal of pain. The remaining five went to the Grini concentration camp near Oslo and on 18 January 1943, two months after they had landed in Norway, they were shot without ceremony.

The Germans' conduct broke every rule in the book and their behaviour was indefensible. This was not killing in the heat of battle or even immediately afterwards, but calculated cruelty which, sadly, can still be found between guards and captives. The families of the Scots who died knew only that their relative was 'Missing in Action'. Only when the war came to its end did they learn their loved ones had indeed met their end.

In June 1942, a book by a former member of 603 Squadron caused a sensation. It was by a pilot called Richard Hope Hillary, an Australian brought up and educated in England. *The Last Enemy* opens with a powerful telling of his final combat flight in the Battle of Britain on 3 September 1940. Hillary was shot down and baled out of his blazing Spitfire. He survived, badly burned about the hands and face, to spend many months in hospital in the care of Archibald Hector McIndoe, the New Zealand surgeon of Scottish descent and pioneer of remedial plastic surgery. In a series of long and delicate surgical operations, Hillary received new upper eyelids as well as a new upper lip, but his hands, savaged by the flames, remained weakened and wasted.

Hillary pestered the Air Ministry to send him back to operational flying. He wanted, he said, to keep faith with his dead comrades. He finally went before a medical board that, surprisingly, passed him for operations. After a spell at Montrose, Hillary went to 54 OTU at Charter Hall in Berwickshire to become a night fighter pilot. Ominously, the trainees nick-named it 'Slaughter Hall'. On 8 January 1943, in Blenheim BA194, Hillary spiralled into the ground at Crunklaw Farm, Edrom, and he and his navigator, Walter Fison, died. It seems probable that Hillary, orbiting a flashing beacon, succumbed to vertigo and lost control for vital seconds.

In January 1943 Errol, near Dundee, saw the formation of a highly secretive and secret unit with the innocent title of 305 Ferry Training Unit. The first trainees arrived on 11 February 1943 to convert to the Armstrong Whitworth Albemarle, a twin-engined bomber with a crew of six, designed as a replacement for the Whitley. The new arrivals kept to themselves. They had been selected with some care for they were all members of the Red Air Force. Only fourteen Albemarles, from 500 ordered, reached Russia, along with twenty crews. The first left on 3 March 1943 and three others followed on 11 March. Deliveries continued until 30 April, when 305 FTU closed. Two of the Albemarles crashed on the way to Russia and one aircraft, captained by a Hero of the Soviet Union, a Captain Gruzdin, hit a hill near Kenmore in Perthshire, the crash wiping out the entire crew.

At 1639, on the sunny afternoon of 27 March 1943, HMS *Dasher* was sailing up the Firth of Clyde, close to Little Cumbrae Island. She was an aircraft carrier, converted from a merchant ship, and had begun life in the United States as the *Rio de Janeiro*. In April 1941, before she was finished, the Sun Shipbuilding yard in Philadelphia changed her into an escort carrier. Handed over to the Royal Navy on 1 July 1942, gracefulness of line was not her outstanding attribute, since she displaced 14,500 tons when fully loaded. Her flight deck measured 480 feet in length and 70 feet in width. As she was 492 feet and 3 inches long and 69 feet 6 inches in the beam, *Dasher* looked like a huge flat floating slab.

En route to Greenock, as is the way with carriers, the Sea Hurricane pilots of 891 Squadron spent time flying off and on *Dasher*. Below decks, in the ship's hangar, aircraft were refuelling while one Hurricane sat patiently on the lift, waiting to go down from the flight deck. At 1640 a huge explosion tore through the ship. The two tons of *Dasher's* aircraft lift rocketed into the air, reaching about 60 feet before it came back down to plunge into the chill Clyde waters. With the lift no longer blocking the shaft, flames and smoke roared out from below decks and holes appeared magically along the starboard side of the carrier. Flames and smoke pushed through them and the ship took on a 10-degree list to starboard. The flight deck buckled for about half the length of the hangar below, every light blinked out and all electric motors on board ground to a halt. *Dasher's* bows began to rise as water flooded into her stern. Captain Lennox Albert Knox Boswell, commander of *Dasher* for only a few weeks, ordered the crew to abandon ship. Men jumped overboard, some with life-jackets, others without, while below decks, stokers, mechanics, stewards scrambled up ladders. *Dasher* exploded.

Twenty thousand gallons of aviation fuel and 75,000 gallons of diesel ignited to create an enormous fireball. Blazing oil splashed across the water, burning and killing many of the men who had jumped for their lives. Two coastal vessels, *Gragsman* and *Lithium*, together with a radar training vessel, *Isle of Sark*, and a French boat, *La Capricieuse*, entered the inferno. *Gragsman* rescued 14 men, 3 of whom later died, while *Lithium* pulled out 60 oil-covered survivors. *Isle of Sark* returned to shore with 32 live ratings and 3 bodies and the French ship collected 26 men from the sea.

At 1648, as the rescue boats grappled with slippery oil-soaked survivors, *Dasher* slipped beneath the surface of the Clyde to fall 500 feet to the sea-bed. In all, 149 survivors came ashore. Twenty-three iden-tified dead received burial. Thirteen were laid to rest at Ardrossan Cemet-ery to be joined 13 days later by one survivor who had succumbed to his injuries. Seven men were buried in Greenock Cemetery and 4 bodies were claimed by the families for private burial. In all, 346 Royal Navy men died, along with 27 Merchant Navy seamen, 3 RAF men and 3 employees of the NAAFI. For weeks afterwards, bodies of the 379 who perished were washed ashore on the Ayrshire coast.

The official inquiry into the disaster questioned 34 witnesses. They decided that the explosion had probably occurred in the aft depth charge magazine or the main petrol stowage close by. They finally concluded that the ship sank 'following petrol fire and explosion thought to have been caused by an aircraft attempting to land'. Conspiracy theorists set to work yet again without delay, their cause much aided by the Admiralty putting tight wraps on the incident. A tale of sabotage by a mysteriously well-spoken dockyard worker at Dundee attracted many adherents. Others preferred the simple explanation that a cunning U-boat had entered the Clyde Estuary to torpedo the carrier. Others, more cynical, suggested a British submarine had made a costly error. In more recent years, speculation has grown that one of the dead provided the body for *Operation Mincemeat*, more popularly known as 'The Man Who Never Was'.

At the end of April 1943 the *London Gazette* promulgated the award of the third Victoria Cross to go to a Scottish flyer when Wing Commander Hugh Gordon Malcolm of 18 Squadron won the highest military gallantry award in Tunisia on 4 December 1942.

Malcolm was a regular officer, a product of the Cadet College at Cranwell. Born at Broughty Ferry, Dundee, on 2 May 1917, he completed the two-year course in December 1937. Posted to 26 Squadron, equipped with Lysanders, he had a serious crash in May 1939. Amongst other injuries, he suffered a fractured skull. Four months passed before he was fit to fly again. After a series of postings on Lysanders, and a spell at 17 OTU, Malcolm went to 18 Squadron with its Blenheim IV aircraft in April 1942.

Over the next months, the squadron flew an increasing amount of night intruder sorties over occupied Europe in support of bombing raids. At the end of August, 18 Squadron began to receive new aircraft and, to accompany them, a new commanding officer. The aircraft were Blenheim Vs and the new CO was Malcolm himself, now promoted to wing commander. The squadron joined three other Blenheim-equipped squadrons to form 326 Wing. In early November 1942 the Wing moved to North Africa and they were soon in action, losing four aircraft on their first sortie against an enemy airfield at Bizerta. Two fell to enemy fighters while two collided on the way home. The Blenheims were simple prey for the voracious Luftwaffe fighter pilots from Gruppe I and Gruppe II of Jagdgeschwader 2 who claimed squatter's rights around Bizerta.

On 4 December 1942 part of the Wing, eleven aircraft in all, were at an advanced airstrip at Souk-el-Arba to support army units in the front line. In the morning nine Blenheims attacked a German landing strip and returned without loss in the early afternoon. Within an hour, 1st Army asked for another raid in the same area but fighter cover was not immediately available.

Malcolm tasked all eleven aircraft for the raid. Despite the clear odds against its success, he was determined to fly in support of the hard-pressed ground troops. At 1515, Malcolm led out the group. He took off, but the next aircraft burst its tailwheel tyre as it started down the runway and promptly ground-looped out of the way. The remaining nine aircraft got off safely. All ten Blenheims, flying at low level, took up a tight formation so that every gunner covered a neighbouring aircraft. Twenty minutes passed. One Blenheim went down with engine trouble but the crew survived the teeth-shattering forced landing in the desert, 15 miles away from their base.

As the Blenheims approached their target, Jagdgeschwader 2 rose to meet them. The Blenheims circled, ready to bomb, and the sky rained Bf109 fighters. Some fifty Messerschmitts slaughtered the Blenheims, the Luftwaffe polishing off the ten British aircraft within five minutes. The fifty or so German pilots claimed twelve kills between them. Three of the ten actually made it back to the Allied territory before they crashed. Two still had their bombs on board. Four of the twelve aircrew were injured but Malcolm's aircraft was not amongst them, since his Blenheim, BA875, crashed into the sand 15 miles west of the target. It burned and Malcolm and his two crew members perished.

Prestwick expanded and on 25 March 1943 Ferry Command became 45 (Atlantic Ferry) Group in the newly created Transport Command. Aircraft from US and Canadian factories arrived within days of leaving the production line and by the war's end about 38,000 aircraft had been flown across the Atlantic to join the forces. Hudsons, Liberators, Fortresses, Mitchells, along with Canadian-built Mosquitoes and Lancasters, made up the majority of movements. On 8 August 1943 a Mosquito raised some eyebrows when it flew from Gander to Prestwick in 5 hours and 37 minutes.

In contrast, an RAF Dakota or DC-3, designed by the company founded by the descendant of Scots immigrants, towed a Hadrian glider across the big ocean in July 1943. The Hadrian, stuffed full with 3,000 lb of supplies, meekly followed its tug from Montreal to Labrador. The next stage saw the pair land in Greenland, after which, they went to Iceland. The final leg was a triumphant flight to Prestwick with a total time airborne of some 28 hours.

Returning ferry crews originally travelled back to Canada by ship. In the latter half of 1941, however, three Liberators, originally intended for Coastal Command, were converted as rough-and-ready transports and handed to British Overseas Airways Corporation. Twenty or more returning crew could be shoe-horned into the fuselage. The return flights fell short on normal civilised amenities and sophistication.

The entry of the United States into the war had greatly increased Prestwick traffic and several US airlines became 'contract carriers'. Radio Range navigation systems were quickly established at Stornoway and Prestwick to complete a transatlantic system, and in due course, the USAAF Air Transport Command began operations together with the US Naval Air Transport Service. Almost unnoticed, Trans World Airlines and American Airlines ran daily services from Washington and New York. Money could buy comfort.

If most of Scotland's aviation concentrated on training crews for active service, one unit worked to a slightly different agenda. On 28 April 1943 at Dundonald, a small airfield near Troon in Ayrshire, a mixed bag of eight Mustangs, eight Hurricanes, two Blenheims, two Ansons and a light aeroplane, a single-engined Percival Proctor, became 516 Squadron. The previous day, they had been 1441 Combined Operations Flight.

The squadron played its part in training army and navy units in fighter control, smoke laying, ground attack on troops landing on beaches and any other job that came to hand in the business of combined operations. The squadron flew whenever the weather allowed it and sometimes when it didn't. Many exercises were both elaborate and carefully controlled. Soldiers and airmen both used live ammunition, an exciting prospect when 25-pounder field guns and 3-inch mortars were in play, let alone aircraft cannon and rockets.

Quiet spots on the west coast, such as Ardrossan and Brodick, became the scenes of realistic assault landings. Birds were a continual hazard to the ultra- low-flying pilots who took risks that would normally result in an appearance with polished shoes and best uniform in front of the commanding officer. Fatalities happened and one pilot was killed when he hit the ramp of a landing craft.

On the Moray Firth, Banff opened and the first users of the airfield

were 14 Pilot Advanced Flying Unit. One of the early arrivals was wireless
operator Harry Gummer, freshly released from hospital after a crash:

> a brand new airfield, right on the coast, new Nissen huts and the
> NAAFI staff, very new!
>
> When off duty we would walk along the coast to Banff and
> Macduff and often be invited in to have tea and scones. We had
> a few WAAFs on the unit, so rare in the area, the local children
> used to walk behind and giggle and cheer at these girls in uniform.
>
> Although a fishing port, the fish and chip shop used to sell
> fried eggs and chips. I can still see in my mind, the large sweet
> jars, full of broken eggs which were poured into a frying pan.
>
> At Boyndie or Portsoy, there was a hotel where you could eat
> as much as you liked for two and sixpence (12½ pence). The price
> soon increased due to the airmen!

Aberdeen had suffered air raids since 1940. The German occupation
of Norway and Denmark placed it neatly within range of the Luftwaffe's
Scandinavian bases. Most were 'hit-and-run' attacks which caused
comparatively little damage and casualties, although 12 July 1940 saw
a serious attempt in an apparent bid to hit the shipyard.

On 21 April 1943 came the 34th attack on Aberdeen, which was not
only the most severe raid on the city but also proved to be the last air
raid on Scotland during the war. The Luftwaffe sent around 20 Dornier
217E twin-engined bombers, which sneaked in from their base near
Stavanger as dusk fell, catching the defences on the hop. German air
raids had tailed away over the previous months and night attacks had
all but ceased. By the time the nearest fighter unit, 165 Squadron at
Peterhead, had scrambled, the Dorniers were high-tailing it back to
base. They left behind 98 dead civilians and 235 wounded. All told, 178
Aberdonians lost their lives to Luftwaffe bombing while many more
were injured. Number 13 Group detached a flight of 165 Squadron from
Peterhead to Dyce to be nearer Aberdeen, and on Sunday 9 May 1943
they took part in one of the curious incidents that peppered the war.

At 1748, two Spitfires at Dyce scrambled. Radar had picked up a
fast-moving aircraft heading straight for them. They intercepted the
intruder, a Junkers 88 that sprouted an amazing aerial array, the very
latest in the Luftwaffe's range of night fighting aids. As soon as the fighters
approached, the Junkers dropped its undercarriage, the international sign

of aeronautical surrender. White flares sprouted from the intruder. The flight leader spoke to the controller and received the immediate instruction to shoot down the enemy aircraft. The Junkers continued, wheels down, as more flares curled into the air. The flight leader ignored his orders and the Spitfires took up position on either side and escorted the German to Dyce.

The Junkers 88 landed safely. The fuselage markings, D5+EV, quickly identified the aircraft as a Junkers Ju88R-1 from 10/NJG3, based at Kristiansand. It carried the very latest version of the Lichtenstein airborne radar, together with a fine collection of maps and other information. Although British scientists had worked out the theoretical properties of the Lichtenstein, they now had a real one with which to play. They quickly evolved counter-measures, nothing more complicated than strips of aluminium foil, that were used to blind the German defences for the first time when 746 RAF aircraft dropped 2,300 tons of bombs on Hamburg in 48 minutes. The foil simply filled German radar screens with clutter. It worked extremely well and only twelve Bomber Command aircraft failed to return. Many assumed the Junkers was stolen by a British agent. The crew, however, were Oberleutnant Herbert Schmid, Oberfeldwebel Paul Rosenberger and Oberfeldwebel Erich Kanteill. The population of Hamburg paid a bitter price for their defection.

The Moray Firth became the scene of large-scale invasion exercises in 1943. Amongst other inconveniences, they forced temporary closures of the low-flying area set aside for the use of Dalcross and the Pilots' Advanced Flying Unit, since close support gunnery practice for the Royal Navy took precedence. If an absent-minded instructor or, more frequently, a pupil appeared on the scene, every available warship burst into a frenzy of signalling. Aldis lamps blinked furiously at the intruder, couching requests to leave the area forthwith in short, salty non-diplomatic phrases.

The invasion exercises had a dual purpose. As Mustangs shot up the landing beaches with live ammunition, Blenheims dropped phosphorus bombs and Lysanders laid carpets of smoke. *Operation Tyndall* came into play in August 1943, its aim being to persuade the enemy that the invasion of Norway was just around the corner. This would stop enemy units there moving south when Italy was invaded. Simulated invasion preparations included two Horsa gliders prominently displayed at Banff and a collection of bogus aircraft scattered around airfields on the east coast. German high-flying reconnaissance aircraft carefully photographed the realistic canvas and wood dummies but little evidence exists to show that the Germans fell for the ruse.

Out to the west, Tiree soldiered on. Amongst its many tasks it had the vital duty from September 1943 onward of supplying long-range meteorological forecasts. Number 518 Squadron, equipped with the Halifax V, reached out 700 miles into the Atlantic or ranged north to the Arctic Circle. As an antidote to boredom, the crews also carried depth charges for use on lurking U-boats. The pilot officer with his saxophone had left and the station staff still felt they lived at the edge of the known world. Leave to the big island 'across' sometimes emphasised the cosmopolitan nature of the services as Flight Sergeant Frank Fitzpatrick recalled:

It was the custom to collect all those who were due for leave so that they could be ferried to the mainland together. I was on such a crossing with a motley collection of ranks, trades and sexes. Amongst us was a sergeant cook who seemed very popular with some of the crowd.

When we disembarked and started off on our various ways, we were passing a very smart hotel with notices announcing 'Officers' Mess'. The sergeant cook left us and started up the drive.

We stood still, wondering. He hadn't gone far when an irate officer came storming down the drive, shooing him away.

'Are you blind, sergeant? This hotel is the Officers' Mess'.

The sergeant gave him a smart salute. 'Yes, sir. I know. I own it.' He then continued down the drive and into the main entrance.

Warfare costs lives. Not only those of the enemy killed. Accidents happen. Engines fail. Six Wellingtons from 20 OTU at Lossiemouth vanished over the sea, disappearing without trace. In bad weather, aircraft flew into hills or simply crashed. Isaac waited patiently each time. But the rescue services got better, since they had faster boats. Radio aids made a difference and sometimes, fortune smiled on men who thought they had exhausted their luck.

On 11 October 1943 one of Sullom Voe's Catalinas from 190 Squadron ditched in rough seas, 60 miles from land. It had not been the best of trips, since towards the end of the 22-hour patrol, the radio failed in sympathy with the engines. At 0800, the autumn sea is cold and forbidding, and the Catalina, without power, pitched and rolled with the waves.

The water smashed at the hull while a fierce wind snatched at the wings. Dark grey, almost black cloud threatened harsh rain to come and visibility was down to a mere 100 yards. Rescue seemed a long way off. The weather indeed prevented a proper search, since no aircraft could take off in such conditions. The Air Sea Rescue launches fought their way through towering seas but found nothing.

At 1700 hours, an all-white hen pigeon, White Vision, one of the two on board the Catalina, fluttered into her loft. Bred by the Fleming brothers of Motherwell, White Vision had a message container tied to her leg, giving the position of the Catalina. The rescue launches had information they could use, and at five minutes after midnight on 12 October, sixteen hours after the Catalina smacked down on the angry sea, a High Speed Rescue Launch sighted the drifting boat. All eleven crew were taken on board. The Catalina was abandoned, hatches open, and she sank minutes after the last man, the captain, Flying Officer Ronald Vaughan, jumped onto the launch. Released at 0820, White Vision had flown steadily into a 25-knot headwind, in appalling visibility. Her companion pigeon, also launched with a message, never made it to safety. White Vision received the Dickin Medal. Her name also changed. She became White Saviour.

On 14 December 1943 the *London Gazette* carried the notice that the Victoria Cross had been awarded to Flight Lieutenant William Reid of the Royal Air Force Volunteer Reserve. A Glasgow man, Reid won his VC for his heroism during a raid on Düsseldorf on 3 November 1943. Born at Ballieston on 21 December 1921, he went for initial training in August 1941 before going to Canada and the United States for flying instruction. He was back in England in August 1942, and after his conversion course as a bomber pilot, he found himself as an instructor with the promise of an eventual posting to an operational squadron. He finally reached 61 Squadron at Syerston in September 1943.

On the night of 3 November 1943 Flight Lieutenant William Reid started out on his ninth operation as captain. At 1659, the wheels of Lancaster LM360 lifted from the concrete of Syerston's in-use runway. The mid-upper gunner and rear gunner settled down for a cold ride, since the heating system in both turrets had failed. The Lancaster droned on until breakers in the sea below heralded the Dutch coast – on course for the target at 21,000 feet.

The windscreen vanished in a maelstrom of Perspex as the 20-mm cannon and five 7.9-mm machine-guns of a prowling Messerschmitt

Bf 110 with its deer-horn radar antenna poking from its nose had joined the party. Each gun turret took hits although both gunners escaped injury. Reid was in a worse state: shrapnel splinters penetrated his head and shoulder and jagged shards of perspex lacerated his face. With the windscreen gone, the icy blast into the cockpit had one redeeming feature, since it swiftly coagulated the blood from his wounds.

Reid pulled his goggles over his eyes and set about regaining control of the Lancaster that had started to dive. It took 2,000 feet to get it back under some sort of control. The Messerschmitt's pass not only smashed the gun turrets, it also tore the port elevator to pieces, wrecked the trim tab, destroying the compass and other instruments as well as damaging the hydraulics. Flight Sergeant Alan Jeffries, the navigator, asked Reid how he was, and the pilot nodded. 'Yes, I feel all right,' he answered. He asked about the crew. Hearing that they were uninjured, he settled down to fly to Düsseldorf. The damage to the tail caused the Lancaster to yaw but Reid tamed it with a bootful of left rudder.

A Focke Wulf Fw 190 took up where the Messerschmitt had finished. In one swift, brutal assault from the left, cannon shells rattled into the Lancaster and the navigator died at once. The wireless operator, Flight Sergeant John James Mann, crumpled, badly wounded, while the flight engineer took a hit in his left arm and Reid was hit again. The hydraulics suffered more damage, both gun turrets took another hammering and the oxygen system collapsed along with the intercom. The rear-gunner sprayed the night fighter with his one working Browning. Norris, the flight engineer, found an emergency oxygen bottle and clipped it to Reid's supply tube as the Lancaster shed height. Together, both men struggled to level the aircraft at 17,000 feet. Reid flew on, and with no compass and missing instruments he lined up on the Pole Star, worked out a rough course and continued, with 200 miles still to fly.

It took almost sixty minutes after the Focke Wulf attack for LM360 to reach Düsseldorf via Cologne. Reid folded his arms around the control column to hold it rigid. The Lancaster flew steadily across the target. The bomb-aimer, Flight Sergeant Les Rolton, with no communication between him and the pilot, released when he recognised the objective. Still holding the Lancaster steady with hard left rudder, Reid finally headed home. Rolton joined Norris and Reid in the cockpit and between them, using the moon and stars as a guide, they steered towards England. Reid grew weaker as each minute passed.

They were nearly back at the Dutch coast when the flak started. But the three managed to escape without further damage and cleared the coast. The emergency oxygen supply petered out. All four engines spluttered into silence and the Lancaster floundered into a flat spin. But Reid hardly reacted, since lack of oxygen, wounds, exhaustion left him slow to think while Norris was in little better shape. Training reminded him that he had not switched the petrol cocks to a full tank. The Merlins throated into life. With the hydraulics gone, the bomb doors had stayed open and the fuel needles marched relentlessly towards empty.

A cone of searchlights lit up the night: it was an unknown airfield. William Reid circled and flashed the landing lights to show the aircraft was in distress. With his strength draining away, he used the emergency pressure bottle to lower the undercarriage. With the effort and the warmth as the Lancaster dropped down from the freezing higher levels, blood began to ooze from his wounds, his head injury dripping red towards his eyes.

Reid lined up the Lancaster on the runway, crossed the boundary, and cut the power. He steadily pulled back on the stick until the wheels touched. As the weight bore on the undercarriage, one leg collapsed and the Lancaster slithered on its belly for some fifty or sixty yards. They had landed at Shipdham in Norfolk, three miles south of East Dereham, home of the USAAF 44th Bombardment Group. Released from hospital, the Glaswegian's war had not ended as he went to 617 Squadron. On 31 July 1944 a falling bomb from another Lancaster passed through his aircraft, severing all the control cables and weakening the fuselage. Reid ordered the crew to bale out and escaped as the aircraft broke up. Only he and the wireless operator survived.

Flight Lieutenant William Reid finally came home in May 1945. He had won the fourth Victoria Cross awarded to a Scottish airman.

13

U-Boats and Flak Ships

Scotland saw more combined service operations training and exercises as the invasion of Europe edged towards reality. For any who doubted, the news that General Dwight David Eisenhower had become Supreme Commander of the Allied Expeditionary Force on 16 January 1944 gave notice that it was now a question of 'when' the Allies invaded Continental Europe, rather than 'if'.

For the pessimists, the weather had not improved. Bowmore, Strathclyde, served as a practice alighting area and diversion base for flying boats. No hangars existed and precious little else as crew comforts. In January 1944 a 422 Squadron Sunderland diverted to Loch Indaal, riding serenely at anchor until a gale came along when she sank. The four men of the onboard crew launched a dinghy as the Sunderland slowly disappeared beneath the surface. The second pilot did not reach it in time and the dinghy, blown by the wind, slowly moved away, despite frantic efforts with paddles. Fortunately, the tailplane stayed clear of the water and a motor launch finally rescued the pilot from a watery end.

The winter of 1943 had been another cold experience for many airmen and airwomen. Cynthia Routh, then a WAAF sergeant, was posted to Brackla towards the end of 1943:

> Brackla was back to basics. We had iron beds and 'biscuits' which were three hard squares that, laid end to end, were the length of a mattress. The ablutions were in one of the farm sheds which had been fitted up with metal wash basins along one wall. The waste water ran straight down into a trough where the farm ducks would come to paddle as it drained away. We had to be careful not to get into their way!

The winters were very cold. There was no heating in the sleeping quarters. I often went to bed with my greatcoat, socks and scarves over my pyjamas. There was ice on the blankets where we had breathed in our sleep. Even the water in my hot water bottle froze. At one time, the only running water was in the latrines. We caught the flush in our mugs to clean our teeth!

In March 1944 a detachment of the US 492nd Bomb Group, nick-named the 'Carpetbaggers', arrived at Leuchars. They had Liberators and C-47 aircraft, some painted green, some painted grey with civil markings as part of Operation *Sonnie*. The aircrew wore civilian clothes when flying. Its nominal role was to transport from Sweden to Britain Norwegian volunteers and any American interned aircrew that the Swedes released. The unit came under the command of Colonel Bernt Balchen, a Polar flier of some fame. Norwegian-born, Balchen was a natural adventurer, having served as a Finnish cavalryman during the First World War, then joining the Royal Norwegian Naval Air Service. In 1926 he emigrated to the United States, where he piloted the first aircraft to carry the US mail across the Atlantic in a Fokker tri-motor *America*, and in 1929, he became the first man to pilot an aircraft over the South Pole.

Sonnie lasted fifteen months, although the 492nd left Leuchars in November 1944. By the end of the war, they had ferried more than 4,304 passengers to Britain. They also carried spare parts, supplies and equipment to repair two-thirds of the American combat aircraft that had force-landed in Sweden. Only one *Sonnie* aircraft was lost when it hit a Swedish mountain. Balchen also commanded Operation *Ball* which used 6 black-painted war-weary Liberators to drop supplies and agents to the Resistance in Norway. They made 64 missions and two aircraft and twelve crew were lost.

At Dounreay in the Highlands, the airfield originally intended for Coastal Command finally reached completion. Neither runway aligned properly with the prevailing wind. The approach was poor because of the surrounding hills and apart from the concrete, the airfield had no facilities.

'This aerodrome', stated an inspecting officer, 'is on the extreme north coast of Scotland and is unsheltered from very strong gales, low cloud and very heavy rain, making it unfit for use consistently when the weather at Skitten about thirty miles away is fit. The prevailing wind is down the short runway which ends at the face of a cliff and would require extending.'

The airfield went immediately into 'care and maintenance' status and the Air Ministry hurriedly transferred Dounreay to Naval hands on 15 May 1944. The Admiralty needed an airfield with a Class B repair yard to support Scapa Flow, and it took no time at all for the Royal Navy to realise they had been offered a pup of decidedly uncertain parentage. Dounreay was never commissioned into naval service and returned to C&M status. In 1954 it fell once again into Air Ministry hands. They gratefully handed it over as the site for a nuclear power station.

Sergeant Alf Allsop, at Peterhead, served with a squadron that had more than ordinary enthusiasm for the invasion. Alf was a fitter and rigger with 350 Squadron, the first Belgian-manned fighter squadron, who had come to Scotland for a rest. They had recently converted to the Spitfire Vc:

We'd only been there a couple of days before we had two Spits badly damaged beyond repair. They landed together and the last one to touch down caught up with the first. His propeller chewed up the fuselage and only stopped when it hit the armour plating behind the pilot's head.

The other incident occurred when a pilot was flying very low – they liked to do that – over a loch and his engine cut dead, and in he went and sank to the bottom.

Now a Spitfire hood is jettisonable with the aid of a lightweight crowbar clipped to the inside of the cockpit door. Unfortunately, there wasn't one! However, this particular pilot carried a commando dagger in his flying boot. Using the oxygen mask as a breathing mask, he managed to escape from the Spitfire and swam to safety.

We painted a mermaid on his replacement aircraft.

They salvaged the aircraft from the bottom of the loch and found the cause of the engine failure. The vertical drive shaft to the two magnetos had sheared. Some engineering inspector had missed that one.

The squadron stayed in Scotland for only six weeks. Before they returned south, one further incident marked their stay:

The hut that the lads were billeted in was not too clean so one of the Belgian ground crew decided to wash the floor with 100 octane petrol, stood back, admired his efforts and lit a cigarette.

Goodbye, billet!

High-octane aviation fuel played a similar part at Kinloss when Whitley LA819 went up in flames. An electrician decided to test the magnetos shortly after the engines were washed down with petrol. One spark was all it took. Number 45 Maintenance Unit had opened in Kinloss alongside the OTU in 1939. Responsible for the testing, the servicing and the storage of a range of aircraft types, it had a busy time modifying Halifax aircraft to serve as glider tugs for the invasion.

On the night of 5 June 1944 the aircraft they handled set out as part of the initial assault on Hitler's Fortress Europe. With troops and aircraft now fully committed to the fighting on the Continent, Scotland's role changed. The RAF station at Annan, in Dumfries and Galloway, became a storage depot for 14 MU at Carlisle in July 1944. Originally used by 55 Operational Training Unit, first with Hurricanes and then Typhoons, the station was far from ideal. Operational for two years, it suffered from a spate of bad weather as the station record book for 30 April states:

the weather – not suitable for publication – no flying whatsoever. It is better to draw a blanket over the whole day as everyone is hopping mad. The gentlemen who selected the site for the aerodrome must find their ears burning today!

On 24 June 1944 a seven-man crew from 162 Squadron of the Royal Canadian Air Force, flying from Wick, met the Kriegsmarine's U1225 north of the Shetland Islands. They flew a Consolidated Canso amphibian, a version of the Catalina flying boat with an undercarriage so that it could use both land and water. The captain, 34-year-old Flight Lieutenant David Ernest Hornell, was on his 61st operational sortie.

The Canso took off at 0930 from Wick to head north over the vast stretch of grey sea. After ten hours of searching, from the port side gun blister Flight Sergeant Israel Joseph Bodnoff and Flight Sergeant Sydney Reginald Cole, two of the three wireless operators/air gunners, saw the sight of which every U-boat hunter dreamed. Five miles away, fully surfaced, minding its own business, was a U-boat. Cole told the captain and then relieved the man at the radio set, Flying Officer Graham Campbell. He, the third WOP/AG, went to man the nose guns and Hornell turned the Canso into the attack, lining up with the boat's bow to drop his depth charges along the whole length of the U-boat.

Oberleutnant zur See Ekkehard Scherraus, the 24-year-old captain of U1225 decided to tough it out and fight. Even the swiftest crash-dive would not get him deep enough, fast enough, to escape. At 4 miles distance, the U-boat opened fire with her battery of 20-mm and 37-mm cannon, mounted by the conning tower on a special platform known as the 'Wintergarten'.

Hornell jinked as the shells hurried towards him, and the first burst of fire smashed the wireless aerials. Cole's signals to base died in mid-stutter as the Catalina took 2 minutes to cover the 4 miles, steady on the attack heading. The U-boat gunners kept their nerve and their aim. Flak smashed into the flying boat, chewing at the starboard wing. Shells tore into the fuselage, exploding inside, scattering shrapnel in a devil's pattern.

Fire streamed out of the starboard engine as shrapnel scattered along the wing. The metal burned, flames licking across the surface. The second pilot, Flying Officer Bernard Charles Denomy, fought to feather the engine as Hornell struggled to keep the Canso on its attack run. At less than a mile to go, the Canso returned fire. The nose guns spat a few rounds before one jammed. The side blister gunners did their unsighted best. The Canso shuddered as cannon shells smacked into her hull.

Half a mile to run and Scherraus turned U1225 broadside on to the approaching danger. The water was just 50 feet below as Hornell approached the U-boat. Bombs and depth charges do not drop in a straight line. They leave the aircraft with the same forward speed, losing momentum as they fall through the air. At low level, precise judgement hits the bull's-eye.

Two depth charges straddled the U-boat. Her bows lifted. The pressure hull punctured. Clear of the sea for long seconds, the broken bow finally smacked onto the water and the sea flooded into the 1,545 tons of U1225, a class IXC/40 boat, built at Hamburg the previous year. The Canso fought for height. The starboard engine, blazing furiously, fell away to hiss into the water below. Broken fuel lines fed the flames while inside the aircraft, thick smoke curled ominously through the fuselage. At 250 feet, Flight Lieutenant David Ernest Hornell persuaded the Canso to turn into wind. The time had come to ditch.

The controls barely responded. Flames licked hungrily at the starboard wing and much of the right hand fuselage. The aircraft smacked on to the sea, bounced, hit the water again, and bounced once more before it finally stayed down. The two pilots left hurriedly through their escape hatch. Behind them, the other crew members scrambled out through the port blister.

One of the two flight engineers, Sergeant Fernand St Laurent, threw one four-man dinghy out, then dived after it. The dinghy inflated upside down and Bodnoff and the second engineer, Flight Sergeant Donald Stuart Scott, pitched out the other. Cole grabbed the emergency ration packs and water bottles to become the last man out as water lapped at his toes.

Ten minutes later the Canso sank. Seven men sat or clung to one dinghy. Thirty yards away, St Laurent fought to right the other dinghy as Campbell and the navigator, Flying Officer Sidney Edward Matheson, swam to help. Between them they turned the dinghy upright and struggled on board. The air blew out and all three men splashed back into the water as the dinghy collapsed. The eight-man crew now had one single dinghy and Sumburgh lay 200 miles to the south. Two hundred miles to the east sat the Norwegian coast. Hornell used his trousers, a knot tied in each leg, to bale out the water that threatened to sink the dinghy. Finally, four men sat in it while the other four clung to the sides, neck deep in the Atlantic. The crew quickly dumped the original plan to take turns; after an hour, all eight were on board although Scott's legs trailed in the water.

The weather worsened as a cutting wind, racing across the ocean, taunted the sea into a 40-foot swell. The dinghy pitched and rolled, rose and fell. Four hours passed and midnight came closer without darkness in the northern latitude. The eight men heard a distant droning – in the sky above, a Catalina plodded homeward. Campbell frantically fired three red distress flares which rose into the sky, bursting into two bright scarlet stars.

The first flare died and the Catalina continued on its course. The second flare had no effect. The third exploded into the sky. The Catalina, on routine patrol, banked, headed for the dinghy. It belonged to 'A' Detachment of 333 (Norwegian) Squadron from Woodhaven on the Tay. The rescue party not only found the Canso crew, they also saw a collection of dinghies filled with survivors from U1225. The Catalina dropped markers and flame floats, radioed base and circled to look for more dinghies. After thirty long minutes, it returned to Hornell's men. Its Aldis lamp blinked the cheerful news that a high speed launch was on its way. Another circuit, another message to tell the Canso crew they had killed their U-boat.

The Catalina did not leave. Leaning the fuel mixture for maximum endurance, Lieutenant Johannsen, the captain, stayed on station for the next fourteen hours. Although he flew a flying boat, he dared not land on the mountains of water that passed as waves, and several times the Catalina crew saw the dinghy capsize. Each time, the Canadians righted it and struggled back on board. Fernand St Laurent died, since summer is never too warm on the North Atlantic. With a vicious wind and swamping seas, even the strong weaken.

The morning wore on, and at about 1100, an ASR Warwick, a direct descendant of the Vickers Wellington, arrived. Flying in low from the south, it parachuted a lifeboat to the men in the dinghy. The release gear failed to work correctly and the lifeboat hit the water 500 yards away. Nearly blind, exhausted, suffering from exposure to the relentless sea, Hornell tried to swim to the lifeboat but Denomy held him back. In the early afternoon, Scott died. Hornell, Campbell and Matheson were close to death and the three others, Bernard Denomy, Sydney Cole and 'Joe' Bodnoff fought to keep them alive. Hornell lost consciousness. Matheson and Campbell were little better off.

There was more engine roar and a Short Sunderland flew low over the sea. Behind it, in the distance, came an Air Sea Rescue launch, spray foaming at the bow as it cut through the waves. It arrived 20 hours and 35 minutes after the Canso crashed. David Ernest Hornell died on board the launch, at some time during the 14 hours it took to reach Lerwick. The others survived.

The *London Gazette* announced Hornell's posthumous Victoria Cross on 28 July 1944. Denomy received a DSO. The Distinguished Flying Cross went to both Campbell and Matheson and the two surviving NCOs received the Distinguished Flying Medal. The rules on posthumous awards meant that St Laurent and Scott, the flight engineers, received only a Mention in Despatches.

The summer was warm and fine in 1944 and at Brackla, used as a satellite airfield for Kinloss and as a Relief Landing Ground for Dalcross, it became so hot that Sergeant Cynthia Routh negotiated a special concession for her airwomen. After some discussion, she received permission for them to remove their jackets at work. The privilege was so remarkable that someone with a camera took a photograph to mark the event.

Brackla changed its role and in late 1944 it became an Aircrew Allocation Centre. Many men, sometimes freshly returned from tropical areas, arrived in excellent time to endure the Highland winter. One Australian officer, tour-expired from Bomber Command, gloomily recorded that 'the hut was as cold as a morgue'. He found it impossible to sleep, so gave up. The next morning, he strode into Nairn and booked himself into the Highland Hotel.

In July 1944 Flying Officer John Alexander Cruickshank of 210 Squadron became the fifth Scottish airman to win the Victoria Cross. Born in Aberdeen on 20 May 1920, Cruickshank joined the Commercial Bank at the age of eighteen. A year later, on 10 May 1939, he enlisted as a 'Saturday Night Soldier' in 129 Field Regiment, Royal Artillery. In September Gunner Cruickshank became a full-time warrior when his Territorial Unit was called up as part of the second line 15th (Scottish) Division. In early 1941 Cruickshank decided he wanted a more active war and applied for aircrew training. After the usual paper-filling and selection tests, he began training in July and by the middle of September he was in Canada for pilot instruction and completed his advanced tuition at Pensacola in Florida. By the time he finished his operational training and crewing at Invergordon on Catalina flying boats, it was March 1943. He and his crew joined 210 Squadron on the 25th of the month.

By 10 July 1944, when his promotion to flight lieutenant came through, Cruickshank and his men had completed 47 operational patrols over the featureless Atlantic. On the morning of 17 July 1944, John Cruickshank took off in Catalina JV928 from Sullom Voe at 1345 on another patrol, his normal nine-man crew augmented by an extra pilot, along to gain experience.

Eight hours later, JV928 rumbled along steadily at 2,000 feet, some 300 miles west of Norway and 600 miles north of Sullom Voe. There was nothing in sight and only the ocean below. Then, the radar plot showed a contact, forty-three miles distant. The Catalina was both out of sight and out of hearing of the vessel on the surface. Cruickshank headed straight for it in the strong Arctic evening light. Minutes ticked away as a smudge, dark in the distance, looked like a submarine – on the surface, water breaking at the bow as she ploughed through the sea. The Catalina closed, since it had to be friendly, and she blinked a challenge, fired a recognition flare and flew nearer.

The contact erupted flak for she was U361 under the command of Kapitänleutnant Hans Seidel. For many years, U347 has been named as the U-boat. In fact, she tangled with a Liberator on the same day, some miles away. Eric Zimmerman's painstaking research has established that U361 fought Cruickshank.

The Catalina hastily pulled away. The flak shells followed.

Cruickshank bled off height and lined up for his attack run. The advantage of surprise had vanished, but a U-boat on the surface, even with its guns in action, was a target worth chasing. At 50 feet, the Catalina skimmed across the water towards Seidel and his crew, and as the range dropped, the Catalina bit back. The bow gun opened fire, followed by the fuselage blister guns, and machine gun bullets, mixed with tracer, hurried towards the 'Wintergarden'. One thousand yards became 500. The range dropped, and as the U-boat grew larger, Flying Officer John Charles Dickson, the navigator, clicked the depth charge release. Nothing happened and they stayed firmly in place. Cruickshank kicked the rudder, hauled back on the stick in a climbing turn to port. The Catalina reached 800 feet, followed by more irritated bursts of flak that lashed into the fuselage. There was a crew check. No casualties, so Cruickshank went in again.

U361 had slowed to give her gunners a better aim, and as the Catalina roared in once more, a flak shell smashed into the fuselage and exploded inside the flying boat. Dickson died instantly, while the flight engineer received wounds in both legs. Flight Sergeant Jack Garnett's windshield shattered with the blast and behind him a fire started.

Cruickshank was in worse shape, since he had wounds in his chest and both legs. But he carried on, 50 feet above the water, aiming straight at the U-boat and releasing the six depth charges. This time they pitched in a perfect pattern and the Catalina soared over Seidel's command, climbing into a providential bank of sea fog directly ahead. Below, the depth charges exploded to tear out the life of U361. One thousand tons of steel fashioned by the Flensburg Shipyard into a Type VIIC U-boat went to the bottom of the Arctic Ocean. None of the fifty-two crew survived.

Cruickshank and his men had no chance to confirm their success, since the enemy anti-aircraft fire had badly damaged the Catalina. Holes peppered her hull but pride of place went to a one-foot long gash. The radar was dead. A petrol line leaked fuel. With a minimum five-hour flight to safety, any loss of fuel could tip the balance against survival. While some of the crew did their best to patch up the hull,

Jack Garnett took control of the aircraft, and one of the two gunners, Flight Sergeant Appleton, came forward to take care of Cruickshank. As Appleton cut away his skipper's blood-soaked trousers, Cruickshank fainted.

Appleton, helped by Garnett, lugged the captain to the only undamaged rest bunk. Garnett returned to fly the aeroplane and Appleton did his best to treat Cruickshank's wounds. The pilot came round and immediately tried to go forward, but Appleton restrained him. Cruickshank refused morphia in case it stopped him from carrying on. He continually fell unconscious as his blood seeped through the emergency dressings, but he came round each time with a grim determination to continue. It took over five hours to reach Sullom Voe and in a quirk of fortune, the Catalina arrived in the middle of the short northern night, with dawn a full hour away.

John Alexander Cruickshank insisted on going forward. While the Catalina described great circles around Sullom Voe, the crew tossed out everything they could to lighten the aeroplane, since the lighter the Catalina, the better the chance of it staying afloat when it touched down on the water. As the grey light of morning spread from the east, Cruickshank and Garnett eased the flying boat onto the water. As she settled, the fuselage flooded as water hurried in through the hastily patched holes. Quick thinking pushed the throttles forward and the engines roared. The Catalina ran up on to the beach and flopped to a halt and the medical team climbed on board. The doctor, Patrick O'Connor, immediately realised that Cruickshank's only chance of survival depended on a blood transfusion without delay. Like any exceedingly good doctor, he improvised, using anything to hand, including a chamber pot.

When the condition of John Alexander Cruickshank at last stabilised and he reached hospital, the doctors counted seventy-two wounds. His Victoria Cross was gazetted on 1 September 1944. Three weeks later, at Holyrood House, he received the medal in person from King George VI. Jack Garnett was with him to collect his Distinguished Flying Medal for the same action.

Prestwick grew and became one of the few airfields in the whole of the United Kingdom to have a radio range facility so that incoming aircraft could let down through cloud. This proved a life-saving service in capricious weather.

From June onwards, US C-47 transports shuttled in with American casualties direct from France. At Prestwick, they were transferred to the

C-47's big brother, the four-engined C-54, known in civilian circles as the DC-4 Skymaster, for onward carriage to the USA. In August 1944 Prestwick logged no fewer than 7,847 aircraft movements. The Tiger Moths with their primitive silencers were a distant memory for the inhabitants who lived under the flight paths.

The inexplicable still happened and at Lossiemouth, on a clear, bright day with little wind and excellent visibility, a Beaufighter took off on a test flight from 46 Maintenance Unit. It disappeared into the distance and was never seen again.

In August 1944 Banff prepared for a new owner. Number 14 (Pilot) Advanced Flying Training Unit disbanded after training 1,516 pupils in 113,896 flying hours. On 1 September Banff became a Coastal Command station. The aircraft that flooded in were no patrol aircraft, designed for long flights to search for U-boats in the wide oceans. Coastal Command was about to go on the rampage. Attacks on enemy shipping were nothing new, as Beaufighters had done the job for the previous two years. Wick and Leuchars had both housed Strike Wings and a third operated out of North Coates in England. A dedicated force to harry the enemy out of existence was now in residence at Banff, intended to be bigger, better and more ferocious than anything that went before.

The first two arrivals were 144 Squadron and 404 (Canadian) Squadron with Beaufighters. The first two Mosquitoes for 'B' Flight of 333 (Norwegian) Squadron landed. Banff had become the home of a Strike Wing.

On 6 September nineteen Mosquitoes of 235 Squadron flew up from northern Cornwall to join the Banff Strike Wing. The ground crew, counting carefully, loaded the bomb bays with a total of 235 toilet rolls. On arrival, the exuberant pilots buzzed the harbour then made a low pass over the main runway at Banff and the toilet rolls bounced down onto the tarmac. The following week, 248 Squadron, again with Mosquitoes, joined the throng and in October, the Beaufighters moved to neighbouring Dallachy. Both they and the Mosquitoes would operate in harmony for the next months.

Banff's station commander was Group Captain the Honourable Max Aitken, DSO, DFC, Lord Beaverbrook's son. The station eventually housed six Mosquito squadrons and the six commanders were, at one point, spread evenly between England, Australia, New Zealand, Norway, France and Ireland. Four of them would die on operations. Dallachy held four Beaufighter squadrons, one RAF and one each from Canada,

Australia and New Zealand. The final pieces of jigsaw came from Peter-head, which supplied escorts in the form of Mustang fighters and Fraser-burgh with high-speed rescue launches.

The new wing made its first major sortie with a *Rover* armed recon-naissance on 14 September. Forty-four aircraft took off, twenty-five Mosquitoes and nineteen Beaufighters to find four motor vessels sailing north, protected by two flakships. The wing attacked, scoring hits on every ship and one small trawler was sunk. The larger merchant ships were badly damaged – and all for the cost of one Beaufighter.

More *Rovers* followed at regular intervals, the normal plan being for the Mosquitoes to provide cover for the Beaufighters with their tor-pedoes. This included the distinctly hairy job of smothering any flakships that thought they were in with a chance. The Norwegian crews in 333 Squadron came into their own for they often acted as guides to lead the wing up misty fjords in search of useful prey.

On 26 October the Mosquitoes used rockets for the first time. The Mosquito could carry four under each wing and after early sorties with 60-lb semi-armour-piercing heads, the Wing settled on 25-lb fully armour-piercing warheads that could penetrate a ship's side even if they hit the vessel below the waterline. The rocket not merely beat its way into the ship, it also came out the other side, leaving an eighteen-inch hole in the hull, usually below the waterline. As an additional refinement, the remains of the motor stayed behind in the ship, burning enthusi-astically. The projectiles from one Mosquito were calculated to be the equivalent of a broadside from a light cruiser. The 248 Squadron Mosqui-toes packed an extra bite, since they had seven Mk XVIII on strength, armed with a six-pounder cannon. The barrel poked out some two feet from under the nose and this brute slung a 57-mm calibre shell in the direction of the enemy, usually with devastating results.

The Strike Wing met minimal opposition in the air until 7 December, when twenty-one Mosquitoes and forty Beaufighters, with an escort of Peterhead's Mustangs from 315 Squadron, met up with some twenty Bf 109s and Focke-Wulf Fw190 'butcher birds'. The tenth Polish squadron to be formed in Britain, 315 Squadron had a particular distaste for Germans, and in the brawl that followed, the Strike Wing claimed four Messerschmitt kills, one probable Bf109 and three probable Fw190. In turn, the Luftwaffe initially claimed 13 twin-engined aircraft and two Mustangs as shot down. The Germans, indeed, lost four aircraft, but four Allied aircraft also went down. Two Mosquitoes failed to return as did one Beaufighter and one

Mustang. The Beaufighter crew survived their ditching and arrived at Lerwick on board a fishing trawler three days later. The Banff and Dallachy Strike aircraft would have a busy time until the end of the war. Benbecula had closed down in October 1943 for essential work, and eleven months later, on 21 September 1944, it re-opened. Two squadrons, 19 and 304, equipped with the Wellington XIV, arrived. They had the thankless task of searching for U-boats. In eight sorties made by 304 Squadron during October, the total count of sightings was precisely none. One Benbecula RAF resident noted glumly that he had 'learned to walk at the correct angle in the continuous gale and not to expect more than the occasional glimpse of the sun'.

In September another Dickin Medal went to 'Scotch Lass', a pigeon bred by Collins & Son at Whitecraig, Musselburgh. Radio aids and equipment had improved immensely during the years of war and pigeons no longer went on bombing raids or anti-U-boat patrols. They still had, though, a part to play as the citation for 'Scotch Lass', officially Pigeon NPS 42 2 21610 revealed:

> In the course of her service which commenced at RAF Wick and continued in 1943 at RAF Felixstowe, and included 43 flights from small naval craft in the North Sea, she was dropped with an agent in Holland in September 1944 and although injured by hitting telegraph wires in semi-darkness when released in early dawn, successfully delivered her message and photo films on the same day.

'Scotch Lass' flew approximately 260 miles despite her injuries and was one of at least seven Scots pigeons that won the 'Animals' VC'.

Although radio navigation aids started to make their appearance, aircraft still lost their way. As the summer of 1944 turned to autumn, Flying Officer Peter Payne of 598 Squadron, recently formed in Scotland, cheerfully flying an Oxford from Orkney to Peterhead, found a Flying Fortress off his wingtip. The B-17 was looking for Northern Ireland, and as a courteous gesture, Peter showed him the way to Castletown before carrying on to Peterhead.

In the first days of September, as the first chill winds of autumn bit, the Moray Firth echoed to the growl of Merlin engines as the Lancasters of 9 and 617 Squadrons flew in to Lossiemouth. They were, they believed, the best in the business – and the big boys had a job to do. Sink the *Tirpitz*. Once and for all.

14

Peace and the Cold War

Tirpitz had never realised her potential. She had worried the Admiralty, though, ever, since her keel was laid down on Slipway 2 at the naval dockyard at Wilhelmshaven. Once Britain and Germany were at war, she was an ongoing target. Between 9 July 1940, when fourteen Hampdens set out from England to bomb her under construction, to the Halifax and Lancaster raids at the end of April 1942, there had been 25 attempts to put her out of action. Every one had failed.

In September 1943 the Royal Navy inflicted the first damage on the ship that Churchill called 'The Beast', anchored in Kåfjord in the far north of Norway. Two midget submarines slipped through the defences and exploded charges. The battleship's hull split and buckled, pipework broke and the force dislodged internal machinery, jammed the propeller shafts and even pushed two gun turrets out of position. The blows devastated radar and wireless equipment, the port rudder stuck, the ship's power systems broke down. A Scot from Carluke, Lieutenant Donald Cameron, commanded one of the successful submarines, X6, and he, along with the other skipper, Lieutenant Basil Charles 'Godfrey' Place, received the Victoria Cross.

While *Tirpitz* was under repair, fifteen Red Air Force bombers tried their luck without success on 10 February 1944. When the battleship had started her post-repair trials, the Fleet Air Arm chanced its arm. HMS *Furious* and HMS *Victorious*, supported by escort carriers, a couple of battleships and a drove of destroyers, set out from Scapa Flow on 30 March 1944 on Operation *Tungsten*.

On 3 April 1944, some 140 miles off the Norwegian coast, forty-three Barracuda dive-bombers from 827, 829, 830 and 831 Squadrons, escorted by eighty Hellcat, Wildcat, Seafire and Corsair fighters from 800, 801,

804, 880, 881, 882, 896, 898, 1834 and 1836 Squadrons attacked in the largest air strike ever mounted by the Fleet Air Arm. At 0416, the first Corsairs left *Victorious*. Eight minutes later, the Barracudas followed. *Furious* launched her Barracudas while the escort carriers despatched their fighters and by 0437, the first wave of raiders headed south-east towards the unsuspecting *Tirpitz*, anchored in Altenfjord.

By 0528, they had the target in sight, and light flak began as they closed to within three miles of the battleship. The Wildcats and Hellcats flew low, machine-gunning the decks, as the Barracudas peeled off in their bombing dives. In theory, the dive-bomber released no lower than 3,000 feet to be certain their bomb gouged through the ship's armoured decks but several pilots went lower to ensure they were bang on target. It took one minute to score six direct hits.

One hour later, at 0635, just as the luckless Germans had made some progress in clearing up, Hellcats and Wildcats appeared out of the morning sky to machine-gun the ship. A minute passed, Barracudas hurtled down and nine bombs smashed into *Tirpitz*. By 0758, all first wave aircraft had returned bar two Barracudas, shot down by the minimal anti-aircraft fire. The Luftwaffe never appeared. One Hellcat ditched on the journey home. Three Barracudas went down from the second attack. Amongst the nine dead crewmen was Sub Lieutenant Robert Norman Drennan of Aberdeen. His pilot, another Scot, Sub Lieutenant Thomas Charles Bell, came from Glasgow.

It took two minutes to undo the six months of repair work. The upper deck was a mass of twisted metal and splintered steel and the radar and wireless had suffered once again. The ship was flooded. In human terms, 122 men had died with 316 wounded, amongst them the captain, Kapitän Hans Meyer. The Fleet Air Arm originally planned to return the next day. Satisfied with the damage caused and concerned about aircrew fatigue, Vice Admiral Sir Henry Ruthven Moore headed back in triumph to Scotland.

By 22 June 1944 *Tirpitz* was ready to recommence trials. The Admiralty's Operation *Mascot* swung into operation on 17 July 1944. *Tirpitz* had become a tougher proposition, since an observation and fire control post now sat on top of a neighbouring mountain which meant attacking aircraft would face a wall of flak in addition to shells from the ship's formidable 38-centimetre guns.

The three carriers, HMS *Furious*, *Formidable* and *Indefatigable*, sent off 44 Barracudas, armed with 1,000-lb and 500-lb bombs, with an escort of 18 Corsairs, 18 Hellcats and 12 Fairey Fireflies. At 0204, the alarm klaxons wailed and the flak crews rushed into position. A smoke-screen, lit from the shore, drifted across the battleship and by 0215, *Tirpitz* was almost entirely obscured from the air. The first Barracuda started its attack at 0220. One minute later, a near miss shook the teeth of the flak gunners. After that, they relaxed as smoke hid *Tirpitz* from view. The Navy lost one Corsair and one Barracuda. The Fleet Air Arm attacked again on 22 August, 24 August and 29 August. Three attacks brought two hits that caused only superficial damage.

The Lancasters that crowded into Lossiemouth on 11 September did not stay. They departed the next day for Yagodnik, near Murmansk in northern Russia. On 15 September twenty-one Lancasters from 9 and 617 Squadrons scored two direct hits on the forecastle to put *Tirpitz* out of action once again. The engineers patched her battered bows and painfully, she moved to a fjord near Tromso. Crippled, and able only to make at best 10 knots, she was a long way from menacing Allied shipping. Ultra intercepts told Whitehall *Tirpitz* was out of the war for a long time to come.

At Tromso, *Tirpitz* was close enough for the RAF to reach her without a detour to Russia. On 29 October thirty-nine Lancasters, twenty from 9 Squadron and nineteen from 617 Squadron, flew from Kinloss, Mill-town and Lossiemouth. Fitted with uprated engines and extra fuel tanks, they managed one near miss from 13,000 feet. Cloud rolled in to obscure the ship while they were on the way. The near miss did more damage than the bomber crews realised. It distorted the port propeller shaft, as well as flooding the ship fore and aft. *Tirpitz* was trapped. She could no longer move under her own power, nor could she fight back. Downing Street and Whitehall were determined to utterly destroy the potent symbol of German power. To sink her would capsize German morale and lift Allied spirits.

On 12 November 32 Lancasters took off from Lossiemouth for Tromso Fjord on Operation *Catechism*, each aircraft carrying a 12,000-lb Tallboy bomb. They had crippled *Tirpitz* on 15 September and 29 October. The first aircraft became airborne at 0300 and the others followed, one by one, into the dark winter sky.

As the sun came up, it unveiled perfect flying weather. Snowy mountains etched themselves against a powder-blue sky that stretched into the distance. None of the Lancasters had a problem in finding their assembly point 15,000 feet above a frozen lake in Sweden. It was clear, calm and cloudless as the Lancasters headed for *Tirpitz*. On board, alarms sounded, the blue and yellow warning flag ran up the halyards to hang limply in the windless morning. The water around the ship was blue-tinted glass as the sound of Merlin engines drifted across the sky.

The approaching Lancasters caught their first sight of their quarry some thirty miles out. She looked like a model ship on a painted ocean, sitting naked and unprotected. No fighter swarms rose to meet the enemy. Bomb doors opened and one after another, thirty-two Tallboys plummeted towards the ship. One hit, then another – both on the port side, one close to the bridge, the other by the massive 'C' gun turret, 1,000 tons of steel. The first strike gave *Tirpitz* a 20-degree list to port while the second bomb pushed her further over. Near misses along her sides sent her some seventy degrees from true.

The handful of guns fired on until their crews could no longer keep their feet against the list. *Tirpitz* shuddered, and at 0950 the rumbling of the Merlin engines faded as the Lancasters headed for Scotland and the main magazine blew up. The explosion lifted 'C' Turret into the air to crash into the water 40 yards away. Slowly, reluctantly, *Tirpitz* rolled to her left, turning turtle. In her hull, nearly 1,000 gradually suffocated or drowned. A fortunate 87 crew members, trapped in the very bottom of the ship, were rescued by cutting holes in the ship's keel. The Beast was conquered.

On the first day of the new year, 1945, the son of a Perthshire ploughman won the sixth Victoria Cross awarded to a Scot for gallantry in the air during the Second World War. George Thompson, the son of James and Jessie, was born on 23 October 1920 at Trinity Gask. At the age of fifteen, he left school to start a four year apprenticeship in Kinross as a grocer. He obtained his certificate weeks after the war started, applying to join the Royal Air Force in the summer of 1940, along with many others. Like them, he was given deferred service. Like them, he joined the Local Defence Volunteers, since he wanted to obtain something with which to fight and receive realistic training.

A few months later, George Thompson volunteered once more. He went to aircrew selection in January 1941 but was not chosen and he enlisted instead as ground crew. A boyhood interest in wireless led to formal training and in February 1942, after a short spell at Coningsby in Lincolnshire, Thompson went to Iraq. Service in a hot and dusty land, in a base removed from the fighting line, did not appeal to George, so after eighteen months of a humdrum daily round, he applied again for flying duties. With a trade behind him, allied with the growing need by Bomber Command for wireless operators and gunners, Thompson was accepted for training. By August 1943 he was back in England, and by the end of April 1944 he had remustered to wireless operator/air gunner with sergeant's stripes on his arms.

He reported to 14 OTU at Market Harborough on 2 May 1944 for operational training and crewing up. George Thompson quickly received an invite to join a crew already half-formed. The 'beauty contest' started with the pilot who was then always the captain, irrespective of rank. Flying Officer Harry Denton, a New Zealand farmer, had already recruited a bomb aimer and a navigator. Denton completed the list with two air gunners from Wales.

They trained in Wellingtons and then in Stirlings where the final crew member, the flight engineer, joined them. On 29 September 1944, Flying Officer Harry Denton with an all NCO crew, Ron Goebel as bomb aimer, Ted Kneebone the navigator, flight engineer Wilf Hartshorn, the two Welsh gunners Haydn Price and Ernest Potts, and George Thompson, joined 9 Squadron at Bardney in Lincolnshire. They flew on operations three times during October. In November, the squadron did little operational flying and December saw only one trip for Harry Denton and his men. George Thompson 'put up his crown' on 30 November when Bardney's personnel occurrence reports promulgated his promotion to flight sergeant.

On 31 December 1944 as the Hogmanay celebrations wound up, ten Lancaster crews, amongst them Harry Denton's, found their evening disrupted. They were briefed for an attack at dawn the next day on the Dortmund-Ems canal. On the hard cold morning of 1 January 1945, bitter with frost, dark as the plague, the seven men clambered into Lancaster PD377. The engines wheezed into life, one after another: starboard inner, port inner, starboard outer, port outer. As each engine started, flame belched from its exhausts, scarring the darkness. At 0735, Harry Denton released the brakes and the Lancaster trundled carefully to the take-off point. At 0745, PD377 began her take-off run. With twelve 1,000-lb bombs on board and a full fuel load, the aircraft eased into the air only as the boundary hedge approached. At 500 feet, Harry Denton began to turn, only to see the next aircraft hurtle off the runway to explode in a cataclysm of flame. The third Lancaster also failed to get away, sliding across the grass at the side of the runway before slithering to a halt.

More than one hundred Lancasters joined up over northern France in a loose formation to cruise to the target. At 10,000 feet, visibility was good as the winter skies cleared. The attack was a daylight raid and the target was clear and bold in Goebel's bombsight. Denton made a text-book run, bomb doors open as Goebel guided him. One after another, the twelve bombs fell away. As the last one released, an 88-mm shell smacked into the aeroplane in front of the mid-upper turret while a second round demolished the nose. The bomb-aimer's Perspex vanished in a storm of splinters, the port inner engine caught fire and the pilot's canopy shattered. Denton blacked out fleetingly but he came to, punched the fire extinguisher button, put on full right rudder to counteract the Lancaster's sudden desire to turn to the left and fought off a stall. The slipstream roared in through the shattered Perspex, taking the navigator's charts with it as it rushed to the rear of the fuselage, where matters were even worse.

The fresh air fanned the fire that broke out immediately the mid-upper was hit. A six-foot-square hole in the floor marked where the shell came in. The flak gunners had severed the hydraulic lines, the aircraft intercom and the trim controls. Hydraulic fluid squirted into the blaze which roared more hungrily as it gobbled up the liquid. In the mid-upper turret, Ernie Potts sat engulfed by fire. Denton fought to keep control. Lancasters could absorb a great deal of punishment. Human strength was the weakness, but with Wilf Hartshorn standing by, Harry Denton imposed his will on the aeroplane. As a final fillip, Ron Goebel appeared, blackened by smoke, clutching what was once a parachute pack, looking dazed but uninjured.

Flame now licked at both gun turrets. Ernie Potts was unconscious, unable to help himself, and George Thompson – without gloves, for wireless operators do not operate keys and twist dials with thick-clad fingers – moved to help his mate. His first problem was the hole in the floor and so he edged past it, clinging to the side of the fuselage, and reached the gun turret, where Potts was on fire. Thompson pulled him clear, his own clothing smouldering as he put the unconscious gunner over his shoulder before he inched back, past the gaping hole, to the comparative safety of the forward fuselage. He then beat out the gunner's burning clothing.

In the rear gunner's berth, Haydn Price was trapped. When the intercom died and the flames began, he had to bale out. He rotated his turret, disconnected the leads to his electrically heated flying suit, took off his helmet, opened the turret doors behind him to fall out backwards to safety. Except fire roared in. Flames scorched off his hair and burned his ears and face. Price shut the doors, rotated his turret to its normal position and waited to die. His clothes were ablaze as flames, smoke and fumes pushed him towards oblivion. But he heard banging on the doors that dragged him back to consciousness – George Thompson had arrived.

Thompson had eased himself back past the gaping hole when he realised that Price was trapped. His own clothing was tattered rags, his trousers had burned away and blisters and blackened skin seared by fire ravaged his legs, hands and face. Thompson helped the burned rear gunner out of his turret, beat out the blazing clothing again with his bare hands, assisted Price along the fuselage, helped him past the hole where Germany still slid by beneath, to finally join Ernie Potts.

Burned, blistered, exhausted, Thompson had not finished and the ice-wind of the slipstream tore at his burns, creating an exquisite agony. Frostbite gnawed at his fingers, but despite this Flight Sergeant George Thompson forced his way up to the front cockpit to tell Denton that the two gunners lay injured, unable to bale out. The Scot was so badly battered that Denton did not recognise him.

The Lancaster reached the Rhine and German flak gunners sighted the cripple. More shells curved their way into the sky and the starboard inner engine coughed, then fell silent. With two engines only, the Lancaster, already losing height, had not long to last. Avoiding some high tension cables, Denton managed to put down the Lancaster in a field, where it smacked through a hedge. The fuselage broke in two but both parts stopped before they reached the next hedge. Forty minutes had passed since the flak shells had hit PD377 over the Dortmund-Ems Canal. Every member of the crew escaped from the aircraft. Ernie Potts died the next day and Haydn Price needed months of plastic surgery, but he made a full recovery. George Thompson began to mend and penicillin helped as he endured pain without complaint and stayed cheerful. Hopes were high until pneumonia struck. In his weakened state he had no chance and died on 23 January 1943. On 20 February 1945 the *London Gazette* announced the award of the Victoria Cross 'in recognition of most conspicuous bravery'. The citation concluded that Thompson's 'signal courage and self-sacrifice will ever be an inspiration to the Service'.

The winter months that led to 1945 had a harsh coldness that had not been felt for many years and temperatures fell to well below zero. With the creeping feeling that the European war was slowly moving towards its end, many of the training units let the weather have its way. At Banff, the Strike Wing continued to pound German shipping but they took losses for the enemy fought back with some stubbornness and no little skill. On 15 January 1945, on a day that became known as 'Black Monday', the Wing lost five Mosquitoes in a raid on Leirvik harbour. Flak and the 'butcher birds', snub-nosed Focke-Wulfs from Herla, showed the enemy remained defiant. The Mosquitoes destroyed their target, two merchant ships, but the losses worried 18 Group Headquarters.

On 9 February 1945, Dallachy's Beaufighters suffered their 'Black Friday' when nine of them, together with a single Mustang, failed to return from an operation in which thirty-one Beaufighters and twelve Mustangs took on a German destroyer with escorts. Six of the losses came from 404 Squadron alone.

Occasionally, pure chance brought success. On 21 April 1945 forty-two Mosquitoes, on their way home from an abortive mission, found an unsuspecting enemy. Cloud scowled at 600 feet, rain streamed across windshields and visibility was wretched. The astonished Mosquito crews glimpsed eighteen unwary aircraft on a reciprocal course. Junkers 88 and 188 torpedo-bombers, in line astern, neatly spaced in six Vics of three. The unfortunate Germans came from Kampfgeschwader 26. In the ensuing melee, the Junkers headed rapidly for cloud and safety, the Mosquitoes tripping over each other as they made for the enemy. Seven German aircraft went down. Twenty-eight men lost their lives.

The final shipping strike of the war came from the Banff Mosquitoes. On 4 May 1945 the war was all but over. Hitler was dead and Germany had nothing left. Everybody who could beg, steal or find a serviceable aircraft wanted to take part in the last sortie. Nearly fifty Mosquitoes flew out, escorted by eighteen Mustangs. Anything was grist to their mill and they sank three merchant ships in two separate attacks. Two Mustangs collided and their pilots died. Another was hit by flak although the pilot escaped. One Mosquito crash-landed in Sweden, the pilot killed.

The Banff Strike Wing had lost seventy-three aircraft in eight months. Number 603 (City of Edinburgh) Squadron came home from the war to Drem. On 11 May 1945 two Junkers Ju52 transport aircraft, painted in bright white, landed at the airfield. The Ju52, with its three engines, bombed Spanish towns for Franco in the Civil War, dropped German paratroopers over the Netherlands and Crete, flew in supplies to the Wehrmacht fighting to hold Stalingrad and had been the workhorse of the Luftwaffe. Like all long-serving aeroplanes, the Junkers had a nickname: 'Tante Ju, Auntie Ju. Always there, always dependable'. Now she carried high-ranking German officers to Scotland to sign the formal capitulation of all German forces in Nazi-occupied Norway. Scotland's war had ended.

The Royal Air Force had reached its manpower peak with 1,079,835 personnel, of whom 193,313 were aircrew. The indispensable ground crew covered every trade and skill imaginable from the determined gunners of the Royal Air Force Regiment to dedicated mechanics at wind-swept radar stations. The WAAF made up almost 10 per cent of the RAF strength, serving in eighty trades. Women were flight mechanics, fitters and electricians. They re-armed and refuelled aeroplanes, kept radar working and controlled aircraft from the ground. C. G. Grey would not have approved.

Scotland was far more than simply a stores depot, warehouse, arsenal and training area in the long years of conflict. She had been home to airfields from which men flew to seek out U-boats, to hunt down enemy convoys, to drop resistance fighters in a struggle against an implacable foe. The country, once again, had played its part.

Airfields and depots, as in 1919, closed and ninety-five airfields shrank to a couple of dozen. The Air Ministry dissolved squadrons without hesitation. Edinburgh's Own, 603 Squadron, disbanded on 15 August 1945, three months after the Glasgow squadron, 602, ceased operating, only to re-form the following year. The forty or more radar stations that looked out over the Atlantic on the west coast and the North Sea on the east coast began to close, one after the other. Depots and maintenance units shut, and by the end of the year, it seemed that all military flying in Scotland had disappeared. Kinloss remained and became a Coastal Command Station. Leuchars survived, going to Fighter Command. Lossiemouth became a Fleet Air Arm base as HMS *Fulmar*. On 10 May 1946 the Auxiliary Air Force re-formed. One of the first squadrons to start again was 603 Squadron at Turnhouse, and three months later, 602 Squadron began operating at Renfrew. After another three months, in November 1945, Aberdeen's 612 Squadron opened its doors. All three squadrons were day fighter units, equipped with Spitfires. In 1947 the Auxiliary Air Force received the honorific prefix 'Royal' in recognition of its gallant and devoted service throughout the Second World War.

All three services had a distinct desire to return to pre-1939 standards, since wartime had diluted morals and values. Social distinctions had blurred, especially amongst aircrew on multi-engined aircraft. As one writer on Service etiquette warned: 'During the last war inexperienced officers drank in public bars with the rank and file; this was an undesirable practice and had many unfortunate results. Let the men enjoy their liquor in their own company.'

In September 1947 John Wears, later a flight lieutenant, completed his recruit training at Innsworth. His first posting was to the other end of Britain, and when he went to 63 Maintenance Unit at Royal Air Force Montrose:

As was the custom in those days, new arrivals soon found themselves on guard duty. I was no exception. Three days later I was on guard on the south west of the airfield, on the pathway below the old 1914–18 hangars. My first duty was from 1800 to 2000, a lovely autumn evening, and no problems. My second duty was from midnight to 0200.

At about 0045 I saw a strange glow appear, moving along the front of the old hangars. As I watched, it turned left and started to come down the path towards me. At it came closer I could hear the sound of footsteps, and then I saw the figure of a man.

I shouted, 'Halt! Who goes there?'

No reply. Again I shouted, 'Halt! Who goes there?' No reply, so I cocked the rifle and shouted, 'Halt or I will fire!'

Back came the reply 'Orderly Officer'.

I told him to 'advance and be recognised', but there was something strange about him. As he came nearer to me I could see what appeared to be the two rings of a flight lieutenant. I then gave him a butt salute, slapping the rifle on the butt while in the slope arms position, which he returned as a normal salute. I then saw he was wearing a Sam Browne belt. Strange, I thought, but I had only been in the RAF a short time.

He then said to me, 'Have you seen the patrol?' Not an expression the air force used, but I presumed he meant the fire picket.

I said, 'Yes, sir.'

'Which way did they go?' he asked.

I turned and pointed in the direction they had gone and said, 'That way, sir.'

When I turned around there was no sign of him. I searched the surrounding area but there was no place for anyone to go.

The guard was changed at 0200 and I reported to the guard commander. I was asked if I had anything to report.

'Only the Orderly Officer,' I said.

'Who was that?' I was asked.

'I don't know. Some flight lieutenant.'

I was then told that the orderly officer that night was a warrant officer. I then heard a whisper from somewhere 'Flight Lieutenant Arthur!' but this meant nothing to me.

I didn't hear about Arthur and the ghost of Montrose until many years later in the Officers' Mess at Scampton. I was rather pleased I didn't know about it when I went on guard that night!

A talkative Desmond Arthur, or a kindred spirit, walked abroad once more.

Scottish Aviation Limited under the leadership of David McIntyre, the Everest flier, had survived the war in reasonably good shape. They had agreed licence deals with the Douglas Company and Consolidated Aircraft to convert the military versions of the faithful Dakota, the C-54 Skymaster and the B-24 Liberator bomber aircraft for civilian use. Scottish Aviation had spent much of the war overhauling Dakotas and Liberators. Conversion was a simple add-on process and in all, nearly 300 Douglas Aircraft received a Prestwick makeover.

The company turned its thoughts to designing and making its own aeroplanes. An Air Ministry Specification A4/45 for a light, high-wing three-passenger monoplane able to use makeshift landing grounds and absorb rough treatment attracted their attention. The prototype flew on 5 November 1947. Not overpowered, the aptly named Prestwick Pioneer won no military contract but a swift redesign, incorporating an engine of twice the power and an extra seat inside the cabin did win approval: the Pioneer II. A total of fifty-nine aircraft left the production line for military use.

The Pioneer, with its excellent short take-off and landing ability, did extremely valuable service in Malaya during the euphemistically described Emergency against Communist terrorists, since it could climb out steeply from short jungle airstrips surrounded by trees. The Pioneer went on to serve in Borneo and Aden with conspicuous success, and the last example retired from military service in 1969.

One thing stopped the post-1945 run-down from being a carbon copy of that following the First War. The world was an uncertain place. The swastika, kicked into the rubble of a defeated Germany, gave way to a new threat with a red star in its fur hat. The Cold War, with the occasional hot flush such as the Korean War, lasted until the fall of the Berlin Wall in 1989. Scotland, once again, found herself in the front line and National Service scooped up conscripts to keep numbers stable.

An early consequence of the stand-off between Russia and the Western Allies after the defeat of Nazi Germany came on 24 June 1948. The beaten nation was divided by the Soviet Union, France, the United States and the United Kingdom into four occupation zones. Berlin, buried deep within the Russian Sector, was similarly carved into quarters under a Four Power Allied Control Council. The Russians dearly wanted Berlin under their own full control and took every opportunity to harass the supply routes into the city. Road and rail transport from outside the Soviet Zone became subject to a barrage of regulations as did the authorised air corridors into the city.

Further disagreement on post-war development quickly surfaced. The Russians, with long, bitter memories of Prussian aggression, wanted an emasculated Germany; the other three Powers saw Germany, no matter what its faults, as an economically successful essential component of a post-war Europe. On 6 March 1948, the three Western Powers formally agreed, at the London Conference, to join their zones into a single federal republic, a resolution that included their areas of Berlin. This ran entirely against Russian desires and just two weeks after the declaration in London, on 20 March 1948, infuriated Russian representatives stormed out of a meeting of the Allied Control Authority. They followed this with a flat demand for the immediate removal of British, American, and French troops from Berlin. When no withdrawal resulted, a terse announcement stated that 'the Soviet administration is compelled to halt all passenger and freight traffic to and from Berlin tomorrow at 0600 because of technical difficulties'.

In the euphoria of the 1945 victory, guaranteed access by road and rail routes into Berlin had been ignored, and the Soviet authorities now made it crystal clear that occupation rights in Berlin and the previous use of the routes did not allow unfettered access through the Soviet Zone of Occupation. That left only one choice. At the end of the war, the Four Powers had agreed to create six air corridors into Berlin. Three went westward, deep into Iron Curtain country, while the remaining three connected Berlin with Hamburg and Hanover in the British Zone and with Frankfurt in the American Zone. The Americans decided they would supply Berlin by air. On 28 June 1948, a gaggle of hastily gathered Douglas C-47 aircraft left Wiesbaden, close to Frankfurt, with 80 tons of medicine, flour, and milk for Tempelhof Airport in Berlin. The Berlin Airlift had begun.

The Royal Air Force was quickly involved. By the middle of June, American aircraft were flying a daily total of 1,500 tons into Berlin while the British effort, with a much smaller transport element of Avro Yorks, a derivative of the Lancaster, and Dakota C-47 aircraft flew in 500 tons every day. The Americans named their effort 'Operation Vittles'. The British, equally realistic, called it 'Operation Plainfare'. The Berliners, with a certain humour, nicknamed the American, British and French aircraft that roared over the city in a seemingly unending stream, 'Rosinenbomber', the 'Raisin bombers'.

Scots who had flown operations over the Third Reich repeated the trip to bring food to a desperate city. The Soviet authorities, incensed at the Western response, put fighter aircraft into and across the corridors. Barrage balloons appeared. Target towing aircraft flew in front of incoming transports and near misses became the order of the day.

By August, every flight into Berlin, in good weather or bad, by day or by night, was made under instrument flight rules. A pilot who missed his approach did not go round to try again: he took his cargo back to base. Take-off times were assigned precisely. At Tempelhof, an aircraft took off or departed every ninety seconds. British pilots concentrated initially on Gatow, the airfield in the British Zone. In the middle of July, Berliners who gazed skyward rubbed their eyes in wonder. A Short Sunderland flying boat swept majestically across the countryside to touch down on the Havel river. A fleet of ten boats joined the operation to fly in that essential commodity, salt. One Scottish pilot, who had received a Distinguished Flying Cross for his efforts to destroy Berlin a mere four years earlier, was bemused to see the leader of a gang of

German workers thoughtfully pat the side of the aircraft they were unloading.

'Different times, Tommy,' he said cheerfully. 'Not so long ago, I flew night fighters to shoot you out of the sky.'

On Easter Sunday, 16 April 1949, the Western Powers decided on an all-out effort. Careful planning to ensure as many crews and aircraft, including civilians, were on hand resulted in 1,398 flights taking in 12,941 tons of supplies. One aircraft touched down somewhere in Berlin every minute, and it was probably this effort that persuaded the Russians that the game was up. They lifted their blockade on 11 May 1949. The Americans, British, and French flew on to build up a reserve stock of 300,000 tons by 30 September 1949. Berlin would not suffer again.

On 4 April 1949, the Western Powers signed into being the North Atlantic Treaty Organisation, its members agreeing that 'an armed attack against one or more of them in Europe or North America shall be considered an attack against them all and consequently they agree that, if such an armed attack occurs, each of them . . . will assist the Party or Parties so attacked by taking forthwith, individually and in concert with the other Parties, such action as it deems necessary, including the use of armed force, to restore and maintain the security of the North Atlantic area'.

Scotland was thrust into line, if not as an immediate major player, as the country that held the coat of Norway on the northern flank of the Alliance. The RAF Maritime Headquarters at Pitreavie Castle took on new responsibilities and became the Headquarters of the North Atlantic Area, or HQNORLANT in NATO-speak with its air marshal taking on the role of COMAIRNORLANT while the admiral rejoiced in the acronym of COMNAVNORLANT.

The Royal Air Force found themselves key defenders against Soviet air attack from northern Russia. This task was important only if an old-fashioned conventional war was on the cards but a missile-generated nuclear conflict was a very different matter. For NATO itself, the northern flank was merely one area where aggression lurked. Planners viewed the long border of what had become the German Democratic Republic with concern as they did the eastern flank and the Greek–Turkish hinge.

Even so, the men and women who served the Royal Air Force and Fleet Air Arm in Scotland could console themselves they were part of NATO's defensive shield, democracy's guardian, as they shivered in the biting winds of winter that howled across desolate airfields while luckier ones faced down the same enemy in the warmer climes of the Mediterranean.

The jet age arrived in force. The Spitfire gave way to the Meteor 4 and the Vampire, supplanted in their turn by the Meteor 8 and the Venom. The passing years saw continual development with faster aircraft, guided missiles, electronics and computers. Radar and other tools of the trade improved. The Royal Air Force and the Royal Navy changed to meet the new requirements.

Scottish Aviation, buoyed up by the success of the Pioneer, produced a two-engined design named the Twin Pioneer. Despite its name, it was a totally new concept. The prototype flew on 25 July 1955. The RAF ordered thirty-nine, the first of which arrived in the late summer of 1957. Immediately dubbed the 'Twin Pin', the aeroplane had the same outstanding short field ability. Like its predecessor, it served with distinction in tropical conditions in Borneo, Aden, Bahrein and Kenya as well as in the United Kingdom.

A savage blow struck Scottish Aviation Limited on 7 December 1957. David McIntyre, along with the crew, died when the Twin Pioneer he was demonstrating crashed in North Africa and nobody survived.

By 1954, the total of radar units in Scotland had dropped to eleven, and four years later fell to six. More powerful, better designed radars, the first stumbling computers and improved electronics meant fewer stations. At airfields, technology also improved. The primitive homing procedure where a pilot asked for a course to steer, then made a long transmission – Mary continually had lambs on the frequency – gave ground control the bearing of the incoming aircraft. This, ideally, was then converted into the heading that the aircraft should steer – an aircraft due south or 180 degrees from home needed to be told to steer due north or 360 degrees. Inexperienced or overworked operators sometimes passed the original bearing, not the reciprocal, a mistake that could prove fatal. In the early 1950s, this manual system gave way to a cathode ray tube display that gave faster and more accurate control. Subsequent years saw still more improvements.

The Royal Air Force signals system was a vast enterprise under the control of 90 Group. Independent of the main RAF Commands, the Group had the simple task of controlling the design, manufacture, installation, operation and maintenance of the RAF signals system. Various mysterious stations came under their control as did the private telephone network that linked together every station and unit in the Service. Travelling supervisors roamed the country to inspect operations and administrative efficiency at regular intervals. Amongst them was Flight Sergeant Harold Watling, based at Haydock in Lancashire, close to Liverpool, whose beat covered all of Scotland and the Isles, Northern Ireland and the Isle of Man, a total of 72 stations to visit regularly:

> I was paying a visit to RAF Edzell, in Angus, a small flying station, which rarely had any flying activity. It was not all that far from Aberdeen and the Balmoral area. The signals section was under the charge of a warrant officer, a friendly chap who told me that rarely was there anything to do on the station.
>
> He and I were going through the Form 2107, Schedule of Tie Lines and Private Wires. Most were straightforward Air Traffic Control Circuits to the airfield and to Leuchars. One circuit, though, had apparently no termination shown against it and was never used. At least, no calls had appeared on the board. Neither was it labelled on the gate panel. The GPO at Aberdeen had suggested ceasing it. The warrant officer asked my opinion. 'I should cease it,' I replied, 'why pay rental for something never used?'
>
> Some time later, all hell broke loose. Prince Philip tried to access the line from Balmoral to use the airfield for a Royal Flight.
>
> The circuit was speedily restored.

In 1955, the Royal Auxiliary Air Force squadrons fell out of favour. All three Scottish Squadrons 602, 603 and 612 flew the de Havilland Vampire and they went because, some argued, the growing complexity of military aircraft and the increase in airline traffic caused difficulties in operation. This weasel-worded approach blithely ignored the example of the part-time Swiss air guard who flew jet fighters in the most crowded skies in Europe and that of the USA amongst others. It did, apparently, save money but the reasons were political not military.

The arrival of the ballistic missile persuaded some that the manned fighter had come to the end of its useful role. The 1957 White Paper, presented by Duncan Sandys, hatchet man to the Prime Minister Harold Macmillan, proposed wholesale reductions in all three services. The Government scrapped a series of military development projects. Sandys also wanted to dump all manned fighters for missiles and furious opposition saved only half the existing fighter squadrons. The Sandys doctrine of an all-missile defence made no allowance for intruders who merely intended to cock a snook or were simply lost. Taking out a civilian airliner with a guided missile is not a sensible option, even in modern turbulent times, since mistakes cannot be rectified.

The missile mania that gripped the Government, with its corollary of all-out nuclear war, led to an interesting schizophrenic phase in defence policy. On one hand, vast sums of money provided underground bunkers to preserve a chosen elect from slaughter should the worst befall. The facilities included functioning operations rooms for the Royal Air Force although how many men and machines would be able to fight on after a first atomic strike by the massed missile divisions of the Red Air Force was never apparently analysed in depth.

In 1958, the RAF had 269,200 uniformed personnel spread amongst 185 squadrons who operated 2,000 first-line aircraft. More change was on the way. The Government decided to end National Service. The 'call-up' finally ended on 31 December 1960 and men born in 1941 or later escaped the obligation entirely. In real terms, the Services shrank to about half of their 1958 size within a decade.

The Soviet Air Force developed the jolly habit of flying legally in international air space before diverting gently towards more strategic areas. A favourite ploy was to fly down the North Sea route, edging ever closer to the United Kingdom. NATO responded by demonstrating the ability both to intercept and destroy any intruder. As far as the RAF was concerned, this meant a 24-hour, 365-day Quick Reaction Alert with aircraft and crew continuously at readiness. The incursions were not occasional affairs and they happened several times a day as the 'potential enemy' probed for weaknesses.

Sergeant Roy Evans was a Javelin navigator with 25 Squadron, the first formed in Scotland, at Leuchars in 1960. His pilot was Flight Sergeant Bob Kelly, an elite 'Driver Airframe', later promoted to Master Pilot, and they formed one of the few non-officer fighter combinations in the RAF:

We are in our Gloster Javelin Mark 9 N/AW fighter, watching as the rain lashes down in a typical late-summer edition of the weather at Leuchars, Fife. We have sat here for an hour now. Only another 30 minutes until we are relieved. We are on two minutes readiness on the Operational Readiness Platform, the ORP.

The thought of that next mug of coffee gets more attractive the longer we sit. Suddenly, over the Telescramble line, we hear 'Mission 301. Scramble! Scramble!' My pilot, Bob, immediately hits the two starter buttons for the Armstrong Siddeley 'Sapphire' engines. They wind up as the controller gives me the course to steer, or vector, for our climb-out, confirms the radio control channel, and tells us that we have a 'Hostile target x 1'.

As we lurch forward off the brakes, the scramble-line connection automatically breaks and we are on the tower frequency. I check in. Confirmed clear for take off.

Bob swings onto the glistening runway. We accelerate towards the gloomy hills and murky cloud of a dismal afternoon. The speed increases. In the cockpit we hardly hear the Sapphires as they hurl us along the runway. At thirty seconds, Bob rotates the aeroplane. We lift off, clean up the undercarriage gear and flaps, and immediately enter cloud. My Airborne Interception (AI) radar is warming up, the Navigation box glows comfortingly. Everything in order.

We pull through 3,000 feet, then turn right in a tight turn onto our climb vector of 050°. We are steady on that when Ground Control Interception (GCI) confirm we have one target, 130 nautical miles ahead of us, on a southwest heading at about 30,000 feet. We both check fuel, instruments and oxygen. All normal, no problems. I concentrate on my AI set, generally called the 'weapon', listen to the stream of information from the GCI controller. When passing 15,000 feet, I am aware that peripheral light has increased. Bob confirms we are in '8/8 Blue', brilliant sunshine, with no cloud above.

After 4 minutes we level off at 40,000 feet. The target is now about 50 nautical miles distant so we arm the outboard pair of the four Firestreak missiles on our underwing pylons. At 30 miles range, I see a faint blip on my AI, painting at 10° port. It fades momentarily, then comes in strongly at 28 miles. It must be big, I think, and transmit 'contact' on the radio. At 20 miles range, with the target at 15° port, I assess the interception as a 'Head-on', so that we approach at 180° with a five mile displacement. Displacement is the difference in position. With no displacement, and no separation which is the height difference, we would meet nose to nose if neither of us changed course. We also have a few thousand feet in hand as we are higher than him.

I call 'Judy' to tell the ground controller that I am happy and need no further (distracting) information from GCI. I tell Bob that we will throw a Rate One turn to port at 12 miles. Rate One means 30 degrees of bank. This will give us a rollout range of 1.5–2.0 nautical miles, ideal for a missile attack. At 12 miles, with the target now 25° off, we turn, descending slowly to maintain our attack speed of Mach 0.93. I notice that the range closes faster than expected so I tell Bob to 'Speed back', for a 20 knot reduction. He acknowledges then tells me we have caught a *Bear*, the NATO codename for a huge Soviet bomber, with multi jets and turbo-props. It also has lots of defensive armament! We roll out with the *Bear* 1.6 miles ahead. We close in. Bob confirms the missiles are locked-on – 'acquired' in the jargon – so we radio 'Splash', to tell GCI that interception is completed and we are ready to open fire.

Control replies. 'Do not fire! Do not fire!' He stresses 'not'.

We adjust speed to come alongside on the port side of the *Bear* where we can see the Soviet gunners in the dorsal, ventral, lateral and tail turrets. As we converge, some of the gunners wave, which I acknowledge. As we pull slowly ahead, we waggle our wings and gently turn to starboard.

The Russki commander, or most probably the on-board Commissar (political man), decides that it's game over. The giant *Bear* slowly turns onto a north-east heading back home. We stay on the west side to escort him out.

We again check fuel, systems and oxygen and follow the bomber for around another 50 miles until GCI advise 'RTB' – return to base. They confirm our Pigeons, or homeward course and distance to be 230°/150 miles.

Twenty minutes later, we land with a 'DCO' – detail carried out to our credit. After a debriefing by the CO, the flight commander and the operations officer, we return to the crew room to the inquisitive questions from our fellow aircrew. At least they have the coffee waiting.

Not your conventional day at the office maybe, but that is what we continually trained for!

The stand-off between the NATO Powers and the Warsaw Pact kept several Scottish airfields alive. Britain's strategic bomber V-force – the Valiant, the Victor and the Vulcan – needed dispersal airfields. Soviet missiles could reach Britain in minutes and so it made sense, if danger threatened, to send bombers to distant bases. Kinloss, Lossiemouth, Prestwick, Macrahanish and Leuchars were earmarked as diversion airfields but even then, a paper calculated that 150 missiles would completely eliminate the bomber force.

On 23 January 1963 the last National Serviceman in the Royal Air Force took his discharge. Senior Aircraftman John Wallace from Glasgow, an instrument mechanic, completed his service at Kinloss. The station did him proud. On his last weekend in the RAF, a Shackleton flew him to Gibraltar and back. The Air Officer Commanding 18 Group presented him with a commemorative scroll and the station commander gave him a plaque of the station badge.

He, and eleven of his friends, received a special lunch in the Airmen's Mess, served by waiters from the Officers' Mess. He collected a large iced cake with an inscription to take home. A group of airwomen chaired him to a waiting Shackleton from 120 Squadron as the Station Pipe Band piped him aboard. The Shackleton, with the Air Officer Commanding as co-pilot, then flew him to Renfrew where an RAF staff car waited to take him home to Glasgow. With his departure, the Royal Air Force became an all-regular service for the first time since 1939.

In 1968, Fighter Command joined Bomber Command in something of a forced marriage to form Strike Command. Like a python, the new command soon swallowed lesser creatures and seven months after its formation, Strike Command gobbled up Coastal Command on 28 November which took the name of 18 (Maritime) Group. The former 18 Group at Pitreavie Castle transformed itself into the Northern Maritime Region. For practical purposes, at squadron level, nothing much changed, and reconnaissance aircraft continued to fly long sorties to deter ambitious Soviet submarines or to cause panic in the stomachs of Iron Curtain spy-ships, masquerading as fishing trawlers. These found it essential to anchor two yards outside the three-mile limit in visual and listening range of military installations.

Strike Command swallowed more. The Signals organisation, the slightly secretive 90 Group, became a Command in its own right on 3 November 1958. Signals Command was to be a tasty snack shortly after its tenth birthday, on 1 January 1969. Transport Command, which had changed its name to Air Support Command, entered the fold on 1 September 1972 and that became two Groups, 38 (Tactical Support) and 46 (Strategic Support).

Flying Training Command and Technical Training Command, divorced in 1940 when they were both large and unwieldy, remarried on 1 June 1968. Flying Training Command had already swallowed up Home Command, responsible for air cadets, reserves and miscellaneous matters, in 1959. They failed to see that Maintenance Command, which had renamed itself Support Command, was also a predator. On 1 June 1977 the Training Commands fell prey, and with a slight change of name to RAF Support Command, the new tiger controlled two organisations. To confuse the onlooker, one was named Personnel and Training Command, the other Logistics Command.

More changes would follow.

15

A Changing Age

In 1946, the Air Ministry needed a new long-range maritime patrol aircraft. U-boats had come close to victory in two wars and a future enemy would undoubtedly use similar tactics. Roy Chadwick, the outstandingly talented designer at Avro, had produced an improved Lancaster design that became the Lincoln. The blueprints evolved into a land-based maritime aircraft that flew in Scottish skies for four decades: the Shackleton.

The four Merlin engines of the Second World War bomber gave way to Rolls-Royce Griffons, each of which drove a pair of contra-rotating propellers. With memories of fighting U-boats on the surface, the Shackleton had two 20-mm cannon in front, one each side of the nose, two more cannon in a dorsal turret and two machine-guns in the tail. Depth charges and bombs to suit filled up an extensive bomb bay while a crew of ten operated the aeroplane. The first ones entered service with 120 Squadron and 236 Operational Conversion Unit at Kinloss in February 1951.

Tweaking of the design followed over subsequent years, and by the middle of the sixties, the Shackleton had gained a clear-view canopy and a sound-proofed wardroom for a relief crew when the aircraft went on extended patrols. The aircraft had grown heavier so a tricycle under-carriage came into use. The mid-upper turret vanished. A nacelle sprouted on each outer wing, each containing a Viper jet engine that delivered 2,500 lb of thrust, an extremely useful accessory to assist the take-off and climb with a heavy load or in high temperatures.

Bernie Donders, then a flight lieutenant and later a squadron leader, found that the new nose-wheel undercarriage did not always behave according to plan. He received a complimentary green endorsement in his flying logbook, signed by the station commander on 5 January 1960:

In accordance with the instructions of the Air Officer Commanding 18 Group Coastal Command, the following endorsement is made in respect of Flt Lt B Donders.

On the 16th October, 1959, Flight Lieutenant B Donders was the captain of Shackleton MR Mk 3 WR988 airborne from Kinloss on a training detail. During the flight the nosewheel failed to lock down despite the use of the emergency system. For three hours Flt Lt Donders calmly and efficiently attempted to lock the nosewheel down by rocking and stalling the aircraft and by following technical instructions from the ground. The nosewheel could not be locked down and as the light was fading Flt Lt Donders was instructed to carry out an emergency landing on a foam path. A most skilful landing was made resulting in the minimum possible damage to the aircraft. No injuries were sustained by the crew.

As Bernie carefully explains, the endorsement did not quite tell the complete story:

The reason for the failure was a broken hydraulic jack that was used by both the main and emergency systems in those days.

A couple of days after the event, my crew and I were having a drink together when the flight engineer said that he had since been studying his crash landing drills very carefully and they stated clearly that when the aircraft came to rest, the captain would order 'Out! Out!' and not 'For ****'s sake, get out quick!'

By the late 1960s, it was apparent a pressing need existed to detect low-level attackers approaching Britain, since conventional radar heads had difficulty in picking out aeroplanes from ground clutter. Even without that complication, the maximum detection range was only about twenty-five miles and incoming raiders comfortably covered that distance in three minutes. An airborne system could look much further afield.

The Maritime Reconnaissance Mark 2 version of the Shackleton, which had a tailwheel rather than the tricycle undercarriage, was chosen for the job. Its MR role had gone to the Nimrod but two other reasons won the day. The tailwheel gave nose clearance for the vital radar fit. On top of that, the Mark 3 Shackleton was, in a technical phrase, clapped out, since its heavier weight plus extra stresses caused by its Vipers, considerably aged the airframe. Shackletons had come in only one colour, a pure sparkling white, until that date. The new role demanded a new paint job. The MR2 appeared in a tasteful shade of grey.

In 1972 Lossiemouth came back to the Royal Air Force with the demise of the old fixed-wing conventional Fleet Air Arm. It soon became the new home of the Shackleton AEW and 8 Squadron. Lossiemouth's naval terminology and habits lived on as Geoff Cooper discovered:

At the beginning of September 1974 I was posted up to RAF Lossiemouth to fly the Shackleton, the Old Grey Lady as she became known later on.

After a long long drive up the old A9 on a Sunday night, I finally reached Lossiemouth at 1am and stumbled into the Officers' Mess where I woke up the hall porter. He assigned me a 'cabin' and I lurched off to get some sleep before the start of my Shack conversion course in about 7hrs time.

The following morning passed by in a haze and lunchtime couldn't come soon enough. I drove over to the mess and went into the bar for a coke and a bar snack. They operated a 'chit' system whereby no money changed hands. The chap in front of me at the bar was writing out a chit and I couldn't help noticing that he'd written '1 Grouse'.

I remember thinking to myself – now that's a pretty up-market bar snack . . . the glorious twelfth, Scottish grouse moors, yep, makes sense – I'll try one of those and so instead of ordering a ham and cheese toastie, I too ordered '1 Grouse'.

Sam, our dour old Scottish barman, put a glass in front of me containing a generous measure of something that looked and smelt like whisky.

I said, 'Sam, I ordered a Grouse . . .'

'Aye,' he said, 'and that's what I've given ye,' pointing to the bottle.

In my defence, I have to say that in 1974, The Famous Grouse was virtually unknown south of the border.

I must be honest, it was the start of a beautiful friendship with both Sam and the Famous Grouse.

Scottish Aviation Limited continued to prosper, with a series of maintenance contracts for Royal Canadian Air Force jet fighters, trainers and transports. In 1966, they had the job of making centre panel sections for the Lockheed Hercules military transport, known as 'Fat Albert' to its crews.

Their success attracted a take-over. The ship-building firm of Cammell-Laird needed to diversify from a declining industry and saw aeroplanes as just the thing. In April 1966 they acquired Scottish Aviation. With more industrial muscle and money behind them, Scottish Aviation successfully tendered for the job of making wings for the Handley Page Jetstream. Unfortunately, Handley Page themselves were not in the best of shape and the company collapsed, first into receivership in 1969 and then into liquidation in 1970. In addition, Rolls-Royce collapsed, an event that hardly helped Scottish Aviation's engine overhaul business. An unlikely saviour of the company came along in the form of another failed business when Beagle Aircraft, having taken over the production of Auster aircraft in 1962, tried to break the growing dominance of American light aircraft in private flying. It was a brave attempt. They created a basic trainer named the Pup that developed into a military basic trainer, the Bulldog. Despite winning an order for fifty-eight aircraft for the Royal Swedish Air Force, Beagle succumbed before the Bulldog completed its flight tests. Scottish Aviation received a British Government contract to build the aeroplanes. Good relations with Sweden were important. Scottish Aviation took over support for all Beagle's original designs and eventually completed 324 Bulldogs, including 132 for the Royal Air Force.

The Jetstream returned in 1970. Scottish Aviation tendered to supply the RAF with twenty-six navigation trainers on the understanding they acquired the necessary rights if they won the contract. They did, and on 26 June 1973 the first Jetstream from Scottish Aviation joined the RAF.

In 1974, politics intervened and with the Labour General Election victory that year, most of the separate parts of the British aircraft industry were forcibly amalgamated and nationalised. Scottish Aviation escaped on the technicality of low turnover – for four years only. On 1 January 1978 Scottish Aviation Limited became one more division of British Aerospace.

The AEW Shackletons of 8 Squadron formed part of 11 Group, the fighter arm of Strike Command. Before converting to the Old Grey Lady, 8 Squadron flew Hunters in Aden, Bahrein and Sharjah, so the

Shackleton quickly acquired fighter-style markings each side of the fuselage roundels.

When things go wrong in fast-jets, they do so with fierce rapidity. Steve Collier, who left the Royal Navy as a lieutenant commander, describes what happened on a perfect day for flying in 1984:

The canopy explodes, projecting glass and lead everywhere; a sudden blast of air in the cockpit, a massive increase in the noise and the aircraft falls away towards the ground. Tumbling, tumbling or was I? Difficult to say really as I was being buffeted around by a 250-knot slipstream having just ejected from a Royal Navy Sea Harrier. I am aware of pain in my face and my right knee. Moments later, a huge fireball erupts. A hemisphere of debris rains down on the Scottish countryside. A sequence of audible mechanical activity from the ejection seat separates me from the seat harness. I feel a jolt on the shoulders as the parachute canopy inflates. Eight seconds later the sheep scatter as I hit the ground wondering what had led up to all this.

HMS *Illustrious* (known to her inhabitants as Lusty), had been steaming off the northwest coast of Scotland for some time. We had been conducting training exercises for a while. Coming up was a joint exercise with some Dutch Marines who were hoping to benefit from training in terrain very different from that in their own native land!

We had disembarked our regular anti-submarine helicopter squadron to make room for a Commando Sea King helicopter force from RNAS Yeovilton in Somerset. 800 Naval Air Squadron was the embarked Sea Harrier squadron, which I had joined while the Ship was in Rosyth about two weeks earlier. Apart from the lengthy training, I did not have a major amount of experience in the Sea Harrier but I was a reasonably experienced aviator generally. We were to support the Marines by attacking bridges and photo recce of some other targets, just ahead of the main assault.

I spent most of the previous day planning the sortie and liaised with our only Army Officer on board to identify the targets and routes we would fly. Making an attack on a target ashore, *on time* is a little more difficult if you take-off from an aircraft carrier at sea. Planning a 'compression spring' to expand or contract your time scale makes life a lot easier. I had used the Caledonian Canal for this technique and was planning to 'turnabout' at the appropriate time. That night, we were in the Wardroom celebrating one of the Squadron pilot's birthday with a little champagne.

The next day was 1 December 1984; a Saturday. As Squadron Duty Officer I was up and about early. Good breakfast. Always had breakfast; well nearly always. Briefing details up, weather reports in, aircraft allocated and plenty of time for me to run through my sortie details. I was to lead a pair of Sea Harriers on this mission with the Senior Pilot as my wingman. We briefed as we normally did, with, in this case, a particular emphasis on bird hazards, as we were flying at low level in the Scottish Hills.

Lots of activity on deck now. We are not the only ones flying. Lots of Marines about too. Deck space limited and busy. 'Aircrew, man the Sea Harriers' booms out over the Flight Deck from 'Flyco' up above. He sits in the bit that sticks out from the Island and has a clear view of the flight deck activity. 'Stand Clear of Jet Pipes and Exhausts. Start Up.' It's past 0900 and we're just waiting for the ship's revised position to come out on a chalkboard so we can update the navigation equipment. It is a more modern process these days.

We are in Loch Linnhe, the seaward loch at the southwestern end of the Caledonian Canal. Soon the ship is manoeuvring into position to establish the Designated Flying Course. We move out onto the centre-line, my wingman ahead of me. Signals from the Flight Deck Officer and 'Flyco' and we're set to go. Power checks and off goes the wingman. Next up is me and we're away. Gear up, nozzles aft and I'm catching up fast. It's 0930. A quick jink manoeuvre and we're in Defensive Battle formation, that's line abreast about a mile apart. This way we can easily see behind each other to warn of approaching enemy aircraft.

We fly at 420 knots at 250 feet above ground level. It's a clear day, the sun still low and behind us as we head up Loch Lochy. I'm enjoying the magnificent view of the surrounding countryside. It's not often we get to fly low level in such spectacular scenery. Must keep one eye on the time and keep the lookout going for other aircraft and birds. A glance at the map and watch tell me it's almost time to turn to make our on target time.

'Turnabout. Go!' We turn towards each other and make our 180 degree turn to go back south east, looking for the next turning point. We roll out. I'm on the left now.

BANG! I must have hit something, I thought. I didn't see any birds. It was either that or the engine had failed. The instruments show a big problem. The engine is losing thrust very quickly. I'm slowing down very quickly too. A big drawback of the Sea Harrier was the size of the air intakes for the engine. Desperately necessary when you are in the hover in order to get lots of air in, but when you've lost the engine they act like air brakes the size of elephant ears. Now the Central Warning Panel is illuminating. Amber captions. Now red captions. OIL PRESSURE LOW! The JPT, the jet pipe temperature, is rising rapidly. The audio warning is shrieking too. As if anyone could miss the warning light show in front of my eyes! This is not good. I call over the radio to my wingman 'Tartan Leader has a bird strike. Standby'

'Where did it hit?' he asks.

'In the engine. I'm trying a relight'

At this point, my only option is to shut the engine down and try and restart it. I close the fuel cock. The engine runs right down and so does the JPT. Let's hope it works out. Emergency drills rattle through the brain. Select 'Manual Fuel On. Open the Fuel Cock.' Must maintain 250 knots to have any chance of a relight. The ground is getting much closer and quickly! I can hear my wingman reminding me 'Don't leave it too late!' It's not looking good. The engine will not relight. No time left to try again.

I hear another call on the radio. 'Director, Tartans are returning. Leader has a bird strike'. The Ship's Director, or Air Traffic Controller, responds. ' Roger, are you declaring an emergency?'

At this point I have no alternative. I make my last transmission. 'Yes, make it a Mayday. Tartan Leader is ejecting!'

I grab the ejection seat handle between my legs and give it a sharp upward tug. A period of time passed which felt like a lifetime but must have been about one second. The Miniature Detonation Cord, or MDC, the grey zigzags in the top of the canopy, explodes firing glass and bits of lead everywhere. It's very windy now. The ejection gun fires and the seat, with me in it, moves up the rail. I can feel the leg restraint lines drawing my legs in tight to the seat and the rocket pack on the bottom of the seat firing to throw me clear of the aircraft. A very short time later and the seat handle is ripped from my hands as the seat separates from the parachute and falls away to the ground.

The parachute opens. I have a quick glance around. I can't see much as my eyes are full of MDC and glass but I couldn't miss the huge fireball as the aircraft ploughed into a barn and caught fire.

I landed amongst scattering sheep a few moments later and could hear the roar of my wingman flying by. I waved to indicate I was OK, well nearly OK. In the descent I hadn't had time to drop my mask and seat survival pack, so I did so now. As I looked down I could see blood covering the stole of my lifejacket and my gloves. I could feel it running down the side of my face. Barely minutes later, I heard the rotor noise of a Sea King helicopter from the ship. I could see them heading for me and it landed about 100 metres away. The aircrewman helped me in to the back. I could see from the way he was looking at me that I must have had some fairly severe facial injuries. The pilot was a Scotsman and was aware that Raigmore Hospital in Inverness had a specialist eye unit and flew me straight there.

Up until that point, I hadn't considered that there was a possibility that I might lose my sight. As the tests progressed, I became more concerned. Fortunately, though, with some professional and skilful attention from the medical staff I was to retain my sight. I had to have a number of operations on my eyes, including an intra-ocular lens implant in my left eye. Some months later I was assigned as an instructor in the Sea Harrier simulator at Yeovilton in Somerset. I did eventually return to flying duties some years afterward but not, unfortunately, to the Sea Harrier. The powers that be considered that it was too risky to let me fly ejection seats again in case I had to repeat the escape and, potentially, lose the sight in my left eye. I continued with my military flying for many years afterwards until I retired from the Royal Navy in 1999.

I believe the name of the farm where the aircraft crashed was Kilmonivaig Farm, although I am not 100% sure of that. I have not been back to the crash site in the 22 years that have passed, but will one day.

Steve continued to fly when he left the Navy. He now pilots corporate jets all over the world.

Ejection is always risky, since sometimes technicalities confuse. One civilian 'MOD spokesman', possibly wearing white gloves and a wonky wristwatch, elicited groans and laughter in equal amounts from fastjet crews when he assured the media that 'once you eject, your parachute opens and you land in the sea still in your seat, which becomes your dinghy, and has a distress beacon attached'.

The most charitable explanation was that the word 'cushion' after 'seat' became lost in the excitement. A solid ejection seat, as one pilot commented, that changes into a dinghy on hitting water presumably turns into a mountain bike with 27 gears on striking solid earth. The Personal Survival Pack, or PSP, a bright yellow cushion sits inside the seat pan. Strapping in fastens the user to the PSP and after ejection, a drogue parachute stabilises the seat. Below 10,000 feet, and within 'g' limits, the harness releases from the seat. The drogue parachute drifts away and the seat falls clear. The parachute opens and the PSP remains firmly attached to the backside until the Automatic Deployment Unit kicks in. The PSP falls away to hang below the pilot and crews flying over tree-infested landscapes often disable the ADU as the hard shell of the PSP can prevent sharp bits of tree skewering the backside.

Despite the ingenuity close to genius that goes into ejection equipment, not everything always goes to plan. Mike Parnell remembers an 8 Squadron sortie:

Joining No. 8 Squadron at RAF Lossiemouth in March 1979 straight out of navigator training was something I did with a mixture of trepidation, at being posted to fly an aircraft from a bygone age. The AN-APS 20 radar we used for air surveillance and control was only slightly younger than the Avro Manchester, an ancestor of the Shackleton itself. The AN-APS 20 traced its roots back to the radars deployed on the ground at Pearl Harbor!

A Jaguar from the Operational Conversion Unit (OCU) at Lossiemouth, where pilots converted from the Hunter to the Jaguar before being posted to an operational squadron, had gone missing. We, being the QRA for the day, were asked to do Scene of Search Commander in the Shackleton. The Nimrods couldn't launch from Kinloss owing to cross-wind limitations, and RAF St Mawgan was too far away for a Nimrod to get north quickly enough.

This was an unusual QRA as the Shack had long since given up SAR as a primary role, although we continued to carry the Lindholme survival gear and flame floats in our bomb bay in case any of the fighters we controlled, or were close by, came to grief.

The RAF Kinloss Mountain Rescue Team (MRT) was already out by the time we took over local search co-ordination. Lossiemouth's Sea King rescue helicopter, the 'Yellow Banana' was busily, and in much danger, literally inching its way up the valleys to the estimated crash location somewhere north of the road between Crianlarich and Dalmally. Everyone in the air and on the ground was working in zero visibility, high winds and blowing snow, risking life and limb to find our downed colleague. We were at about 5,000ft in cloud, heavy turbulence and icing. It was really one of those days when no one in his right mind wanted to be in the air and only the most hardy, or most foolhardy, would be out walking the hills – which I say as both an old aviator and mountaineer.

Much of our time was spent co-ordinating from on high between the Sea King, the MRT and local police, providing the essential 'middle-man' link where terrain obstructed radio communications near the ground. Earnest, professional but relatively routine work. Then came the elated cry of one of the MRT who could see the pilot suspended by his parachute, a little higher than he then was, and in a crevice.

Cheers of joy all round when we relayed the information – the entire radio network audibly lifted, including the Rescue Co-ordination Centre at Pitreavie. It was a moment that made the risk and effort worthwhile. Half an hour later the MRT, though heaven only knows how – and top marks to the man's courage and skill – had reached the pilot. But the next call we had was 'He's in his 'chute; it deployed OK but he's been slammed into the crevice by the wind. A rock's gone through the back of his helmet'. He was dead.

Sadness and silence followed.

Pitreavie Castle effectively passed out of Royal Air Force hands in 1984. Control of the maritime reconnaissance aircraft transferred to Northwood, the home of the old Coastal Command, now comfortably digested by Strike Command. The RAF retained responsibility for search-and-rescue incidents along a line north of Yarmouth and south of the Faeroes, but that too would finally pass away and move to Kinloss.

The public face of the Royal Air Force, aside from low-flying jets hurtling over the countryside, is represented by the Search and Rescue helicopters. Dark mutterings occur in secluded Whitehall armchairs that the whole operation could be handed over to a private company. Some doubt whether that would be a wise move.

Paul Humphreys changed course from 'fish-head', an affectionate RAF term for a Royal Navy officer, to 'crab', an equally complimentary RN word for an RAF member. As poaching pilots was considered slightly bad form by both services, Paul lost eighteen months' seniority, with a reduction in pay, on transfer. As a gentle concession, turncoats could choose the type of posting they wanted first in their new life. Paul, who had happily flown the Wessex helicopter in the RN, plumped for Search and Rescue. Although the Sea King was the new kid on the block, the Wessex soldiered on without gadgets or gizmos. It offered 'seat-of-the-pants' flying.

In December 1987 Paul arrived as the new boy on 'B' Flight of 22 Squadron, based at RAF Leuchars. With two Wessex and four crews, it gave a 24-hour rescue coverage over the North Sea and Central Scotland. As with all service SAR units, its primary job was to rescue downed aircrew although the bulk of the callouts were for civilian incidents. Leuchars handled around 180 callouts every year. Paul arrived as the grand total closed on the milestone of 2,000 rescues:

My first shift, after acceptance training, was on 17 December 1987. Along with my navigator and winchman, we assumed responsibility at the formal handover from the offgoing crew at 0930 in the morning. For the next 24 hours, we were on immediate alert.

A call did not come on that shift, or the next, or the one after that. Rescues happened on the days that I was off shift, but never on mine. As the unit's tally slowly rose towards the 2,000 point, I gave up hope of ever being called out!

December came and went and so did January. The first three weeks of February passed and other crews went out. All Paul did was training flights. Until 21 February:

I assumed the shift with a very experienced winchman and a navigator near to the end of his first tour. Rescue Number 1,999 had happened earlier in the week but, no surprise with me on shift, it was a quiet day.

216

To kill time, I began some of our routine weekly checks on the spare Wessex in the hangar. The engineer shift boss was there, equally bored, washing his car. We exchanged moans about the RAF when a strange warbling sound came from the tannoy.

The engineer stared at me. 'Off you go then!'

'Go where?'

'It's the scramble alarm, stupid!'

During my two months on the unit I had never heard the call. I couldn't believe I was going to finally get my first rescue – and it was going to be Rescue 2,000!

A climber had fallen through a cornice, a snow ledge, on the eastern side of Ben Nevis, and Paul was called out to lift members of the Lochaber Mountain Rescue Team to where the casualty lay. It was deep-winter cold with snow showers along the route, and worse, the light was failing. Paul's first rescue would be in darkness and to add to the mixture, a photographer had clambered on board to record Rescue 2,000 for posterity:

I had never winched in the mountains at night before. Authority had also decreed it was too risky to train in the hills in the dark as this was before SAR aircraft had night vision equipment. The only aid was the 'Mark One Eyeball'. Trepidation smothered me with this thought. I was not overly comfortable with night flying after a crash in a helicopter when I was with the Navy. The idea of learning new skills by trial and error on a high profile night rescue did nothing to help. I suspect my crew had the same thoughts. Their dedication and bravery in trusting their lives to the least experienced pilot on the unit prevented them from voicing their concerns. Instead, they both offered me top tips on how we could successfully complete the rescue.

Not once did they suggest we should give up. Bravery is found in many walks of life, but a Wessex crew trusting a single pilot in an obsolete helicopter, at night in the winter Highlands, a pilot who has never done the job before, rates very highly.

Cloud covered the hilltops as the Wessex reached the eastern entrance to Glen Nevis. The casualty would be hidden in cloud and the mountain rescue team would need to bring him down to the lower slopes. Apart from poor visibility, there was the problem of the Wessex icing up.

Fixed-wing aircraft have heated mats to counter wing icing while helicopters that enter cold clouds find their rotor blades grow ice. The
Wessex rotor blades rotated 233 times per minute and the tips reached
sub-sonic speeds. Even without heated rotor blades, the ice is eventually
thrown off by centrifugal force. One blade shedding ice before the others
puts the whole helicopter out of balance, just as a car with one wheel
out of balance vibrates badly at only 60 mph. Unbalanced rotors,
threshing round at 400 miles per hour, mean instant disaster, so entering
winter cloud was comprehensively forbidden to Wessex pilots:

> At the western end of Glen Nevis are two buttresses that stick
> into the valley, one from the north side and one from the south.
> You could not have designed a better chicane for helicopters if
> you had tried. Our casualty's location was on the eastern side of
> the chicane, with Fort William on the west. As we approached,
> the navigator told me to reduce speed so that we could peer into
> the corrie, where we would deliver the MRT. In the failing light,
> I could work out that it was a 'double bowl' – a lower feature
> with a higher one tucked into the north side. My heart sank as
> I realised that soon I would be expected to be manoeuvring the
> Wessex into the tight, higher corrie. The crew's silence echoed
> my feelings.
>
> My dark thoughts were interrupted by the sight of the looming
> chicane. I jinked and weaved the Wessex through the narrow gap.
> This was good fun – but I still had enough light to help me pick
> my way through.

Clear of the chicane, the Wessex contacted the mountain rescuers
who waited in a car park at Fort William. A bevy of police cars lit up
the landing area with their headlamps as the Wessex touched down in
the low dusk of the winter evening:

> The popular vision of the military is of a dictatorial hierarchy,
> where the senior man tells everyone else what to do, without ques-
> tion. The RAF, and in particular SAR, is quite the opposite. The
> winchman had many SAR tours under his belt. As a flight sergeant,
> he ranked the lowest of the three of us. The navigator, a flight
> lieutenant, was near the end of his first tour. I too was a flight
> lieutenant. I was on my third full tour in the military. Technically

I was the most senior in strictly rank terms but the baby when it came to the job in hand. In SAR, we operate not as a hierarchy, but more as a 'workers co-operative' – a situation that disturbs some passengers from other services!

We immediately agreed to dump the photographer at the car park. He was not only a weight penalty but also a major distraction.

This harsh-sounding decision had a practical reason behind it. Helicopters work on a power to weight ratio. The lighter the aircraft's weight, the more power available in a tight situation or if things start to go wrong. The higher one goes, the thinner the air becomes, which makes it harder for the rotor blades to provide lift and without lift, aeroplanes cease to fly. The casualty was above 3,000 feet and, since the crew wanted to keep the Wessex as light as they could, they decided to take only two of the rescue team on the first lift. Caution is always a SAR crew's best friend in the dark:

As I lifted the Wessex to head for Glen Nevis, my back and arms tingled with apprehension from the pressure of my first callout, it being Rescue 2,000, my first night winching and the thought of failure.

As we approached the chicane, I could just make out a triangle that marked the gap at the top through which I guided the helicopter. With the speed back to 40kts, I took the Wessex to the left to enter the lower bowl. With all the aircraft's spotlights on, I tucked the machine along the side of the rocks to keep clear of any severe winds. As we slowly climbed, I looked up into the higher bowl. To my great relief, I saw bright torches glowing just inside the cloud to mark the position of our casualty. I gently eased the helicopter to just below the position of the lights and brought it to the hover. Power was okay, not a lot in hand, but I had a large drop below so that I could push the nose down if a wind suddenly came round and I couldn't hold position.

Sitting up front, I could not see where we were to winch. The navigator 'pattered' me into position with phrases such as 'Forward 1, Right 1, Steady'. Whilst winching he would keep this going so that there was no danger of our rotor blades striking the rocks.

219

The winchman let down to the rocks below and the two MRT members followed. Paul, with a sense of relief, edged away from the bowl to fly back to Fort William for more rescue team members. The Wessex turned for the chicane and immediately entered cold winter cloud. The navigator instantly called for an instrument turn to head east to take the Wessex away from the chicane. To stay in cloud chanced icing-up with the additional risk of drifting and flying straight into unyielding rocks. The only choice was to reduce height to clear the cloud. The ground below was invisible in the darkness, and Paul had to fly on instruments and use the radio altimeter to give him his precise height above the surface:

If it started to wind down quickly, we would be heading for a hill and need to turn the other way smartly. If it reduced slowly, we would be in the middle of the valley. I had never been a great fan of instrument flying, but suddenly I was a god at the skill. It's amazing what fear does!

The navigator turned all the external lights on. After a minute's flying that felt like an hour, we saw the reflection of the stream in the base of the valley. I brought the helicopter to the hover and turned to face the chicane. This was still covered, hidden in a snow shower. We landed to wait for the shower to pass. It did, after about five minutes.

Airborne again, I picked my way through the chicane and landed on at the car park. The next batch of MRT loaded. The transit back to the casualty was without incident. We soon had another four MRT members on the ground. The winchman called us on the radio to say that he would be ready for lift in about ten minutes.

Paul faced another dilemma. The paper mill at Corpach, about five minutes flying time away, held a fuel dump where the Wessex could top up, but five minutes flying translated into one hour away with engine shut-down, refuelling, start up and return. The casualty did not have an hour; hypothermia meant he had to be in hospital without delay:

The navigator did some quick sums. He reckoned we should just be okay if we landed on the base of the lower bowl rather than stay in the hover. My self preservation instinct made me want to go to Corpach to refuel, to escape the snow showers in the hills but I accepted his experience and guidance. We settled the Wessex on the ground to wait for the call to return.

Five minutes went – no call. The fuel gauges slowly emptied as the two jet engines continued to turn the rotor blades. Shutting down was not an option. Wessex engines had a well known history of being reluctant to start.

Ten minutes – still nothing. I retarded the engines to save fuel. One I brought back to idling; the other I wound back as far as I could without the rotor blades slowing down so much as to cause a dangerous vibration.

Fifteen minutes and the call finally came from the winchman. I slammed the throttles back into their flight gates. Within a couple of minutes we were hauling the winchman and the casualty in a stretcher into the aircraft. As we left the MRT members asked if we could give them a lift home. I had to explain that I was low on fuel and unable to help – much to my relief as the thought of another two trips past the chicane would have completely destroyed my frayed nerves!

When we landed at Fort William, we were greeted by not just our photographer, but by several more, all clicking away. The winchman, with the help of the MRT members who didn't make it up the hill, carried the stretcher to the waiting ambulance.

Two weeks after Rescue 2,000 I was on shift when the mail arrived. In it was a letter addressed to the 'Crew of February 21st'. Inside was a letter from our 'customer' along with a Postal Order for £10.00. It was a wonderful thank you note from an 18-year-old lad that started 'Excuse the handwriting, as it is not easy with two broken arms . . .' and finished with 'have some drinks on me'.

That made the night of anguish all worthwhile.

Although described at the time as a stop-gap, the Shackletons of 8 Squadron continued their patrols. Mike Parnell, the crew navigator/intercept controller, discovered that they did not always behave as staid old ladies should, especially when Flight Lieutenant Ian Weir occupied the left-hand seat. Later a squadron leader, 'Beery' induced a fierce loyalty amongst his crew:

The QRA launch call came in the small hours. Bear 'Deltas' (Ds) were expected to transit UK airspace heading for somewhere exotic like Cuba. We were to intercept them with fighters, identify, shadow and report. The met brief from Cap'n Beery Weir was for utterly foul weather en route the Atlantic heading out over Wester Ross but it would then clear to broken fair weather cumulus with some high cirrus. And so it proved.

It was dark and we were flying into a strong westerly airflow over mountains that were generating huge and highly turbulent cumulo-nimbus clouds. Normally sane aircrew fly around cu-nims but we had to get out to the Atlantic with all haste and went straight through the middle of them. Never before or since have I seen wings flex as much as WR960's did that morning. Fifteen feet tip deflection if it was an inch, I'll swear it! Unfortunately being an aeronautical engineer as well as a navigator, I knew the wings' limit load could not be far off, at which point they would bend, or worse, 'clap' – and that would be the end of Crew 5! By the grace of God we got through it and out into the clear Atlantic air. Not long later I detected two very strong radar returns to the north at a range of 220nm – on a radar calibrated to only 200 and which normally offered rather less!

It was soon clear these tracks were heading south west at a fair pace. Intelligence had been spot on and we had found our intruders. Then Buchan informed us the fighters were delayed.

Quick as a flash the TACO said 'Well we're an 11 Group asset; 11 Group is fighters; let's do it ourselves!' So the RAF's only four piston-engined, eight contra-rotating propellered fighter (uniquely equipped with a bomb bay and SAR gear) set off to intercept the Bears using our air surveillance radar as an air intercept radar – and it worked a treat!

Having spotted them first, as we approached the intercept point with the Bears Cap'n Beery called 'Judy', the term fighters use to indicate they are happy to make the remainder of the intercept unaided by fighter control. I was released to the beam window with a camera to see if I could get a decent photograph as proof we'd done it. A copy of the photo once lived with WR960 in her comfortable retirement home at the Manchester Air and Space Museum, close to the Avro factory where her ancestors were conceived some 70 years ago. Thank heavens they built them strong!

16

Modern Times and After

With the collapse of the Soviet Union and after the first Gulf War, the Government of the day initiated a series of Defence assessments. Under the generic title of 'Front Line First', the scalpel cut deep, not merely into already emaciated flesh but into the bone marrow. Possibly only politicians without a single day of military service in alliance with senior officers untrammelled by memories of the Second World War would have attempted such radical surgery. For the Royal Air Force, it meant a reduction in size to 50,000 bodies and a frontline strength of fewer than 400 aircraft. For Scotland, the result was the steady closure of RAF bases.

At the start of the 1990s, some minor panic and perturbation hit the streets of Arbroath. 'Liner' is not, incidentally, a large ship with four big funnels and a couple clutching the sharp bit at the front and singing. It is a NATO brevity codeword which, used correctly, means to 'fly at speed giving maximum cruising range'. In practice that means in cold power, not reheat, so it often is used incorrectly to mean 'go subsonic'. 'M 1' means Mach One, the speed of sound. 'JVOC', a suitably anonymous RAF controller, describes the incident:

> I was at RAF Boulmer as a fighter controller at the time of the first Gulf War. Tornado F3s rotated between units to enable a common fleet with equal hours to be modified at Leeming.
>
> One day I received a telephone call from a young Navy F3 pilot at Leeming – it was a period when, if an RN pilot wasn't considered ready, yet, for the Sea Harrier, they sent him to the RAF for a tour for experience. He was delivering an F3 to Leuchars and bringing another back. He wanted to see what speed he could get it to and wanted control on the best path up the coast.

At the appointed time he got airborne and coasted and was handed over to me. I cleared him high speed and turned him north parallel to the coast.

M1.0, M1.5, M1.7, M1.8, M1.9, M1.95, M1.96 slowly it continued to accelerate . . .

As it flew north I slowly cleared him to turn left more and more to stay parallel to the coastline till he was pointing at Leuchars. He was still pushing to reach M2.0. Height about Flight Level 400 (40,000 feet). As he reached about 60 miles from the coast I gave the call, '60 miles to the coast, Liner Liner'. Nothing happened.

As he reached 50 miles I repeated the call, 'Wait' was the response.

As he reached 45 miles the fighter allocator behind me became agitated and told me to turn him.

'45 miles to the coast, Liner, Liner or turn right onto 360 feet.'
'Wait' came the reply.

Speed now down to M1.8.

40 miles. 'Immediate right turn 030 and Liner'.
'Wait'.

M1.85.

At 30 miles, he was still heading about 290 and his speed was slowly coming back through M1.7.

20 miles . . . M1.6. 10 miles . . . 1.5. Coastline M1.4.

As he passed overhead Arbroath he was doing about M1.3. At which time he called 'Turning port, Liner', and I handed him to Leuchars Air Traffic Control.

Needless to say, there was slight consternation in the ops room. We waited for the telephone to ring. Nothing.

We discovered later, from an Arbroath newspaper sent from RAF Buchan, that there had been a massive double boom in the town. Windows shattered. The fire brigade and ambulances shot around the town from one end to the other looking for the explosion, before going back to base, puzzled.

Buchan were phoned and asked if they were controlling any supersonic aircraft. They answered they had no flying going on because they were doing a simulated exercise. Leuchars Ops were phoned. They had no sorties airborne. The authorities then gave up and blamed it on a freak thunderstorm.

I got hold of the young Lieutenant on the phone when he got back to Leeming. He had never been above M1.3 on the OCU or Squadron. When the throttle was shut, you were slammed into the straps by the deceleration. On this trip he closed the throttle at M1.99 – and nothing happened. He worked out later the shock wave was detached from the airframe and drag was minimum.

An expert in aerodynamics might sniff warily at the lieutenant's 'working out'. Drag in high speed flight, the expert will explain, rises at Mach 0.98 and reduces from around M1.05 'when the whole flow becomes supersonic, the shock fully established and expansion fans progressively give way to proper shocks'. It is always possible that the pilot simply wanted to see how fast he could go.

Buchan soon suffered the indignity of closure to become an unmanned remote radar head as greater range and satellite communications took over their job. A few years earlier, though, when Buchan was more than a bit player, an 8 Squadron Shackleton trailed its way north. Mike Parnell remembered it well:

We were tasked to fly from Lossiemouth to give AEW support to Neatishead, a large radar station and Sector Operations Centre (SOC) near Norwich. That's quite a long way to travel in the Shackleton, so we set off long before dawn. Our task was cut short due to forecasts of very strong northerly winds for the return journey. We dutifully broke barrier, the galley slave prepared lunch for everyone and we, the radar team, left the banana eaters at the front to get us back home in time for tea – or better still, beer in the Bothy bar – where the real crew debrief took place.

We hit the 120-knot headwind as we entered Boulmer's area near Newcastle. Even flying at range speed of 180 knots – the speed at which the aircraft will travel farthest through the air on its fuel load – we made not much better than 60kts over the ground!

We pottered past Boulmer at about 3,000ft, being overtaken by every car on the A1. We were asked every 10 minutes or so for our estimated time of arrival (ETA) at base. We dawdled on northwards into Buchan's sector, receiving the same relentless checking of our ETA for Lossiemouth.

At about 1300, just past Leuchars, after a further stream of requests to update our ETA – because no one could believe in a fast jet age anything could fly that slow – came one final call of weary incredulity from the Buchan Fighter Marshal, whose job it was to provide an air traffic service to us on the way home.

'55, this is Buchan; say again your ETA base, over.'

Dear old Cap'n Beery, pipe sat on the coaming with his coffee, all good humour about to be lost, growled with not a little indignation and just the slightest hint of his normally very muted Scots accent crackling in the background: 'Buchan, 55. 1600 Zulu . . . Again!!!'

Very quietly and with perfect timing, before Buchan could respond, and even before he had checked in on frequency with the Fighter Marshal, a Hunter from the TWU flying serenely overhead at 30,000 feet or so chipped in:

'Today or tomorrow?'

One by one, the flying stations in Scotland shut down. By the end of the decade, in 1999, only three remained: Lossiemouth, Leuchars and Kinloss. Benbecula in the west joined Buchan as an unmanned site, a Remote Radar Head that sent its information dispassionately to the major operations centre in England. One firing range, at Tain, served the RAF and NATO. Saxa Vord finally closed. On the very tip of the Shetlands, it readily claimed to be the most remote station in the whole of the British Isles as well as one of the smallest in Strike Command. One of its major boasts, during its glory days, was that it organised a 24-hour charity golf competition on the longest day of the year – which, at Saxa, meant daylight all the time.

The Strategic Defence Review of 1998 firmly set a new course for all three British Services. The Royal Air Force produced *RAF Strategy 2002* which provides a 'Vision' that encapsulates the Air Force Board's intention 'to deliver an Air Force that strives to be first and person for person is second to none'. Hard-bitten former members of the Service who read this politely murmur that the RAF always was the best and needs no Mission Statement.

Scottish Royal Auxiliary Air Force units re-formed although they no longer fly. Lossiemouth is home to 2622 (Highland Squadron) of the RAF Regiment and began life in 1979 to help defend the airfield. It now has the enhanced role of reinforcing the regular Regiment. In the 1990s, volunteers served in Bosnia, Cyprus and Kuwait then, in 2003, compulsory mobilisation sent squadron members to Iraq. The squadron still supports British deployments overseas and also maintains, for fun, a voluntary pipe band.

At Leuchars, 612 (County of Aberdeen) Squadron is an Air Transportable Surgical Squadron whose task is to supply field surgical support in times of conflict and, when not involved overseas, to help if a major civilian disaster occurs. The unit has 25 beds available, including two for intensive care, and can hold 25 patients for up to 48 hours. They have also served overseas in Iraq, Cyprus and elsewhere.

Both 602 (City of Glasgow) Squadron and 603 (City of Edinburgh) Squadron are based in Edinburgh. The Glasgow squadron, 602, has the job of supporting the Nimrod at Kinloss and surveillance and reconnaissance aircraft in England with flight operations officers, managers and assistants. Edinburgh's 603 Squadron has a primary role of 'Survive to Operate' or 'Force Protection' which essentially means it provides everybody from cooks to signallers, clerks to gunners in support of the regular Service.

In addition to its Auxiliary Regiment personnel, Lossiemouth is the home of three operational Tornado GR4 squadrons: 12, 14 and 617. Number 15 (Reserve) Squadron is the GR4 Operational Conversion Unit and also supplies the Tornado Display Team. A Search and Rescue facility comes from 'D' Flight of 202 Squadron who were the first RAF unit to move to Lossiemouth in 1972 when the Royal Navy returned it to the RAF. The full-time 51 Field Squadron of the RAF Regiment completes the station's roster.

Leuchars too has a Mountain Rescue Team as well as the air transportable surgical unit. Its flying squadrons include 43 Squadron, who now have the Tornado F3 instead of the BE2 they flew by the walls of Stirling Castle in 1916. Also with the Tornado are 111 Squadron, along with 56 (Reserve) Squadron who form the OCU for the type. Three University Air Squadrons from Aberdeen, Dundee and St Andrew's use the Tutor, a product of Burkhart Grob Luft and Raumfahrt GMBH of Tussenhausen-Mattsies in Germany. It replaced Scottish Aviation's Bulldog. In the new world of the Private Finance Initiative, the aeroplanes are flown and maintained by a civilian company, much as Prestwick's Tiger Moths were in 1936.

Kinloss houses the Nimrod MR2 and two squadrons, 120 and 201, form the frontline and operational spearhead of the Nimrod fleet. Operational conversion is the task of 42 (Reserve) Squadron. The station has a fine collection of lodger units, including the most senior Mountain

Rescue Team in the RAF and a volunteer gliding school. The Nimrod, based upon the civilian de Havilland Comet, the first civilian jet airliner whose fame is commemorated in the international road sign for an airfield or airport, entered service in 1969 as the MR1. The aircraft upgraded to MR2 during the early 1980 period but its successor, the MRA4 is currently seven years behind schedule. Development costs creep inexorably towards four *billion* pounds for a current order of 12 aircraft. Despite its age, the Nimrod MR2, like its predecessor the Shackleton, is a first-rate maritime patrol aircraft with an essential sideline in search and rescue duties.

On 8 November 2005, at 0330 on a cold winter night, the 120 Squadron duty crew responded to an emergency distress call. A trimaran, *Orange Project*, one of 32 yachts in a transatlantic race, had run into trouble, capsizing 250 miles off the Scillies and 265 miles from the French coast.

Nimrods do not scramble like Spitfires in the Battle of Britain. They carry 13 crew and a rescue mission needs briefing before it dashes off into the night and so it requires about 90 minutes to ready the crew and aircraft for what can be a long and difficult flight. The Nimrod took off at 0510, blasting into a headwind of around 140 miles per hour. She needed 2 hours to reach *Orange Project*. Shortly before the Nimrod reached the scene, they learned that another yacht, *Foncia*, had also capsized near *Orange Project* and a third, *Sodebo*, was dismasted about 95 miles further north. Their positions put them at the extreme range for the SAR helicopters, and with the surface wind at 60 knots or more, attempts to winch survivors to safety would be hazardous. A Sea King was on its way to position on the Scillies.

The Nimrod prepared to lose height as it approached the scene at 0710, when a message came in that a French fishing boat was about to take *Sodebo* under tow. That solved one problem; and a second all but disappeared when the coastguard advised that a bulk carrier, the Liberian-registered *Sibotura*, was on her way to assist *Foncia*. One of the Nimrod's navigators takes up the story:

We contacted *Sibotura*. She confirmed she would assist *Foncia*. She was about forty minutes away from the yacht which had two people on board, one of whom was injured. The bulk carrier added that the sea state was such she could do no more than station herself to put *Foncia* in her lee to protect her from the wind.

We investigated three small radar contacts at about ten miles distant. The third of these was *Orange Project,* quickly confirmed by her colour and the photograph we had received. We saw one person on board the dismasted vessel. One of the yacht's outriggers was loose. It later dropped off.

We decided to drop a life raft pair. This consists of two self-inflating rafts joined together by more than 300 yards of rope. With the wind conditions, the rafts would separate on inflation but drift towards the yacht, joined by the rope. The rope had enough spread to cover *Orange Project.*

We calculated the wind speed at 300 feet as coming from almost due west at 35 knots. The seas were high with a considerable swell. The aircraft was set on course for a drop. The Nimrod made visual contact in good time. The life rafts dropped at 0730.

They both inflated as per the maker's guarantee but were upside down, almost undoubtedly because of the high wind. They were also much closer to each other than expected. This may have been caused by the wind or one or both sea anchors had deployed and so slowed the drift rate. Whatever the cause, the rafts were too close together. It looked as if they would miss the yacht entirely.

We decided to drop a single air sea rescue raft with an even longer rope attached to a stores pack. The wind had swung to the north-west but we still assessed it at 35 knots. Once again, the Nimrod set up for the drop and visual contact came along in good time.

As we came back over *Orange Project* we could see that the life raft pair were about 50 yards from the yacht and drifting at the same rate. The ASR raft had inflated but the stores pack had ended up directly behind the raft. Once again, we had too little spread on the rope.

The two drops had attracted no reaction from *Orange Project.* This suggested they did not intend to abandon the vessel. If they did, they now had three life rafts close by. As we had contacted another bulk carrier, *Atlantic Forest,* who had agreed to come on station to protect the yacht from the wind, we left to give assistance to *Foncia.*

The Nimrod quickly closed on the yacht. En route, the coast-guard advised that a French helicopter ship was close enough to send a helicopter to rescue both crews. When we reached the position relayed by Falmouth and *Sibotura*, about 10 nautical miles from *Orange Project*, a radar sweep of the area found no contacts. We checked the position given us, less than an hour old, and set up for a close search of the area. My fear was that the yacht had gone down and that we were looking for two people in the water.

We asked *Sibotura* to search to the east of the reported position as the drift and wind was pushing everything that floated to the east. We set up a clover leaf pattern search east of the original position given to us that also overlapped the last known position of *Foncia*.

Twenty minutes into the clover leaf, Falmouth gave us an updated position. This put *Foncia* some 15 nautical miles west of our search area. As we headed to this new position, we gained radar contact and homed directly to the yacht.

After looking at the condition of the upturned yacht and aware that there was an injured person on board, we decided to drop a life raft pair. The wind remained at 35 knots out of the northwest. We had good visual contact when the life rafts dropped. They deployed correctly but did not drift close to the yacht.

Sibotura was now some 25 nautical miles away. We contacted *Atlantic Forest,* who agreed to shelter *Foncia* in her lee until the French helicopter arrived. This ship subsequently reported that when she arrived, one of the yacht's crew opened a hatch, looked out, then closed the hatch with no other contact.

We learned from Falmouth that the yacht crews had decided to stay with them and wait for the rescue helicopter. We checked on both vessels before climbing out to remain on station.

The Nimrod stayed on station until low fuel forced them to leave at 1240. On their way to St Mawgan, the French helicopter ship called to confirm that one of their aircraft would be on the scene at 1300. The Nimrod then updated the helicopter direct with positions of the yachts and the callsigns of the assisting merchant ships. *Foncia* should take priority as she not only had an injured crew member but was the furthest away. The Nimrod finally landed in Cornwall, after ten hours in the air and a round trip in the region of 1,500 miles.

The pilots in their leather coats who flew from Montrose in 1913, the crew who laboured to take R34 across the Atlantic and home again, the Everest fliers, the men who fought the Junkers and Heinkels over

Scotland or attacked *Tirpitz* would hardly recognise the modern Royal Air Force. The aircraft and crews who tried so many times to destroy *Tirpitz* have given way to a single aeroplane with a laser-guided bomb. Eyeballing the enemy is old hat. 'Asymmetric warfare' to kill a distant, unaware stranger is the modern way.

Aircraft have changed beyond recognition. Electronics make the equipment of the Second World War not merely old-fashioned but archaic. The organisation itself has changed in ways that might perhaps bring a frown to the face of Henderson or Trenchard. The purpose is different. The weapons have changed and Commands that seemed set to last for ever have vanished. Today's Royal Air Force would baffle a Camel pilot or a Whitley navigator – and possibly not be to their liking. 'Company speak' and management methods suitable for profit-making mega-corporations infest a service whose prime function was once the defence of the realm.

The current United Kingdom forces are expected to operate without the tools for the job, although politicians show indecent anxiety to cash in on the achievements of the fighting services, especially if the war is, geographically, respectably far distant. They are distinctly less enthusiastic about opening their chest of treasure. When General Douglas Macarthur faced a recalcitrant President during the 1930s, his retort was blunt. It would not be Macarthur's name on the lips of American soldiers who died with enemy bayonets at their throat but that of the politicians and bureaucrats who clung to the money bag. The answer is simple: either spend the money to support the policy or change the policy to something affordable.

One feature remains constant: the men and the women who wear the uniform. They continue to serve as their predecessors did, be it on the ground or in the air. And the Camel pilot and the Whitley navigator might just feel the slightest twinge of envy at modern flying even if a computer does the work much of the time. But there is still pleasure to be found in the skies although life on a modern front line fighter squadron is a long way from clambering aloft on a rickety biplane to seek the bright sky. The computer-generated 1916 pilot or observer would find some things had changed as Flight Lieutenant Nige Morton, a Weapon Systems Operator with Stirling's own Squadron, 43 (F), the 'Fighting Cocks, reveals:

> Before he can even think about flying in the modern RAF, it is
> off to the medics to ensure that he is fit. There's no longer an open

cockpit and very limited flying altitudes. Easily clearing ears and sinuses is essential in a cockpit that is only partially pressurised. There is none of the comfort of airline travel as that is a weight and power luxury that can't be afforded.

Passed fit to fly, it's now off to get kitted up. The requirement to keep warm, as in the early days of flight, is still there but now it is not so much in the cockpit as outside in the unlikely event of ejection. The coastal waters around our shores are rarely warm. Fast jet crews need an immersion suit, thermal underwear, a kitted coverall, anti G trousers and a life jacket. Our 1916 flyer would feel like a trussed-up chicken as well as overly hot through the exertion of putting on all the kit, (it weighs 20 kgs), but he'll soon adapt. Finally there's the helmet, no longer made of leather, but of Kevlar and fibreglass. It's not only for protection, but essential for the oxygen mask and intercom. At last, the ancillaries are complete and the day of the flight is here.

As our RFC pilot walks up to the squadron he will notice a throw back to another era, the Cold War, with anti-nuclear accommodation for both people and aircraft. The first stop is the crew room for some tea and a chat, catch up on the weekend news, plans for the day, the weather, and the sports results. Then, together with the rest of the formation, it is off to get the official weather brief which supplants the crew room version of 'well the BBC last night said . . .'

All four crews attend. When the met brief has finished the leader stands up to give the big picture overview of the day's mission and divvies out the jobs to the rest of the team. The task is one our RFC pilot would recognise, protecting some lightly armed bombers against adversary fighters. The 'fight' will take place over the Highlands; although place names remain, there are a lot of areas where we can't fly because of civil and military limitations like airways and airport zones, noise sensitive areas and weapon ranges to name but a few. The map is drawn up with the bombers' route and temporary restrictions, and finally photocopied for everyone. At least we only had to draw up one map today. Final co-ordination is completed with the bombers and the opposition; today 111(F) Sqn will be acting as our adversaries to simulate a suitable threat platform. Tomorrow, the roles will be reversed.

Now for something our RFC pilot would recognise – the sortie brief. Although the content and tactics might bewilder, the basic premise of who we are and what we are going to do, the appropriate rules and the friendlies and hostiles. It's over quickly with only the pertinent points being briefed; the rest is 'SOP' or Standard Operating Procedure. Next, off to see the Squadron authoriser, the final link in the safety chain, to find out which aircraft we are going to fly, their recent history and any late changes. There are. Our fighter controllers are not going to be sat in a bunker at RAF Scampton as planned, but will be airborne in one of the E-3D Sentry aircraft from RAF Waddington.

So now it's time to get dressed in all that kit our RFC pilot. It's a little easier to put on this time but still restrictive, then off to the jet. Individual crews walk out together some talking about the sortie, others just idly chatting, all however focused and ready for the sortie. We resemble cavalry officers wearing spurs as we walk, the leg restraints clanging together behind our legs. One of the Squadron navigators will help our visitor to strap in. Though he will be flying in the trainer version of the Tornado F3 so that he can actually fly the aircraft, he will also have to operate all the radar and navigation equipment controllers in the back cockpit. As we enter the HAS, the Hardened Aircraft Shelter, we can see our shiny steed, quiet and formidable, the ground crew waiting. The navigator jumps in to the aircraft, does the initial checks, then clears the ground crew to switch on the ground power. The noise of the electrical motors in the cooling fans is loud, made more intense by the confines of the HAS. Now to get strapped in; straps across the thighs and shoulders, restraints for arms and legs, oxygen and intercom all connected. One piece of safety equipment our RFC pilot would not recognise is the parachute, which in the Tornado F3 is part of the seat. First World War pilots had no escape when things went wrong. Finally don the helmet, put on the oxygen mask and become acquainted with the noise and smell of a modern jet aircraft; a constant electrical hum and slightly air-conditioned rubbery air. The pilot is ready in the front, and signals for clearance from the ground crew to start the engines. The radios burst forth with activity as the rest of the formation checks in with Air Traffic Control. Then the drone starts and vibrations reverberate through the airframe, low at first then getting high in pitch, the sound and feel of a jet engine starting. The drone is replaced by the high pitched whine that indicates the right engine is up and running. A check of flying controls and surfaces and we are ready for the other engine, same again but more distant, hidden by the noise and vibration from the first. Then the canopy is closed and relative peace ensues. The navigation systems and radar are all ready and so is the crew. A sudden jolt runs through the airframe; it's all right, that's the wings moving back to allow for easier taxi-in out of the HAS. Again the radios spring to life with the formation check-in. Everyone is ready. A call to air traffic to request taxi and at last we are off. Pre-flight checks are done, and the ejection seats are made live. A request for clearance is granted by air traffic and we receive permission to line-up and take-off.

Final checks complete, the power comes up, max dry, no after-burner yet, engine checks, and a thumbs up to our leader that we are ready. He gives the signal to light the afterburners, a kick though the airframe as each lights and holds, we look at the leader, signalling that we are ready, he taps his head and as he nods forward we both release brakes for a pairs take-off. Power is increased, speed starts to read, first check at 100 knots, speed keeps building, 140 knots we can go flying, 160 knots and we are. Once airborne the undercarriage travels, then the flaps and finally at 300 knots the afterburners are cancelled. The radio frequency changes to another part of RAF Leuchars air traffic. It's a nice day so just information on other aircraft will be required. There's one in the Dundee circuit, a light civil doing his Private Pilot's Licence, not in our way. We can only climb to 10,000ft as the airway starts there and we need to stay clear. Once clear, it's virtually free airspace ahead, well below 24,500ft that is. There's time to look out the window as we transit north to our RV, the rendezvous with the bombers. This time of year the airspace is fairly quiet, except for some commercial traffic going into Inverness, but come the summer and it will be full of gliders, hang gliders and light private planes, all of which are very difficult to see. The Grampians have a covering of snow and haven't changed in a thousand years, but looking east, the towns on the east coast have certainly grown.

Now for a chance to fly the jet. Yes, there is a stick and throttle, two in fact, but neither is directly connected to the controls, but to computers. Move the controls and the aircraft does as you would expect but with no real feel, and only as far as the computers, and the laws of physics, allow. Even if the computer for the flying control fails and the back-up system of direct links cut in, hydraulics are still needed to move the control services. The force exerted on them by the atmosphere is too much for human muscle alone. A bank of instruments is on the bulkhead in front of our RFC pilot, some familiar such as the altimeter and air speed indicator. The latter shows that we are doing 0.7 mach, almost 7 miles a minute yet at this height there is no sensation of speed, no discernable engine noise, just the constant background white noise of a Tornado F3 though the headphones. Above the instruments sit 2 TV screens. One is the radar display, showing the tracks of both civilian airliners and the bombers approaching the RV. On the other is a representation of the play area, not a moving map, just the vital points that we require. Our position is indicated by an aircraft symbol, which is continually updated by the Global Positioning System or GPS, so there are no excuses for being late or lost. But it's time to stop the tour and start thinking about the fight.

The E3-D controller is now on the radio, checking everyone in. His call sign is 'Magic'. He then starts painting the picture; bandits marshalling to the south, stranger traffic off to the east, no threat though, probably an airliner inbound to Aberdeen. We now have the airspace up to 45,000ft, high enough for the type of fight we want. 'Fights On' and we are off. The fighter starts to accelerate; the pilot moves back the wings. Out the window we see our leader start to climb. We follow. 25,000ft, 30,000ft, finally 35,000ft. We are just below the speed of sound now. Vast trails plume out the back as we streak across a cloudless sky. If the enemy didn't know we were coming, they certainly do now! Radar contact on the targets that Magic is talking about, formation contact is set on who will shoot whom. Magic gives the clearance to engage, 'Fox' is called over the radio, simulating that shots have been taken. We turn partly away from the targets, imaginary missiles winging their way across the divide. Now the missiles are on their own. We turn away hard. The G-pants start to inflate, squeezing the legs and tummy and helping our RFC pilot to avoid 'grey out' as all the blood rushes to his feet. Time-out! The missiles should have reached their targets. Are the opposition dead? Some are. They return to their regeneration point to be a factor again later. The others are mopped up by the second element. Four bad guys all dead, but the only thing we have seen is a blip on the radar screen. The bombers are now on their way, so time for us to flow towards their target. Then Magic talks about a new threat, too close to shoot and leave as we have so far. This time he will have to be dealt with in close combat. Again a call of 'Fox' from our leader. We check of our defensive equipment to see if the bandit's radar is looking at us? Negative. We press towards the radar contact. Then we see him, the pilots talk calmly over the radio. Who can see what? Who will engage? And who will support? Then the G comes on and the dance that is aerial combat begins. The aircraft are manoeuvred to get weapons on, not the luxury of pointing your gun over the side as in the RFC's BE 2. The kill is called and the formation re-established.

All too soon the fight is over. Everyone checks their fuel. Time to go home. We have fuel for a low level recovery, so descend in to the Highlands. A warning sounds, the radio altimeter, set at 5000' to check as we descend. No longer do we have to rely on individual judgment for height on the lines of 'can you see sheep's legs? Yes, too low, can't see cow's legs though, too high!' The paper map is now out, checking ahead for obstructions and avoids. 'Pull Up! Pull Up!' a computerised female voice implores, 'Bitching Betty'. She is part of a system to help prevent crews flying into the ground. False alarm this time, but it is acknowledged by the pilot. Talking to Leuchars air traffic again, Dundee passes below. Tentsmuir Forest off to the right where the first balloon flights from Leuchars took place. The jets are now in close formation, running in towards the airfield. St Andrews off to the south, flying still taking place from West Sands, but now of the kite variety. The jets peel off one by one, pre landing checks complete, it's time to land. Even with all the technology this is still down to pilot skill. The old adage of any landing you walk away from is a good one still rings true. Gear touches down and the thrust reverse is engaged to help us slow down; it's all over!

Well not quite. Time to taxi back, make the ejection seat safe, and complete yet more checks. The ground crew are waiting at the HAS, their final checks complete and we are clear to shut down. Canopy opens, fresh air at last, and peace from the white noise. The usual questions as you get out of the aircraft. I'm sure that our RFC pilot would have been asked the same. 'How did it go? Did you win?' (Not as easy to tell in training rather than for real.) And the one that they are most worried about. 'Have you broken it?' With a negative to the last, it's off to sign the aircraft back to the engineers, and complete all the paperwork.

And now the final act; the debrief. Everyone has changed back in to their flying-suits; cups of coffee and tea have been sought. One thing our RFC pilot will recognise is the need to learn the lessons from what we have done airborne. However, we don't have to rely solely on our memories or notes made airborne, as once again technology comes to the fore. All the TVs in the jet are recorded on to videotape and the position of all players on to solid-state cards. So now we can see if we did as planned? Did we do it to the best of our ability? And how could we improve next time? These I'm sure are the same question that the RFC pilots would have asked of themselves. At the end of the day, technology and weaponry have advanced, but it still is down to man and machine against one another. Fighter crews have always had a camaraderie and respect for each other, no matter what the aircraft, or which side they are on.

It needs a crystal ball of unusually powerful wattage to forecast the future for the Tartan Air Force. In a world of flux, where polar bears drown because the ice floes are melting, where an oil-dependent civilisation finally grasps that the supply is finite, where governments rule by pandering to apprehension rather than tackling problems, where each single Eurofighter Typhoon in RAF service costs the taxpayer about £50,000,000, a Sovereign Parliament in Edinburgh might step back from setting up its own frontline air force. Add in the thirty or more people behind every pilot who service engines, tighten wheelnuts, polish canopies, cook meals, ensure spare parts arrive in time and scrutinise travel claims and the costs mount alarmingly.

Granted some believe the Typhoon will stay in service for fifty years which perhaps makes the arithmetic a little better albeit they may have to be equipped with solar panels or adapted to run on soy sauce or biofuel. Possibly Duncan Sandys will be proved right and missiles will replace crews in cockpits although the need for cooks and clerks, mechanics and electricians will still remain. There is no practical reason why Scotland does not have its own air force if the time ever comes. New Zealand, Norway, Denmark are all roughly equivalent and they all have theirs, albeit sometimes with outside help. As an alternative, an independent Scotland could charge rent for those bases that a future London Government does not close in another cost-cutting and efficiency exercise with a facility fee for using Scottish airspace for low-flying.

A real Tartan Air Force, with its own aeroplanes, would have no problem designing an insignia. It can follow Australia, Canada and New Zealand and replace the red circle in the centre of the famous roundel with a red lion, rampant and proud, the symbol of Scotland.

Epilogue

Memorials to the Tartan Air Force abound. Some are granite, Celtic crosses that look out sombrely across bare landscape or face towns where once young men drank and laughed, while others are simple bronze plaques. A few are elaborate columns, and, always, there are the headstones marking graves, close to where those who flew from Scotland met their ends. Some lie side by side as a crew, eternally united in a fellowship of death.

Other reminders dot the countryside: huts, abandoned control towers with the glass long gone from the windows; one-time runways that occasionally form part of a road on smart housing estates or industrial parks that once were airfields. More recently closed stations are promised a new and useful existence as distilleries or luxury hotels, indoor ski-slopes or fitness centres.

It is still possible for the inquisitive and imaginative to gain a sense of what it was like during two world wars. Montrose Air Station Heritage Centre has the hangars and offices from the days when the young men of 2 Squadron first arrived, and sometimes people believe they see a figure dressed in an old-fashioned uniform or long-obsolete flying gear.

At East Fortune, the Museum of Flight retains its Second World War atmosphere, and as with all proper airfields, somebody has left open a door. The wind bounds across the wide expanse of concrete and grass on a summer day, a faint tremor of a reminder of how it felt to make aircraft ready for war in the sullen cold of a winter night.

The ghosts remain. Isaac still waits. Aviators are always in the front line, be it peace or war. On 2 September 2006 a Nimrod from 120 Squadron with fourteen men on board crashed near Kandahar, in Afghanistan. Nobody survived. And because they live with the knowledge that the

239

bony finger can summon at any moment, those who strive to reach the stars also respect those who share the knowledge of how frail existence can be. Geoff Cooper, navigator, of 8 Squadron, Royal Air Force:

I used to live in Hopeman – a traditional former fishing village midway between RAF Lossiemouth and RAF Kinloss. It was a very tight-knit community and many of the menfolk used to go away to the fishing from ports such as Buckie or Peterhead. In 1978, a fishing boat called *Acacia Wood* was lost at sea with, I think, the loss of six fishermen – all Hopeman folk.

The day of the funeral, all the menfolk (no women present) – dressed in black suits and white shirts – lined up along Harbour Street, the main street of the village with bowed heads as the funeral cortege passed by in silence. I'd never seen anything like this in my life before.

In the distance I heard the unmistakeable growl of a Shack growing louder and louder. Suddenly it appeared at not much above roof top height. It flew low overhead following the line of the main street and out to sea. As it left the land behind, it gently rocked its wings in salute. I don't think I've ever witnessed anything more poignant. Unaccountably, many of us had grit in our eyes.

The flowers of the forest are a' wede away

BIBLIOGRAPHY

Books

Anonymous, *By Air To Battle*, His Majesty's Stationery Office, 1945.

Barnes, Derek Gilpin, *Cloud Cover*, Rich & Cowan, London, 1945.

Berry, Peter, *Prestwick Airport & Scottish Aviation*, Tempus Publishing, Stroud, 2005.

Bird, Andrew D., *A Separate Little War*, Grub Street, London, 2003.

Bowyer, Chaz, *For Valour*, Grub Street, London, 1993.

Boyle, Andrew, *Trenchard*, Collins, London, 1962.

Brown, Malcolm and Meehan, Patricia, *Scapa Flow*, Allen Lane (Penguin), London, 1968.

Bruce, J. M., *The Aeroplanes of the Royal Flying Corps (Military Wing)*, Putnam, London, 1982.

Castle, H. G., *Fire Over England*, Secker & Warburg, London, 1982.

Cole, Christopher, *McCudden VC*, William Kimber, London, 1967.

Compilation, *The Aero Manual 1910*, Temple Press, London, 1910.

Courtney, Frank, *Flight Path*, William Kimber, London, 1973.

Cronin, Dick, *Royal Navy Shipboard Aircraft Developments, 1912–1931*, Air-Britain, Tonbridge, 1990.

Douglas, W. Sholto, *Years of Combat*, Collins, London, 1963.

Driver, Hugh, *The Birth of Military Aviation: Britain 1902–1914*, Royal Historical Society (Boydell Press), London, 1997.

Falconer, Jonathan, *The Bomber Command Handbook 1939–1945*, Sutton Publishing, Stroud, 1998.

Gillies, J. D. and Wood, J. L., *Aviation in Scotland*, Royal Aeronautical Society, Glasgow Branch, 1966.

Gollin, Alfred *No Longer An Island*, Heinemann, London, 1984.

Graham, James, Duke of Montrose, *My Ditty Box*, Cape, London, 1952.

Hayward, James, *Myths & Legends of the Second World War*, Sutton Publishing, Stroud, 2003.

Hering, P. G., *Customs and Traditions of the Royal Air Force*, Gale & Polden, 1961.

King, Brad, *Royal Naval Air Service 1912–1918*, Hikiko Publications, Aldershot, 1997.

Lewis, Peter, *Squadron Histories, RFC, RNAS, RAF 1912–59*, Putnam, London, 1959.

McCafferty, Gerry, *They Had No Choice*, Tempus Publishing, Stroud, 2002.

McKee, Alexander, *Into the Blue*, Souvenir Press, London, 1981.

Mowthorpe, Ces, *Battlebags: British Airships of the First World War*, Sutton Publishing, Stroud, 1995.

Nesbit, Roy Conyers and Van Acker, Georges, *The Flight of Rudolf Hess*, Sutton Publishing, Stroud, 1999.

Northrop, Wing Commander Joe, *Joe: The Autobiography of a Trenchard Brat*, Square One Publications, Worcester, 1993.

Penrose, Harald, *British Aviation: The Pioneer Years*, Putnam, London, 1982.

Peto-Shepherd, Denis, *The Devil Take the Hindmost*, Pentland Press, Durham, 1996.

Prendergast, Curtis, *The First Aviators*, Time-Life Publishing, Alexandria, VA, USA, 1981.

Raleigh, Sir Walter and Jones, H. A., *The War In the Air*, vols 1–6, Oxford University Press, 1922 onwards.

Richards, Denis and Saunders, Hilary St George, *The Royal Air Force* (3 vols), Her Majesty's Stationery Office, London, 1974.

Smith, David J., *Action Stations 7: Military Airfields of Scotland, the North-East and Northern Ireland*, Patrick Stephens, Cambridge, 1983.

Smith, Nigel, *The Tirpitz Raids*, Print on Demand title, ISBN 1871187273.

Springs, Elliott White (ed.), *The Diary of an Unknown Aviator*, John Hamilton, London, 1927.

Stradling, Group Captain A. H., *Customs of the Services*, Gale and Polden, 1954.

Sturtivant, Ray and Page, Gordon, *Royal Navy Aircraft Serials and Units, 1911 to 1919*, Air-Britain, Tonbridge, 1992.

Thompson, Sir Robert, *The Royal Flying Corps*, Hamish Hamilton, London, 1968.

Waite, Ron, *Death or Decoration*, Newton Publishers, Kent, 1991.

Walbank, F. Alan (Editor), *Wings of War*, Batsford, London, 1942.

Warren, Lynn and Smith, Bill (eds), *Montrose Airfield from 1913*, Montrose Air Station Museum Trust, 2001.

Watling, Harold, *A Place In the Ranks Awaits You*, privately published, South Africa, 2003.

Wellham, John, *With Naval Wings*, Spellmount Limited, Staplehurst, Kent, 1995.

Periodicals and articles

The Aeroplane, 29 December 1920.

Historic Scotland, March/April 2004.

Holte, Peter, 'R34: A 1919 Atlantic Airship Exploit', *Aviation History*, May, 2002, USA.

Readers who wish to be fully up to date with the current Royal Air Force should obtain a copy of *Presenting the Royal Air Force*, a well-illustrated booklet that would stun the air and ground crews of 1914 and 1939 and even those of much more recent vintage. The Directorate of Corporate Communication (RAF) can be found at the Ministry of Defence, Room 1/50, Metropole Building, Northumberland Avenue, London WC2N 5BP.

Index

Note
Although BAE have absorbed many of the independent makers of the aircraft mentioned in this book, original designations are retained.

A few non-Scottish locations as well as some persons of peripheral relevance to the main narrative have been omitted for reasons of space.

Aberdeen 142, 166, 200, 227, 254
Achnasheen 13
Air Battalion 16, 59, 68
Airspeed Company
    Horsa 158–160, 167
    Oxford 95, 100, 135, 184
Air Transport Auxiliary, 134–136
Aitken, Gp Capt the Hon Max 182
Allsop, Flt Sgt Alf,174
Amiens 26
Antwer, 118, 120
Antoinette aeroplane 13
Appleton, Flt Sgt 181
Arbroath 223, 224
Ardrossan 162, 165
Armstrong-Whitworth 27, 67
    Albemarle 161
    Whitley 114, 118, 137, 138, 153,
        158, 159, 161, 175,
Army Aircraft Factory 16, 21
    BE2 (all marks) 19, 20–22
    BE5 22
Army Balloon Factory 3–6, 10, 16
Arthur, Lt Desmond 21, 22, 38, 47, 48,
    195
Ascot 74
Auchel,37

A V Roe (Avro) 206, 222
    504C 41
    504K 79
    Anson 92, 96, 97, 100, 106, 109,
        111, 130, 165
    Lancaster 146, 149, 150, 151, 164,
        169, 170, 171, 184, 185, 187–
        190, 191, 197, 206
    Lincoln 206
    Manchester 214
    Shackleton 204, 206–208, 209, 210,
        214, 225, 228, 240
    York 197
Ayr 65
Ayr Observer 65

Bacon, Adml Sir Reginald 33
Balchen, Col. Berndt 173
Balfour, Arthur 44
Ballantyne, William 69, 70
Baring, Capt. Maurice 37
Barnes, Flt Lt Derek Gilpin 110
Barnwell, Frank and Harold 91
Barrow-in-Furness 23
Bawdsey 88
Beagle Aircraft see Scottish Aviation
Beardmore, William & Company 24, 25,

28, 44, 51, 53, 54, 55, 56, 57, 58, 60, 64, 67, 74, 107, 126
R24 45, 57, 58
R27, 58
R34 57, 58, 67ff, 230
R36, 74,
WB I, 44
WB II, 44,
WB III 54, 55
WB IV 55
WB V 55
Beatty, Adml Sir David 33–35
Beatty, Sir Edward 120
Beaverbrook, Lord 120, 182
Becke, Capt. John 19
Bell, Sub Lt Thomas, 186
Bennett, Air Cdre Donald 120, 121, 150, 153
Bergen 114, 113, 131
Berlin Airlift 196ff
Berwick-upon-Tweed 40, 68, 101
Beta airship 12
Billing, Pemberton 47, 48
Binnie, Lt James 45
Blair Atholl 5, 6, 9
Blackburn Aircraft Company 108
Botha 108
Skua 97, 100, 102, 112, 113, 114,
Blacker, Col Stuart 80, 82, 83, 84
Blériot Aviation Company 36
Blériot XI 11
Blériot, Louis 15
Blyth 40
Böcker, Kapitänleutnant, Oskar 40, 41, 43
Bodnoff, Flt Sgt Israel 175, 177, 178
Boeing Aircraft Corporation
B-17 Fortress 136, 184
Boswell, Capt. Lennox 162
Brinckman, Theodore 81
Bristol 123, 124
Bristol Aircraft Company 11, 21, 27
Beaufighter 141, 182–184, 192
Beaufort 122, 128, 129, 136, 145
Blenheim 91, 97, 100, 117, 118, 122, 136, 141, 144, 152, 161, 163–165, 167
Boxkite 12
Pegasus 81
Perseus 113
British Aerospace/BAE 209

Nimrod 207, 214, 227, 228ff, 239
Panavia Tornado 223, 227, 235
Eurofighter Typhoon 237
Bogen Bay 134
Bonar, Flt Sgt Eric Watt 80
Bonnett, Sidney,82, 83, 84
Boulogne 26, 37
Boulton & Paul
Defiant 125, 132,
Overstrand 90
Bramminge 63
Bremen 152, 153
Bremerhaven 40
Brest, 128, 129, 130, 140
Brodick, 165
Brooklands 21, 36
Broomfield 19
Bullock, Air Mech HCS 21
Burke, Maj. Charles 19, 20, 26
Burkhardt Grob Tutor 227
Byron, Fanny see Houston
Byron, Lord George Frederick 81

Cairncross, Cpl James 159
Caithness 153, 155
Calais 14, 16
Cameron, Lt Donald 185
Cammell Laird 32, 33, 209
Capper, Col. JE 4–8, 10, 12, 16
Campbell, L/Cpl Alexander 159
Campbell, Fg Off Graham 176–178
Campbell, Fg Off Kenneth 129, 130
Chadwick, Roy 206
Chamberlain, Neville 85, 92, 94, 105
Chance-Vought Aviation Company
Corsair 185–187
Church, Lt William 114
Churchill, Winston S 12, 18, 25, 28, 44, 75–77, 112, 133, 134, 141, 185
Clappen, Pte Donald 37
Clifden 69, 70
Clyde, River 39, 60, 67, 106, 162, 163
Clydebank 68, 125, 126
Clydesdale, Marquess of Douglas and (cf Duke of Hamilton), 81ff, 89
Clydeside 124, 125, 126
Coastal Class Airships 40, 56
Cody, Samuel 11
Cole, Flt Sgt Sydney 175ff
Collier, Lt Cdr Steve 210
Cologne 152, 170

Connor, Plt Off Clare 118*ff*
Consolidated Aircraft Corporation 195
 Canso 175*ff*
 Catalina 107, 168, 169, 175*ff*
 Liberator 164, 165, 173, 180, 195
Cooper, Geoff 208, 240
Coplawhill 39
Cornelius, Jack 91
Cowdray, Lord 49
Cox, Flt Sub Lt George 41
Craig Castle 43
Crail 105
Cruickshank, Fg Off John 179*ff*
Crosbie, Lt Dudley 26
Cuddie, Plt Off William 132
Culley, Lt Stuart 56
Cunningham, Ptty Off. Hoard 113, 114
Caper 88

Daily Express 6, 8
Daily Mail 3, 14, 15, 30, 28
Daily Graphic 3
Daily Mirror 3
Daily Telegraph 3
Dailmuir 25, 28, 51, 55, 60, 63
Damion, John 42, 43
Daventry 88
Davidson, Sgt Leslie 145, 146
Dawes, Capt George 19
Dawson, Lt Samuel 61, 64
de Havilland Company 86
 DH2 57
 DH9A 78
 DH60 Moth 81, 83
 DH82a Tiger Moth 86, 87, 97, 100, 107, 111, 135, 182, 227
 DH82 'Queen Bee' 107
 DH98 Mosquito 164, 182, 183, 192
 DH100 Vampire 200
 DH106 Comet 228
 DH112 Venom 199
Denomy, Fg Off Bernard 176, 178
Denton, Fg Off. Harry 189–191
Dickin, Maria 146
Dickin Medal 146, 169, 184
Dickson, Capt Bertram 10–13, 17, 21
Dickson, Fg Off. John 180
Dickson, Capt. William 62–64
Dietrich, Kapitänleutnant Martin 40
Dinter, Oberleutnant zur *see* Bernhard, 52

Doig, Sgt Peter 159
Donald, Grahame 11, 56
Donald, Asst Obs Gp Off Graham 133
Donders, Sqn Ldr Bernie 206, 207
Douglas Aircraft Corporation 195
 DC3 (C-47/Dakota/Skytrain) 145, 164, 173, 181, 195, 197,
 C-54 (Skymaster) 182, 195
Douglas, Maj William Sholto 42
Dover 14, 16, 26, 30, 33, 118
Dowding, ACM Sir Hugh 66, 80, 86, 87, 89, 91, 94
Draper, Sqn Cdr Christopher 56
Drennan, Sub Lt Robert 186
Dublin 67
Dunbar 41, 99, 100
Dundee 138, 152, 161, 227, 234 (*see* also RN Air Stations)
Dunne, Genl John Hart Dunne 4
Dunne, Lt John William, 3–7, 10
Dunne Aircraft 5–9
Dunning, Sqn Cdr Edwin 53, 54, 58

Eaglesham 132
Edinburgh 20, 40, 41, 43, 58, 91, 95, 100, 101, 102, 105, 227, 237
Edinburgh Citizen 41
Edwards, Cpl Arthur 12
Eisenhower, Genl Dwight 172
Ellington, ACM Sir Edward 86, 87
Essen 152
Esjberg 64
Evans, Sgt Roy 201
Everest Expedition 80*ff*
Eyemouth 40

Fættenfjord 141, 146, 149, 151
Fairey Aviation Company
 Albacore 95, 146
 Battle 118
 Barracuda 185–187
 Swordfish 95, 100, 109, 116, 127, 146
Fairie, Lt Claud 26
Falconer, Sgt James 159
Falkirk Herald 94
Farman Aeroplanes 11, 12, 19, 21, 58
Farnborough 3, 4, 5, 6, 7, 9, 10, 19, 20, 21, 87
Fellowes, Air Cdre Peregrine 81*ff*
Finse 121, 122

Firth of Clyde 161
Firth of Forth,24, 39, 43, 50, 68, 95, 101
Firth of Tay 21
Fisher, Adml Sir John 7, 30
Fison, Walter 161
Fitzpatrick, Flt Sgt Frank 168
Fleet Air Arm *see* Royal Navy Formations
Fletcher, Lt Cdr Walter 135, 136
Foggin, Capt Cyril 46
Folkestone 30
'Fokker Scourge' 38
Fokker T-VIIIW 127
Fokker America 173
Fresson, Capt Ernest 98
Fundy, Bay of 71

Gander 120, 164
Gann, Earnest 134
Garnett, Flt Sgt Jack 180. 181
George V, King 18, 25
George VI, King 104, 120, 181
German Forces
    First World War
        Albatross 66
        Friedrichshafen F33 54
        Zeppelin Class:
        L13 40
        L14 40*ff*
        L16 40*ff*
        L20 43
        L22 40*ff*
        L23 51, 52
        L33 67
        L49 74
        L53 56
        L54 63
        L60 63
        L64 74
    Second World War
        Kriegsmarine
            *Admiral Scheer,*137, 140, 149, 150
            Admiral Hipper 149, 150
            Altmark 111, 112
            Bismarck 99, 128, 130, 131
            Deutschland 111
            Gneisenau 99, 109, 128–130, 140
            Graf Spee 111
            Köln 112, 113
            Königsberg 112–114
            *Lutzow,*136

Prinz Eugen 128, 130, 131, 140, 144, 149, 150
Scharnhorst 99, 109, 116, 128, 140
Tirpitz 96, 99, 128, 130, 140–143, 146, 147, 149–153, 184–188, 231
U 47 98
U 347 180
U 361 180
U 1225 175–177
Luftwaffe
    Geschwader (squadrons)
        KG26 99, 100, 106, 192
        KG30 100, 104
        KG100 124
        10/NJG3 167
    Aircraft
        Arado 196 115
        Dornier 18, 97
        Dornier 217, 166
        Focke-Wulf Fw109, 170, 183, 192
        Heinkel 111 99, 100, 106, 117, 124, 125
        Heinkel 115, 115, 138
        Junkers 52, 192, 193
        Junkers 88, 100*ff,* 106, 117, 139, 143, 166, 167, 192
        Messerschmitt Bf109, 91, 137, 144, 164, 183
        Messerschmitt Bf110, 132, 169, 170
Gibbs, Lt 6, 9, 12
Gifford, Flt Lt Patrick 102
Gillan, Sqn Ldr John 91
Giles, Flt Cdt 79, 80
Glen Tilt 3
Glasgow, 69, 78, 91, 111, 204
Glen Nevis, 217, 218, 219
Gloster Aircraft Company
    Gladiator 86
    Javelin 201
    Meteor 199
Goddard, Lt Cdr Noel 131
Goebel, Sgt Ron 189, 190,
Göring, Hermann 94, 99
Gosforth Park 19
Goyen, Flt Lt Frank 155
Graham, LAC George 70, 71
Graham, James, later Duke of Montrose 7, 24, 25

Greenock 107, 162
Gretton, Frederick 81
Grey, Charles Grey 46–49, 105, 134–136, 193
Grider, Lt John 65
Grumman Aircraft Corporation
    Hellcat 185, 186, 187
    Wildcat 185, 186
Gruzdin, Capt 161
Gummer, Harry 166
Gurr, Percy 5

Hadden, Maj Genl CF 6
Haig, FM Sir Douglas,28
Haldane, Richard 7, 9, 10, 17
Hamilton, Duke of 133
Handley Page Aircraft Company 209
    Halifax 142, 143, 146ff, 159, 160, 168, 175, 185
    Hampden 112, 118, 119, 141, 185
    Harrow 148
    Heyford 88, 90
    Jetstream 209
    V/1500 75
Hannah, Sgt John 119, 120
Hansen, Herman 78, 104
Hansen, Friedrich Gustav 104
Hare, Lt Cdr Geoffrey 112
Hartshorn, Sgt Wilf 189, 190
Harvey-Kelly, Lt Hubert 24
Hawker Aircraft Company 86, 87
    Hector 92
    Hurricane 87, 91, 92, 93, 94, 144, 145, 165, 175
    Sea Hurricane 162
    Sea Harrier 210–213, 223
    Typhoon 175
Hayhurst, Sgt Douglas 118–120
Henderson, Genl Sir David 17, 18, 19, 26, 29, 36, 59, 60, 76, 231
Henderson, Lt Ian 45, 66
Hendon 25, 37
Hess, Rudolf 133, 136
Herbert, Lt Philip 18,
Hillary, Flt Lt Richard 160, 161
Hillington 92
Hillman, Flt Sgt Ralph 130
Holmsland 64
Hitler, Adolf 85, 92, 94, 101, 112, 118, 123, 127, 140, 141, 157, 158, 192
Holt, Maj. Felton 31

Horn, Hauptmann Alfred see Rudolf Hess
Hornell, Flt Lt David 175–178
Hood, Rear Adml the Hon Horace 34, 35, 36
Hopeman 240
Houston, Sir Robert 81
Houston, Lady 80, 81, 84
Howden 58, 73, 74
Hoy 106
Humphreys, Flt Lt Paul 216
Hunter, Spr John 159

Inchinnan 44, 57, 58, 67, 68, 74
Isbister James, 117

Jackson, Capt. William 61–64
James, Sgt George 119, 120
Jeffries, Flt Sgt Alan 170
Jellicoe, Adml Sir John 29, 32, 33, 34, 35
Johannsen, Lt 178
Johnson, Amy 135
Jolly, Cdr Richard 103, 104

Kanteill, Oberfeldwebel Erich 167
Kelly, Flt Sgt Bob 201
Kent, Duke of 154
Kneebone, Sgt Edward 189
Kidlaw 106
Kiel 130, 136
Kitchener, Lord 18
Kolding 64
Korsfjord 131

Lansdowne, Lt Cdr Zachary 68
Larkhill 12
Larne 30
Latta, Sqn Ldr James 79
Leith 40, 41
Limerick 19
Littlemore 19
Little Wigborough 67
Liverpool 67, 123, 200
Lloyd George, David 33, 49, 75–77
Loch Ness 43, 148
Lockheed Aircraft Corporation 108
    Hercules 209
    Hudson 97, 109, 111, 120, 121, 122, 127, 146, 150, 164
Lodbjerg 53
Lofjord 149

Lofoten Islands 141
London 12, 25, 28, 56, 64, 68, 73, 86, 91,
    105, 121–124, 130–132, 196, 238
London Gazette 10, 56, 64, 79, 104, 130,
    163, 169, 178, 191
Longcroft, Lt Charles 19, 20, 21
Loraine, Robert 12
Lowe, Sqn Ldr Cyril 79
Loveitt, Flt Sgt Raymond 136
Lunan Bay 22
Lyndvig 63

Macarthur, Genl Douglas 231
MacDonald, Ramsey 85
Macfadyen, Flt Cdt Douglas 78
MacInnes, Maj Duncan Sayre 17
MacLean, Sqn Ldr Charles Hector 132,
    133
MacLean, Donald 133
MacMillan, Lt Norman 45
Macmillan, Harold 200
MacRobert, Sir Alexander 143
MacRobert, Sir Alisdair 143, 144
MacRobert, Plt Off Sir Iain 143, 144
MacRobert, Lady Rachel, 143, 144, 145
MacRobert, Flt Lt Sir Roderic 143, 144
MacRobert's Reply 143, 144
McClymont, Cpl John McIntosh 111
McIndoe, Archibald 161
McIntyre, Flt Lt David 81ff, 195, 199
McKechnie, Flt Cdt William 79, 80
McKellar, Fg Off Archie 102, 103
McKelvie, Maj James 79
McMurtrie, Sqn Ldr Richard 122
McPherson, Fg Off Andrew 97
M'Clure, Snd Lt Thomas 66
Mahaddie, Wg Cdr Hamish 153
Maitland, Brig Genl Edward 68, 69, 72
Makepeace, Lt Archibald 66
Malcolm, Wg Cdr Hugh 163ff
Malone, Lt Cecil 24
Man, Isle of, 67, 78, 200
Manchester Guardian 3
Mann, Flt Sgt John 170
Martin, Rudolf,14, 15
Manchester 123
Manchester Air and Space Museum 222
Martin Aircraft Corporation
    Maryland 131
Matheson, Fg Off Sidney 177, 178
Mathieson, Sqn Ldr Alex 137

Mathy, Kapitänleutnant Heinrich 40
Maxwell, Lt Gerald 45, 66
Meyer, Kapitän Hans 186
Mitchell, Reginald 87
Monkton Meadow see RAF Prestwick
Montreal 120, 165
Moore, Vice Adml Sir Henry 186
Moray Firth 89, 95, 148, 153, 165, 167,
    184
Morton, Flt Lt Nige 231
Moseley, Wg Cdr Thomas 155
Mullis, Sgt William 130
Musselburgh 79, 184

Newark 19
Newcastle-upon-Tyne 19, 67, 118, 120,
    225
Newstead 78
Newton, Isaac 22
New York 68, 71, 72, 121, 165
Nicholson, Genl Sir William 15, 16
Nordholz 40
Norman, Spr Robert 159
Norre Havrvig 64
Norris, Flt Sgt 170, 171
North American Aviation Company
    Mustang, 165, 167, 183, 184, 192,
Northrop, Sgt Joe 89

O'Connor, Dr Patrick 181
O'Gorman, Mervyn Joseph Pius 16
Orkney Islands 29, 32, 33, 59, 98, 110,
    114, 136, 148, 184
Oslo 114, 137, 156, 160
Ostend 33

Parnell, Michael 214, 225
Payne, Fg Off Peter 184
Peddie, Prof William 87
Percival Aircraft Company
    Proctor 165
Peterhead 43, 240
Peterson, Kapitänleutnant Werner 40
Petlyakov Pe-8 (TB-7),152
Peto-Shepherd, Flt Lt Denis 148, 153,
    154,
Phillimore, Rear Adml Richard 64
Pinkerton, Flt Lt George 102, 103
Place, Lt Basil 185
Pocock, Sgt Maurice 132
Pohle, Hauptmann Helmut 100–103

Portsmouth 7, 21, 123, 124
Potts, Sgt Ernest 189–191
Price, Sgt Haydn 189
Prien, Kapitänleutnant Gunter 98
Pritchard, Maj. John 68, 71
Pulham 83, 84

Raeder, Admiral Ernst 127, 128, 130, 140
Rees, Lt Col. Lionel 57
Reid, Flt Lt William 169–171
Rolton, Flt Sgt Les 170
Romans, Fg Off David 137
Roosevelt, Franklin 134
Rosenberger, Oberfeldwebel Paul 167
Ross-Hume, Capt. Alexander 26
Rosyth 24, 33, 34, 39, 40, 50, 56, 60, 69, 95, 96, 98, 99, 100–104, 108, 123, 210
Rotherham, Cdr Geoffrey 131
Royal Aircraft Factory 18, 20, 27, 46, 47, 59, 87
    BE2 (all variants), 27, 31, 44, 45, 47, 50, 75, 227
    BE12, 45
    FE2b
RFC/RAF Units and Formations (below Command level)
    4 Group, Bomber Command 114
    13 Group, Fighter Command 87, 118, 132, 166
    15 Group, Coastal Command 116
    18 Group, Coastal Command 96, 116
    29 (Fleet) Group 78
    90 Group 199
    45 (Atlantic Ferry) Group 164
    38 Wing 158
    326 Wing 163
    Central Flying School 18, 21, 27, 36
RAF College Cranwell 78, 79, 163
    No. 1 School of Aerial Fighting 57
    No. 1 School of Aerial Fighting and Gunnery 57, 65
    School of Aerial Gunnery 50
    5 Flying Training School 80
    8 Flying Training School 89, 116
    12 Elementary & Reserve Flying Training School 103
    13 Flying Training School 99
    14 Flying Training School 95, 115

15 Flying Training School 95
236 Operational Conversion Unit 206
14 Operational Training Unit 189
17 Operational Training Unit 163
19 Operational Training Unit 115,136, 137
20 Operational Training Unit 168
54 Operational Training Unit 161
55 Operational Training Unit 175
14 Pilot Advanced Flying Unit 166
305 Ferry Training Unit, 161

Squadrons
    1 20, 23
    2 19, 21, 26, 46, 86, 239
    6 (Reserve), 31
    8 208, 209, 214, 221, 225
    9 187, 189
    10 142, 146, 147, 149
    12 227
    14 227
    15 142, 144
    15 (Reserve) 227
    16 66
    18 163
    18 (Reserve), 46
    19 184
    19 (Reserve) 42
    20 45
    21 117
    22 128, 216
    25 31, 201
    26 163
    26 (Reserve) 43
    35 146, 147, 149, 152
    42 122, 136, 145, 172
    42 (Reserve), 227
    43 42, 43, 227, 231
    44 150
    45 37
    50 141
    56 66
    56 (Reserve) 227
    61 169
    62 91
    72 132
    76 142, 146, 147, 149
    77 50, 114,
    83 118, 119
    90 136

94 144, 145
97 146
101 90
109 114
110 155
111 91, 227
114 136
120 204, 206, 228, 239
139 97
141 132
144 182
149 142
162 175
165 166
190 168
201 110
202 227
203 78
205 78
210 179
224 97, 109
228 155
233 127
235 141, 182
240 110
248 182, 183
254 141
269 96, 122
304 (Polish) 184
315 (Polish) 183
320 (Netherlands) 127
333 (Norwegian) 177, 182, 183
350 (Belgian) 174
404 (Canadian) 141, 182, 192
416 (Canadian) 139
422 (Canadian) 172
516 165
518 168
598 184
602 (City of Glasgow) 79, 81,
    84, 85, 92, 99, 102, 104, 132,
    193, 200, 227
603 (City of Edinburgh) 79, 92,
    99, 102, 104, 106, 160, 192,
    193, 200, 227
608 (North Riding) 144
612 (County of Aberdeen) 79,
    89, 92, 99, 193, 200, 227
614 (County of Glamorgan)
    152
617 171, 184, 187, 227

948 (Balloon) 108
968 (Balloon) 123
*51 Field Squadron, RAF
    Regiment* 227
*2622 (Highland), RAF
    Regiment* 226
2716 RAF Regiment 154
Miscellaneous Units
    18 Balloon Centre 111
    14 Maintenance Unit 175
    45 Maintenance Unit 175
    46 Maintenance Unit 182
    63 Maintenance Unit 194
    1141 (Combined Operations)
        Flight 165
    Photo Reconnaissance Unit
        131
    University Air Squadrons 227

Stations
    Abbotsinch 91, 97, 136
    Aldergrove 120, 121, 127
    Annan 175
    Ayr 57, 156
    Banff 152, 165–167, 182, 184,
        192
    Benbecula 136, 184, 226
    Boulmer 209, 225,
    Bowmore 172
    Brackla 172, 178, 179
    Buchan 222, 224ff
    Castletown 115, 184
    Dalcross 136, 148, 167, 178
    Dallachy 182, 184, 192
    Donibristle 50, 78
    Dornoch 136
    Dounreay 173, 174
    Drem 99, 192
    Drone Hill 98
    Dundonald 165
    Dyce 89. 92, 97, 145, 166, 167
    East Fortune 67, 68, 69, 70, 73,
        239 (see also RNAS East
        Fortune)
    Edzell 200
    Erroll 161
    Fraserburgh 183
    Gullane 99
    Houton Bay 78
    Invergordon 109, 110, 154, 155,
        179

Kinloss 89, 91, 92, 95, 114, 115,
    136, 137, 146, 149, 153, 175,
    178, 187, 193, 204, 206, 207,
    214, 215, 226, 227, 240
Leuchars 17, 78, 97, 99, 109,
    127, 136, 145, 173, 182, 193,
    200, 201, 204, 216, 223, 224,
    225, 226, 227, 234, 236
Loch Doon 50
Lossiemouth 89, 91, 92, 95,
    113, 117, 141, 142, 143, 146,
    149, 168, 182, 184, 187, 193,
    204, 208, 214, 215, 225, 226,
    227, 240
Kirkwall 9
Macmerry 52
Macrahanish 204
Montrose 19, 20, 21, 26, 27, 31,
    42, 46, 48, 49, 58, 86, 89, 96,
    109, 116, 117, 118, 127, 148,
    161, 194, 195, 230, 239
Oban 154, 155
Peterhead 139, 142, 143, 166,
    164, 183, 184
Pitreavie Castle 95, 96, 198,
    204, 215
Prestwick 86, 89, 107, 111, 121,
    132–136, 152, 156, 164, 165,
    181, 182, 195, 204
Renfrew 78, 79, 108, 193, 204
Saxa Vord 226
Scampton 118, 119, 195, 233
Scatsa 117
Skitten 154, 156, 159, 160, 173
Smoogro 78
Stranraer 116
Stornoway 8, 165
Sullom Voe 109, 110, 114, 117,
    148, 168, 179, 181
Sumburgh 117, 141, 147, 148,
    177
Tain 146, 147, 149, 151, 226
Tealing 152
Tiree 139, 168
Turnberry 57, 65, 66
Turnhouse 43, 50, 61, 63, 78,
    79, 91, 99, 102, 118, 193
West Fenton 99
West Freugh 30, 89, 90
Wick 95, 98, 115, 121, 131, 141,
    142, 154, 159, 175, 182, 184

Woodhaven 138, 177
RNAS/FAA Units and Formations
    Naval Air Organisation 16
    RFC Naval Wing 18
    9 Kite Balloon Section 34
    Squadrons
        771 131
        800 112, 210
        803 112
        804 186
        817 146
        827 185
        829 185
        830 185
        831 185
        832 146
        880 186
        881 186
        882 186
        891 162
        896 186
        898 186
        1834 186
        1836 186
    Air Stations
        HMS Condor (Arbroath)
            117, 127
        HMS Fulmar
            (Lossiemouth) 193
        HMS Jackdaw (Crail) 95
        HMS Landrail
            (Macrahanish) 136
        HMS Merlin (Donibristle)
            50, 95, 102
        HMS Sanderling
            (Abbotsinch) 136
        HMS Sparrowhawk
            (Hatston) 98, 112–114,
            116
        HMS Tern (Twatt) 136
        RNAS Campbeltown 115
        RNAS Cromarty 23, 25
        RNAS Dundee 25, 56
        RNAS Eastchurch 16, 18, 23
        RNAS East Fortune 41, 56,
            57, 58 (see also under
            RAF stations)
        RNAS Luce Bay 30
        RNAS Smoogroo 53 (see
            also under RAF
            Stations, Smoogro)

Vessels
  HMS *Africa* 24
  HMS *Arethusa* 112
  HMS *Argus* 25, 78
  HMS *Ark Royal* 7, 99, 101,
    112
  HMS *Caledon* 60
  HMS *Campania* 32-36
  HMS *City of Oxford* 34
  HMS *Cossack* 112
  HMS *Dasher* 161, 162,
  HMS *Edinburgh* 99, 101,
    102
  HMS *Engadine* 34, 35
  HMNS *Formidable* 186
  HMS *Furious* 53, 54, 58, 60,
    61, 62, 64, 78, 92, 101,
    185 186
  HMS *Galatea* 60
  HMS *Haslemere* 135
  HMS *Hermes* 25
  HMS *Hibernia* 24
  HMS *Hood* 99, 100, 131
  HMS *Inconstant* 60
  HMS *Indefatigable* 186
  HMS *Illustrious* 210
  HMS *Invincible* 36
  HMS *Iron Duke* 106
  HMS *Jervis* 100
  HMS *London* 24
  HMS *Mohawk* 103, 104
  HMS *Phaeton* 60
  HMS *Prince* 53
  HMS *Ramillies* 60
  HMS *Redoubt* 56
  HMS *Renown* 68
  HMS *Repulse* 99-101
  HMS *Resolution* 60
  HMS *Revenge* 60
  HMS *Royalist* 60
  HMS *Royal Oak* 60, 98, 99
  HMS *Royal Sovereign* 60
  HMS *Sharpshooter* 105, 106
  HMS *Southampton* 101
  HMS *Tiger* 68
  HMS *Victorious* 146, 185,
    186
  HMS *Violent* 63
  HMS *Yarmouth* 50, 51, 53
Royal Observer Corps 89, 99, 103, 132,
  133

Routh, Cynthia 172, 178
Rutland, Flt Cdr Frederick 50
Ruck, Col. RM 6

Salmond, AM Sir John 85
Samson, Lt Charles 24,
Sandys, Duncan 200, 201, 237
Saunders, Fg Off. George 154
Saunders-Roe
    London 109, 110, 111
Scallinger 63
Scapa Flow 25, 29, 31–34, 40, 53, 54, 98,
    105, 112, 115, 117, 131, 140, 174, 185,
Scherraus, Oberleutnant zur *see* Ekkehard,
  176
Schmid, Oberleutnant Herbert 167
Schneider Cup 11
Schneider Trophy 11, 33, 80, 81
Schneider, Victor 11
'Scotch Lass', 184
Scott, Flt Sgt Donald 177, 178
Scott, Maj. George 69*ff*
Scott, Sgt James 130
Scottish Aviation Ltd 85, 86, 107, 195,
  199, 209
    Bulldog 209, 227
    Pioneer 195, 196, 199
    Pup 199
    Twin Pioneer 199
Seely, Col John 17
Seidel, Kapitänleutnant Hans 180
Seymour, Ptty Off. Bryan 114
Shetland Islands 106, 110, 117, 147, 175,
  226
Short Brothers
    S38 24
    S56 46
    Stirling 142, 143, 144, 153, 189
    Sunderland 108, 110, 111, 178, 197
Sidgreaves, Arthur 92
Slough 88
Smart, Capt Bernard 51-53, 61-64
Smeeton, Sub Lt Bryan 114
Smith, Lt Howard 66
Smith, Fg Off. Sydney 155
Smuts, Lt Gen. Jan 59
Sopwith Aeroplane Company
    1½-Strutter 45
    Camel 55*ff*, 60, 61, 62, 63, 64
    Pup 51*ff*
    Schneider 33

Spithead 25
Squadrons *see* under appropriate Service
    listing
St Andrews 16, 21, 236
Stabbert, Kapitänleutnant Franz 43
Stavanger 114, 137, 166
Stirling 42, 43, 91, 227, 231
Stirling Observer 43
St Laurent, Sgt Fernand 177, 178
Stort, Leutnant Hans 101, 102
Suckling, Fg Off. Michael 131
Supermarine
Seafire 185
Spitfire 87, 92, 93, 94, 97, 99, 102*ff*, 107,
    118, 128, 131, 132, 139, 143, 151, 161,
    166, 167, 174, 194, 199, 228
Stranraer 109
Sykes, Capt Frederick 17, 20

Taylour, Lt Edward 113, 134
Teddington 88
Tentsmuir Forest 17, 236
The Times 3, 85
Thomas, René 13
Thompson, Flt Sgt George 188*ff*
Thyne, Capt Thomas 61, 62, 64
Tondern 52, 61, 62, 63
Towcester 19
Trenchard, MRAF Sir Hugh 36, 37, 66,
    76, 77–79, 85, 87, 92, 231
Trinity Bay 70
Trondheim 114, 141, 146, 147, 151
Tromso, 187
Tuckett, Sgt John, 66
Tullibardine, Marquess of 3, 5, 6, 8, 9
Tupolev TB-7 (Pe-8) 152

United States Forces
    492 Bomb Group 173
Upper Dysar, 19

Vaagsö 141
Vaughan, Fg Off. Ronald 169
Vemork 156-158
Vickers-Armstrong
    Mayfly airship 23, 30
    Warwick 178
    Wellesley 90
    Wellington 112, 118, 168, 178, 184,
    189

Waite, Plt Off Ronald 138, 150, 151
Waldron, Lt Francis 19
Wakefield, Capt .W 55
Watling, Flt Sgt Harold,200
Wallace, SAC John 214
Watkinson, Mdshpmn Frederick 114
Watson-Watt, Rober, 87, 88
Wears, Flt Lt John 194
Weaver Aircraft Company (Waco)
    Hadrian 164
Weir, Flt Lt Ian 221, 222, 226
Weir Ltd., G & J 27, 28
Weir, William 27, 28, 33, 49, 50, 60, 66,
    67, 75, 76, 92, 93
Welham, Lt John 127
Welsh, Flt Lt William 33
Westland Aircraft Company
    PV3 Houston-Westland 81-84
    PV6 Wallace 81-84
    Sea King 210, 213, 215, 216, 228
    Wessex 216, 217*ff*
Westland, Lt Francis 5
'White Vision' 169
Widdowson, Flt Lt Reuben 95
Wile, Frederick 14
Wilhelmshaven 97, 185
Wilkins, Arnold 88
Williams, Dorothy 154
Williams, Lt Norman 61, 63
Willows, Ernest 30
Wilson, Adml Sir Arthur 16
Wilson, Jessie 78, 104
Wilson, Woodrow 81
'Winkie', 146
Wood, Sgt Jack 116
Wood, Flt Sgt Mick 137
'Wopsie' 70, 71
Wright Brothers 4, 5, 6, 9, 10, 15
    Orville Wright 4
    Wilbur Wright 4, 9, 10
    Flyer 4
    Model A 9 10

Yeulett, Lt Walter 61, 64
York 19

Zeebrugge 33
Zeppelins (General) 15, 23, 32, 33, 35,
    39, 43, 51, 54
    Individual - *see* German Forces
Zimmerman, Eric 180